CAVIAR FOR BREAKFAST

THE MISADVENTURES OF AN IRISH DIPLOMATIC WIFE IN REVOLUTIONARY IRAN

Author Felicity Heathcote is a Dublin-based clinical psychologist, teacher and writer who spent several years in Palestine where she conducted workshops for the UN and other non-governmental groups. Born and educated in the UK she has worked in Ireland, Iran, Japan, USA and Saudi Arabia. Official Psychologist to the Irish Olympic team for Barcelona, Sydney and Athens, she applies her adapted zen techniques to mental health issues, sport, business, the arts and education. Her books include Peak Performance: Zen and the Sporting Zone (Wolfhound Press 1996), The Learning Zone (Wolfhound Press 2000) and The Hoopoe Bird Series on Palestine and prisoners of conscience: The Resting Place of the Moon (The Otherworld Press 2007, 2023), The Gaza Diary (The Otherworld Press 2024) and The Man With No Secrets (The Otherworld Press 2010, 2024).

© 2025 Felicity Heathcote All rights reserved

The moral rights of author have been asserted in accordance with the Act. All rights reserved. No part of this publication may be reproduced, stored in a retrieval system, or transmitted, in any form or by any means without the prior written permission of the publisher, nor may it be otherwise circulated in any form of binding or cover other than that in which it is published by this publisher and without a similar condition imposed on a subsequent purchaser.

This edition: Paperback
13-digit ISBN 978-1-0369-6572-3

THE OTHERWORLD PRESS
Cover Design by Eoin Mulcahy

DEDICATED TO THE MEMORY OF

Calligrapher Abdol Rasouli
Kian Zavieh
Jennifer Martin
Otto Bohl
Dr. Ali and Jacqui Haghsenas
Justin and Penny Carroll
Fr. Mulligan

*All of whom made my time in Iran
so memorable and so very special.*

This book was written as a record of a unique time in Iran, during the early years of the Islamic Revolution when very few people had access to this fascinating country. It is a combination of political, historical, sociological events and everyday personal experiences based on dairies I kept during my five years in Iran as the wife of Dr. Niall Holohan, the Head of Mission at the Irish Embassy.

This book is also a tribute to the proud talented nation of Iran, not because of its violent, bloody revolution but because it is a nation which produced literary giants such as Ferdowsi, Hafez and Rumi, the poet Omar Khayyam who was also a mathematician and astronomer, the physician Ibn Sina (Avicenna) and the philosopher Farid ud-Din Attar. A people in whose hearts and minds historical kings and mythological heroes are forever blurred and intertwined.

Felicity Heathcote
October 2025

The photos in this book were taken by Niall, Dr. Joan Mullany, Monica Chambers and myself. I hope they offer the readers a feeling for the places and events I experienced at the time.

CONTENTS

PART 1 - 1981
1. Road to Revolution
2. The Giant Packing Machine
3. Ten Pieces of Luggage
4. East German Guards
5. Confidential Documents
6. Passport Control
7. Red Square
8. Lubianka Prison
9. Soft Class
10. Revolutionary Guards
11. Zam Zam Men
12. Murder Mystery
13. Bodies in the Teapot
14. Headscarf in the Soup
15. Death on a Summer Afternoon
16. Toad Alert
17. Canadian Hostages
18. Where is President Banisadr?
19. Brown Sugar
20. Tea on the Embassy Steps
21. Caviar for Breakfast
22. The Big Cover-up
23. AK-47
24. Aladdin's Cave
25. Arabian Nights
26. 'Half the World'
27. Land of Sufi Poets
28. Persepolis
29. Leprosy Clinic

1982 – PART 2
30. Six–Fingered Yousef
31. Mount Ararat
32. Night Caller
33. Bus to Aleppo

34. Human Rights
35. Valley of The Kings
36. White Handkerchief
37. Omar Khayyam
38. Rabies Scare

1983 – PART 3
39. Ball on a Wire
40. Ministry of Potatoes
41. Planning an Escape
42. Now Ruz
43. The Forest of Philipopolis
44. The Fiasco of Gallipili
45. The Diplomatic Bag is Leaking

1984 – PART 4
46. Cat Killer
47. Cyrus the Great
48. IranAir Flight 655
49. The Pink City
50. Gin and Tonic
51. Baby in a Peg Basket
52. Sleeping on the Roof
53. An Undiplomatic Lunch
54. The Skull
55. Tehran Clinic
56. 'In the Hands of Allah'
57. Gratitude

1985 – PART 5
58. The Iraqis are Coming
59. Mysterious Poet
60. A White House
61. Rumi
62. Helicopters in the Desert
63. Bobby Sands Street
64. Black Flags
65. Sultaniyeh

66. Fly Swatting in Ardebil
67. Evin Prison
68. Blood Fountain
69. Faces at the Window
70. Maidan-e-Shah
71. Shah Abbas

1986 – PART 6
72. Winding Down
73. Towers of Silence
74. A Form of Closure
75. Worsening Situation
76. Plastic Plates
77. Burning Candles
78. Diplomatic Circus
79. Caspian Coast
80. The Grand Hotel
81. Tea Factory
82. Football-Bosomed Goddess
83. Conspiracy Theories
84. Trip to Rey
85. Fath Ali Shah
86. Varamin
87. Visa Problems
88. Valley of The Assassins
89. Turkish Cafe
90. Island of Rhodes
91. Death of Father Mulligan
92. Return to Reality
93. Uncertain Future

Note: Some of the Persian names may be spelt in different ways such as Rey or Ray. Names before and after the revolution may also be different such as Shah Mosque or Imam Mosque, Maidan-e-Shah or Maidan-e-Imami.

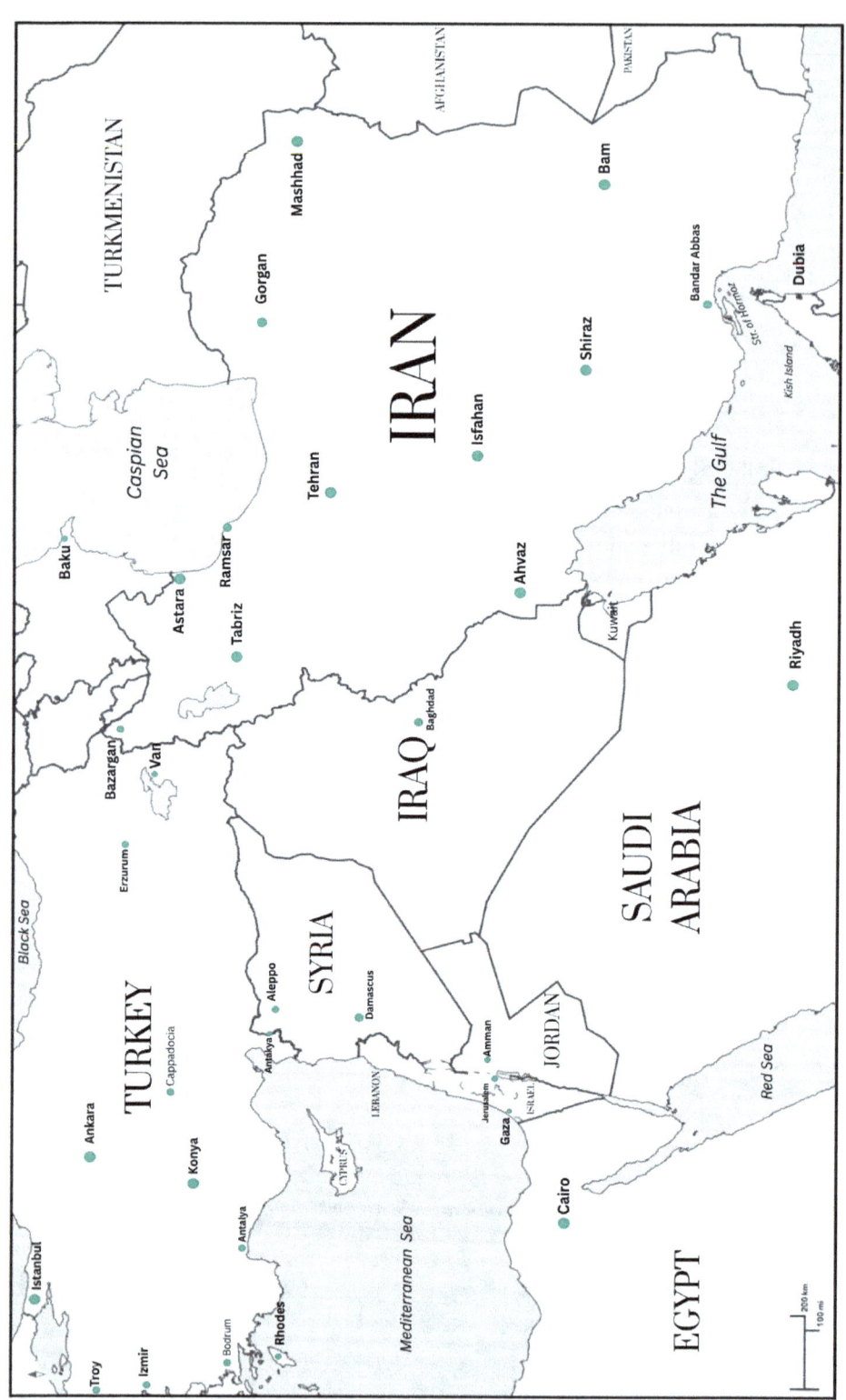

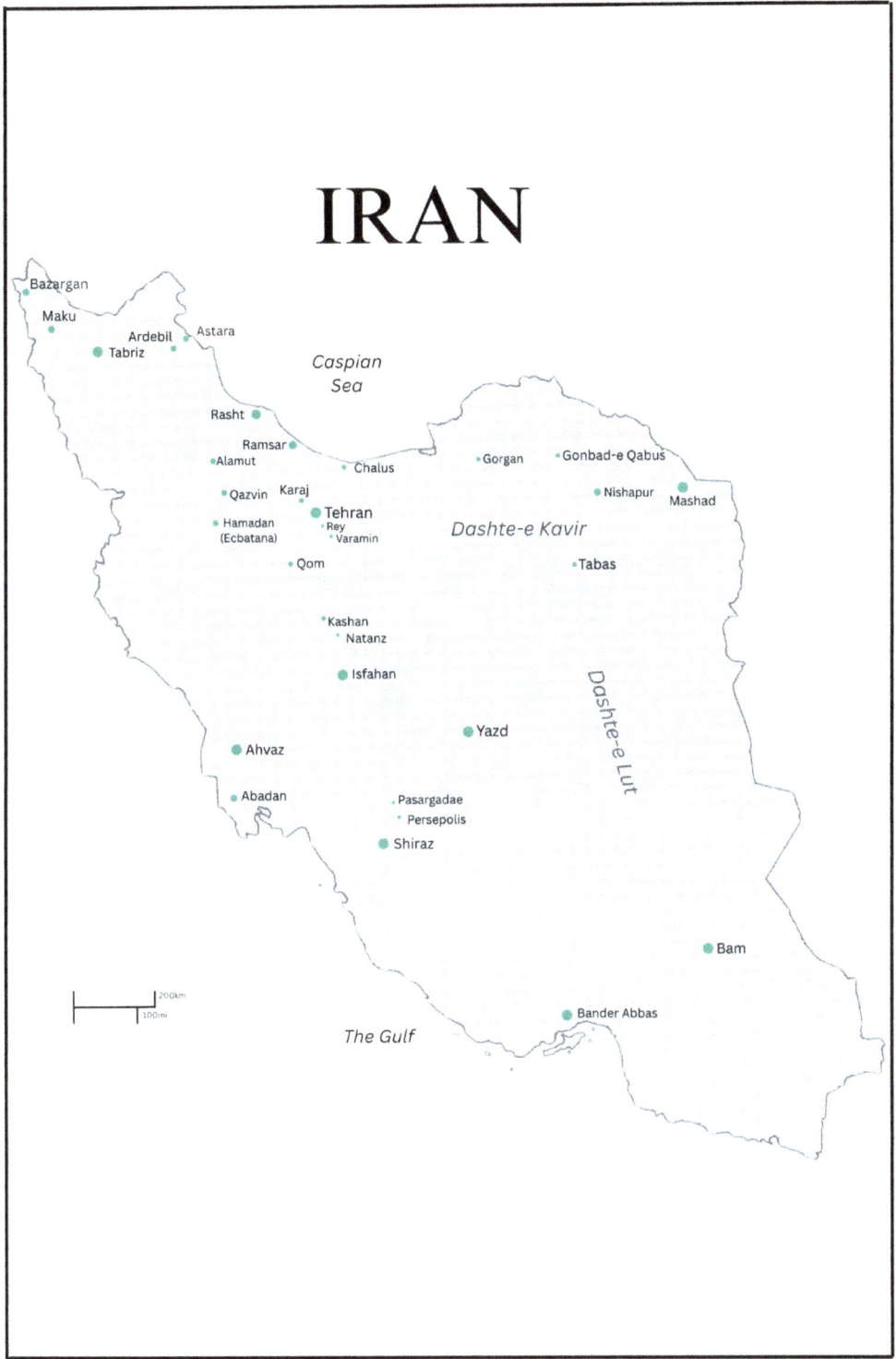

PART 1
- 1981 -

1. ROAD TO REVOLUTION

Saturday June 20th 1981

The embassy car almost slammed into a line of vehicles as they all came to a sudden halt across the road from the Armenian Church. We were completely blocked in. Suddenly, shooting broke out all around us. Anxious-looking Iranians got out of their cars checking what was going on and returning quickly to their seats as groups of demonstrators were running towards them. As the cars started to move forwards slowly, we realised to our horror that we were heading towards the shooting and were unable to reverse.

Continuing to edge forward to an intersection we heard the sound of bursts, like firecrackers, all around us. Hundreds of shots rang out as mobs of black–shrouded women and bearded male protesters ran past the cars, screaming in terror.

Now at the end of another traffic jam we slide down in our seats. Pretty useless really, the bullets would slice through the car anyway. A girl in a black chador with a big rock in hand bangs on window and tells us to "get out quickly." We gesture that we are unable to move and she runs away.

The girl is making a selfless gesture by trying to warn us of danger and she probably thought that as Westerners we were at great risk. To be caught in a stampede of terrified demonstrators, however, seemed much more dangerous. We discovered later that the crowd was trying to escape from the Pasdaran or Revolutionary Guards who were shooting all over the centre of the city at groups of anti-government leftist protesters and Mujahideen-e-Khalq (MEK).

We stayed for some time on the floor of the car while the car rocked from side to side swaying, as if held in the grip of a giant earthquake. Holding our breath it seemed that we were suspended in time, as bodies pushed and shoved their way past the cars.

Finally, the world appeared quite calm as the shooting faded away although signs of the terrible panic remained. Broken plastic bottles, flattened cigarette boxes and torn headscarves lay crushed and crumpled on the ground, where they had been dropped and trampled on in the confusion. That afternoon many people lay dead in the streets of Tehran.

We heaved ourselves back into our seats as the shooting died down, clambering back up from the floor of the car and just sat there in a state of shock trying to decide what to do next. This experience had been quite traumatic and it took some time to think straight again.

Attempting to drive back to the Embassy seemed to be the best plan of action but even that was not going to be easy. The taxi in front started to back into us and managed to turn and speed off in the direction from which we had just come. The searing screech of a siren broke the unnatural silence as an ambulance came up from behind and attempted to pass us. Once again we held our breath as we watched the driver desperately try to negotiate a narrow path between the surrounding mass of cars. Eventually he managed to find a way through but to our distress he was blocked in a little way ahead. The thought that an ambulance might be unable to reach an injured or dying person in time to save them, was even more upsetting than the violence itself.

Now the demonstrators were beginning to regroup and our only way of escape seemed to be by turning left into Pahlavi Street. Great clouds of toxic smoke were wafting across the road, coming from piles of tyres, which burned like symbolic funeral pyres in the centre of the avenue. At this point we decided that the nearby Intercontinental Hotel might be a safe location, away from the shooting and rioting so we headed in that direction. Unfortunately, we ran into a fresh group of demonstrators, carrying rocks and roughly hewn wooden planks, who were being chased by bands of pro-regime Hezbollah militants standing in open trucks screaming and shooting into the air. (Hezbollah means *Party of God* and is a term used by Shia militants around the world - especially in Lebanon.)

This was not quite the scenario I had envisioned for a genteel afternoon in the French Institute listening to a lecture on Ferdowsi, the great Persian poet. Nevertheless we tried to continue, mainly I suppose, because we did not know what else to do. This was not a great decision either. Trouble loomed as we encountered even more frantic demonstrators running around attempting to block the road by heaving three huge rocks into place. Feeling we would definitely not escape from this latest assault I covered my eyes unable to face our would-be attackers. Of course Niall had no intention of coming face to face with any potential attackers so he put his foot on the accelerator and swerved around the huge rock at the edge of the road, barely managing to get through the tiny space without scraping the car. Other cars followed us and as the demonstrators ran around gesticulating wildly, I opened my eyes to watch the anxious faces of occupants in the surrounding cars.

This was obviously getting more and more serious, so we abandoned any idea of reaching the hotel and turned onto the highway heading back to the embassy as quickly as we could. Welcome to the Iranian revolution. My thoughts were pretty grim as I finally realised what lay in store.

February 1981
Our adventure in the Islamic Republic started one rainy wintry day in Dublin in 1981. I was working in St James's Hospital on a Japanese Zen meditation therapy or mindfulness programme, which, on my return from Japan, I had developed for concentration and stress-reduction in Olympic athletes and psychiatric patients. The programme was going very well and I was just about to develop it for the general public when Niall asked me to meet him in the Department of Foreign Affairs because there was something he wished to discuss with me. That sounded very ominous and as I rode my bicycle into St. Stephen's Green, my wet hair plastered against my head, I began to think that it could be something to do with another posting.

I really did not want to leave my work so soon again. I had previously been running the psychology department in a Dublin teaching hospital and had to leave that post when I married Niall and he was sent to Japan. I did not regret it as I found Japan fascinating. Lecturing at the famous Jesuit University Sophia, where I had also studied Zen Meditation and the art of being mindful had completely changed my life and opened up a career in Olympic sport. On that rainy day, however, I was not yet ready to move anywhere again, however interesting it might be.

I walked through the beautiful foyer of the building with its lovely ceilings, sparkling chandeliers and sweeping staircase. Niall was in the Middle-East section and his room was at the back of this building, which had been donated to the state by the Guinness family. As I entered his room, I could see that Niall was looking a little tense. When he asked me to sit down, I really knew trouble was brewing so I decided to pre-empt him and put him out of his misery by asking him where the posting would be. 'Tehran', he blurted out, looking very uncomfortable. Seeing the rain running down my face he added: 'lovely weather over there.' This was beginning to seem more like a Monty Python sketch every minute. 'You mean Iran! Hostages, Assassinations, Mad Mullahs, War With Iraq – that Iran?' That was just the beginning of my list, I could have gone on but I stopped to take a breath. At this point Niall jumped in again 'We can turn the posting down' he said 'in fact lots of people at a higher level have turned it down already.' 'I'm not surprised.' I muttered, with a sour expression on my face, in the vain hope of intimidating him. Not a chance!

Niall decided to try a new path and started in his usual calm, measured and often extremely annoying way, to remind me of my deep affection for Japan and how I had not wanted to go there either. He was right, I tend to love wherever I am and never want to change. He then reminded me of our trip to Iran on the way back from Japan where we stayed with his colleague Peter in the Irish Embassy. I had not been too keen on the mindless, luxurious lifestyle of the wealthy Iranians. The waste of food at receptions had upset me when there were so many hungry people around. Another point was that the Shah's secret police (Savak) were extremely brutal and as a result many people lived in fear of their lives.

Niall suggested that maybe life under the new regime would be better for everyone. Sadly that would turn out not to be true; but they were all arguments that convinced me it would be an interesting posting. I had one request-that we travel there by train through Russia which would give us time to see the countryside and acclimatise ourselves to the idea of landing in the middle of an on-going Islamic revolution.

We were going to be working in the embassy on our own, which was a bit daunting but Niall saw it as a great challenge and he was always clear-headed enough to cope with any difficulties that might arise. I, on the other hand, would get too emotional and would be liable to say exactly what I thought, probably getting both of us into trouble because of that. Hopefully Niall could pull me back from the brink of disaster when necessary. So started our exciting adventure in revolutionary Iran.

2. THE GIANT PACKING MACHINE

Thursday May 14th 1981

The next few months flew by and packing our possessions began to seem much more stressful than the idea of the journey itself. Two days before we were due to set off the house was in a terribly chaotic state and we were afraid of packing anything that we might need to leave in the house. As an expert on 'piles' of belongings I had heaps of clothes and suitcases lying around everywhere. Consequently there was a momentary panic as the big metal diplomatic box, which was filled with a telex machine and a top secret, enigma-style coding device, disappeared from view. It was finally found, after a desperate search, under a pile of sweaters. Unfortunately I think I must have missed out on the tidy gene!

Our neighbour Mrs O'Leary came in for coffee early in the morning and her son John came in from next door to help me finish off painting the walls in the front bedroom. Not a great job I'm afraid but the best we could do in the circumstances. I did not do too well on cleaning myself up either and when Niall rushed in at seven thirty my hair, face and hands were covered with patches of cream paint.

Still smelling of paint-remover we went to meet Eamon O'Tuathail, who was the Irish Ambassador in Saudi Arabia and who suggested he might come over to Iran at Christmas. It was comforting to think that there might be contact with someone from the outside world next Christmas.

We moved on to see Niall's sister Renagh for a late dinner. Renagh was a journalist and she and Niall were interested in discussing the forthcoming election but I was so tired I fell asleep. Exhaustion had been a similar story over the previous weeks. The removal company was on my mind rather than any election.

Friday May 15th 1981

I was up early to try to make sure everything was sorted for packing knowing, from painful, past experience that any object not nailed down would be packed and removed! Four burly packers from the removal company arrived and the giant packing machine moved into action. Crystal and porcelain were scooped up and wrapped with great speed in tissue and cardboard wrapping, as bubble wrap was not yet available. Clothes on hangers were hauled from wardrobes and pulled onto metal frames and books were piled into large cardboard boxes.

At the peak of all this frenetic activity two, much too cheerful, carpet men arrived to lay new carpets in one of the bedrooms. Although I was always very good at cutting things as close as possible, on that occasion it was the fault of the carpet people who were supposed to have laid the carpet two weeks previously.

Then it was all over, everyone disappeared as suddenly as they had arrived. Only at this point was the true state of the house revealed - plastic floor coverings, rolls of packing tape off-cuts of carpets and empty paint tins. An even bigger distraction was provided by the constant ringing of the phone as I rather unsuccessfully tried to tidy up the place.

The coach of the Olympic Archery Team, Tom Shakespeare, phoned up to ask how he could contact me over the next year. He was anxious to keep up the training for the Los Angeles Olympics in three years time. The diplomatic bag was really the only method of contact and hopefully it would arrive once a week, although in the midst of a revolution no-one could be quite sure. Anyway I had already laid out a plan for the team and knew that Richard Delaney, the Irish crossbow champion would help them execute it until I returned.

When Niall came back from the bank we tried to carry out a cosmetic job on the house and pack our bags at the same time. Our tempers were already frayed when suddenly the doorbell rang which signaled that the Japanese contingent had arrived.

Our friend Yoshi Ushioda, the Japanese Curator of the Chester Beatty Museum, had been helping us to find tenants who would rent our house while we were away. After our three years in Japan we continued to study Japanese with Yoshi for several years and just spending time with her was a wonderful experience because of the depth of her knowledge on Japanese history and culture.

Yoshi had recommended that we rent our house to employees of a Japanese business that had recently started up in Ireland. The Japanese Director and his wife were on the doorstep to introduce us to the young couple who hopefully would rent the house. To make them feel more at home we had left several Japanese objects for them including a slender porcelain Japanese doll kneeling calmly in a glass case and various blue and white teacups. To our amazement, despite the disarray everyone seemed very happy with the house so we took them all to meet our neighbours - the O'Learys.

The director, Hamida-san, asked the neighbours to help the Hayashis as their English was not too good which was very helpful but, unfortunately, he then asked Mrs O' Leary, in true Japanese style, to let him know if they caused any trouble. That seemed very much like the paternalistic business approach that we had got to know so well during our time in Japan. Mrs Hayashi looked upset, her husband, however remained impassive as he looked at the floor, presumably very au fait with this kind of authoritarian behaviour. In order to break the awkward silence I started to chat away inanely about feeding my budgerigars and asked Mrs Hayashi to keep an eye on them while I was in Iran.

When they all had left we started our round of farewells, amazed at how lovely people were when they knew we were leaving the country for a few years. It was always the same and seemed a bit like an obituary as people suddenly decided that we were great, mainly because we were not going to be around for some time.

3. TEN PIECES OF LUGGAGE

Saturday May 16th 1981

As our towels and sheets had been packed we spent the night at the home of our friend Sheelagh whom we knew from our time in Japan and who very kindly offered to help when we had left the country. Unlike myself, Sheelagh was great at organisation and I knew everything would be in very good hands. The next morning I went back to the house to say goodbye to the budgerigars. They did not look too upset at our departure - much to my disappointment.

We set off with a small group of anxious friends including Hamida-san and Khairat (the Deputy Head of Mission from the Egyptian Embassy) for Dublin Port and the Jetfoil ferry where we had another tearful farewell. As a diplomat, Khairat was allowed to come on board with us for a few minutes before we left and I felt that he, more than most people, realised the potential seriousness of the situation into which we were getting ourselves. It was sad to leave our friends but now I was beginning to get really excited at the idea of the long journey ahead into the unknown. My disquiet was not to make its appearance again until a little closer to the Iranian border.

On our arrival at Holyhead in Wales we were treated with some suspicion by the customs men because of the amount of luggage we were carrying. This consisted of nine pieces including a metal box with 'Diplomatic' written on it. We explained we were travelling to Tehran by train and an incredulous look of "rather you than me" passed over their faces. My uncle collected us from the port and we went to see my great aunt who had prepared a meal for us. Niall was exhausted and went to bed while I went to meet my father to discuss a new book on chromatography that he had been commissioned to write.

On our return from Japan in the late seventies, he had told us that he thought there had been a travesty of justice in the case of the Irish people convicted in the Guildford Four bombings. An expert in chromatography, he suggested that any first year biochemistry student would have failed their exams if they had used the methods, by which the suspects had been convicted. In an attempt to achieve some justice in the case he had written letters to Cardinal Basil Hume and the Belfast politician Gerry Fitt - but had received no reply. This was the first I had heard of this argument; indeed most people had seemed glad to have seemingly plausible scientific evidence leading to the imprisonment of the suspects for such a terrible crime. My father's views were to be vindicated many years later when the convictions were overturned in their entirety.

When I met my father on the way to Iran he appeared to have lost interest in writing his latest scientific book on chromatography and wanted to talk about a peace conference he was attending in Portugal the following week. It was really good to see that he was still as interested in the peace movement as he had been as a young conscientious objector during the second world war.

On our arrival in London we went straight to the house of a colleague at the Irish Embassy to collect our new passports containing Iranian visas and we then went to stay with my friend Aiveen for the night. In the morning after a superb breakfast - which felt a bit like the Last Supper - we piled all our bags and cases into her car and headed for Liverpool Street Station. We had by then collected yet another bag as Aiveen had given us a large amount of food for the trip. In true Aiveen style, the bag was a medley of tins of ham, pats of butter, watercress, biscuits and cheeses, plus a selection of chocolates, crisps, beer, sandwiches, knives, forks and a bottle of mayonnaise in case we might be hungry!

At the station Aiveen gave me a beautiful silver necklace she had bought in Bombay. Originally from Armagh in Northern Ireland, she had qualified with me in clinical psychology at Glasgow University and it was our close friendship that had led me to apply for a post in the Department of Mental Health at Queen's University in Belfast.

I will always remember when I met her, in the late sixties, at the Crichton Royal Hospital in Dumfries where we spent the first year of our university course. She had just driven over on the boat from Larne and emerged from her car wearing thigh high sage green suede boots, a tartan mini-skirt and a rust-coloured sweater. Full of good humour she stepped forward, a vision of smiles and long auburn hair, a marked contrast to my student mode of public transport, jeans and a duffel coat. When we met in London she was working at the Tavistock Clinic and was engaged to Manek, a psychiatrist from India.

The Harwich train appeared crowded and we rushed to the front. Fortunately there were seats in the first class and we had a compartment to ourselves and our ten pieces of luggage. Farewells were made out of the window and tears mingled with the fine rain that had begun to fall. Settling down we watched as the train moved smoothly by the back gardens of endless rows of suburban houses squatting bleakly in the rain. By now my tears were falling freely as reality started to kick in. Even the gloomy sky and the rain took on a rosy glow when friends and family were left behind, especially when the intended destination was such an uncertain place as Iran. From time to time throughout the journey my mood swung between feelings of excitement and apprehension.

Once again there was some trouble when the boat train reached Harwich because we had too much baggage; finally managing to find a trolley we boarded just in time. The sky was very dark and overcast as we stood on deck shivering in the rain and watching the pretty shoreline disappear from view. To pass the time we wandered through the Duty Free area where I bought a bottle of French perfume. In an attempt to lighten our mood a little, we then went downstairs to watch Goldie Hawn in the film 'Private Benjamin'. At least the film took my mind off the uncertain journey ahead.

Of course Dutch Customs stopped us but on learning of our destination they soon let us go. I was beginning to think we were seen as a bit of a liability by customs officers everywhere.

Seeing the train with the destination marked on each carriage was such an exciting experience although we were a little nervous when we had to walk to the front to find our carriage. The Hook of Holland to Moscow carriage was quite different from the rest, with Russian characters strung across the side. A group of burly Russians gathered on the platform and viewed our ten pieces of luggage with interest – the luggage really was beginning to be a star attraction. We were shown to our compartment by two attendants who occupied a small office at the far end of the carriage.

We surveyed the space with horror, noting that our luggage was taking over and we could barely move. It felt very oppressive. We placed some bags under the lower bunk and attempted to stack the rest, but it did not appear to make much difference. Despondently we perched on the bunk. Our passports and tickets had already been taken away, so we really were in the hands of the Russians. The train jerked into life and set off.

On the platform, small groups of Russians waved to departing friends leaving us to wonder with great interest who were our travelling companions. At that time of the cold war, Russia was an unknown quantity - a communist state, feared by most people. We felt that Iran was, probably, more of a threat but nevertheless I was a little anxious, in spite of my excitement, at the prospect of travelling through Russia.

4. EAST GERMAN GUARDS

We turned our attention to the scenery, watching the flat Dutch countryside glide by. The view of the ordered landscape with its neat houses, windmills and little fields bordered, not by fences or walls but by channels of water, seemed a safe haven compared with thoughts of Russian spies and Revolutionary Guards. Occasionally a little water pump stood beside the canal. The houses were lit up and reminded me of our previous visit there in February, the day after we heard that we might be going to Tehran.

I was shaken from my reverie when the compartment door opened and a diffident attendant brought us tea in lovely glass cups and silver Russian styled holders.

My big mistake proved to be taking the lower bunk. During the night the attendant had returned our passports and an hour later the East German guards boarded the train. To my surprise they were much gentler and more polite than on my previous trips to Warsaw in the early seventies. At that time the guards strode arrogantly through the train like mechanised robots barking out orders and checking passports with expressionless faces. Maybe on this occasion the fact that our carriage was a first class sleeping carriage destined for Moscow made a difference; anyway I could not sleep or really settle in case I missed something out the window.

When I looked out I could see the barbed wire, the river, the area just beside the infamous Berlin Wall and the East German guards in their lookout posts. The guards on the train may have looked a little friendlier but it was still a chilling experience to cross the border between East and West Berlin. (Now that the Berlin Wall has been pulled down and the breakup of the Soviet Union has occurred, it is difficult to imagine how anxiety-provoking the crossing of the so-called Iron Curtain used to be.) This was indeed a huge psychological and physical barrier that kept the east and west of Europe apart for ideological reasons. Anyone crossing these borders was regarded with suspicion by both sides. I had made the journey to Prague and Warsaw on two occasions when working at Queen's University in Belfast. I booked through the British travel agency Thomas Cook and was immediately put on the list of the Special Branch in Northern Ireland; such was the paranoia about communism at that time. I loved the beauty of Warsaw and Prague with their fascinating and tragic histories and I am glad that I managed to visit those counties at that unique time. I was not at all impressed with their governments but like many students of the sixties era I was not really too keen on any government. (At the time of writing, there is a risk of the Iron Curtain descending once again. Tragically, President Putin with his abhorrent and vicious attack on Ukraine appears to be attempting to return Ukraine back under Russian control. Where this cruel campaign will lead, no one knows.)

As we crossed the River Oder on our way into Poland, more guards lined the platform and our passports were checked again. The Polish customs arrived, more officious and less friendly than I remembered. (I wondered if politically speaking we were in the wrong carriage with destination Moscow; or did their current insecurity mean that they had to act in a heavy-handed manner anyway?)

We ate some more of Aiveen's food, as we had searched for a dining car but there was none. At that point we really appreciated Aiveen's considerate actions and thought that perhaps at Warsaw we could get a hot meal. Passing through the city of Poznan once again we could see large groups of people standing on the station platform and then continued through the Polish countryside to Warsaw.

Two more cups of tea appeared that day. It was quite a hot day and there was no air conditioning, so we decided to conserve our two remaining cans of beer. We arrived in Warsaw on time at 4pm in the afternoon and we waited to join up with other carriages bound for Moscow, arriving in from Vienna and Paris.

5. CONFIDENTIAL DOCUMENTS

The Paris train was late and so we had nothing better to do than watch a group of young Russians parade up and down the platform. They were dressed in mis-matched tracksuits, which was apparently the compulsory socialist wear for travelling expeditions. Their clothes certainly seemed dated and dowdy compared to their western counterparts and in those days young Russians would often try to buy clothes off westerners. Sadly I received no offers for my jeans!

We would have loved a hot meal and the friendly Russian lady from two compartments down told us that we should be at the station for at least one more hour and could cross the tracks to get some food. Carefully taking our passports and three envelopes for the embassy in Moscow, which contained coding instructions, we set off looking for food. The Russian carriage was just the right atmosphere for inducing and maintaining paranoia so we did not want to leave any confidential documents behind. I was not quite sure, at this stage, whether the situation was shades of John le Carré or a comedy film. No one would change money for us in the station, the man in the information kiosk, smiled with great glee as he refused to help either us or the Russian passengers. At this point it was definitely a comedy moment rather than a spy experience.

Wandering back to the train, thirstier and hotter than ever, we spotted a small Polish man wearing a red builder's helmet surrounded by a group of Russian youth. He was gleefully folding handfuls of money as the Russians rushed away with their zlotys. Before we could even approach him, he had stepped off to another platform perhaps to stash away his loot like a squirrel with his piles of nuts. We resigned ourselves to tea and our last beer, as we watched the Russians sauntering along the platform in groups like young people everywhere. One carried a blaring transistor, another a tape recorder, a little like Europe twenty years earlier.

At last, to our relief the long overdue Paris carriage made its appearance and after a noisy crash and shudder the train was complete and everyone jumped aboard for one of the most interesting but stressful parts of the journey.

We tried to recognise bits of Warsaw as we passed through but it was not really possible. Niall thought he might have seen Stalin's wedding cake building but again he was not sure. We asked for tea and as we had broken the key of the ham tin, the attendant opened it for us. Niall went to sleep but I did not really sleep that night because of fear of the Russian customs which I was sure would involve some major upheaval.

6. PASSPORT CONTROL

Wednesday, at 2 a.m. in the morning Russian time, there was a knock at the door and the attendant appeared. He warned us that passport control was coming up. He was all decked out in his blue jacket which was festooned with gleaming gilt buttons. There was no sign of the short sleeves and open necked shirt of the previous days. Niall continued to sleep and sometime later the Polish customs officers examined the passports. Once again they were taciturn. I wondered what had happened to the friendly Polish guards of the early 70s.

The train moved on and there was another knock at the door. Two Russians entered, one young with a plump unlined face, the other older man looked a little more serious like Omar Sharif in Dr. Zhivago or maybe I was just thinking of anything to do with Russia. They took our passports and examined our visas and asked for our Russian diplomatic cards but we explained that we were bound for Tehran not the embassy in Moscow. Customs appeared but were also only interested in the word diplomatic. Ironically, this word seemed to work wonders in socialist countries.

Two big blonde Russian women arrived, one speaking French, the other German and they asked if we had any meat or vegetables. We denied both items although in the corner the ham tin quietly let off a meaty odour. The men returned and checked under the bunk. I got out quickly, a sheet wrapped around my pyjamas. They peered in under the bunk before moving off satisfied that we are hiding nothing but half a tin of meat. Meanwhile every other compartment was being examined and all the luggage pored over in minute detail.

The outside of the station at Brest-Litovsk on the Polish border looked like a film set, bright lights glaring down through iron gates. I saw a building a little like a town hall and in front of it a patch of green grass and flowers which looked very pretty. Officials hung around in groups. Our passports were returned and we were shunted back to a siding covered over with a corrugated iron roof where the task of changing the undercarriage to fit the Russian gauge was undertaken. The clock on the wall said 3:30 a.m. I watched as a carriage was shunted parallel to us over a pit as men walked along tampering with the wheels of the train. The Russian workers stared in with wary disinterest. The man in the compartment beside us heaved a sigh of relief as he maintained that thankfully we could now relax and get some sleep, all of the checking was over for the moment. The customs had spent a long time going through his things and those of all the other Russians. In the compartment on the other side of us, two Russian officials who boarded the train at Warsaw appeared to be working on some papers.

The following morning as the train rushed through the thickly forested countryside the atmosphere on the train had lightened considerably. The radio was blaring out Russian music and people gathered in the corridor staring out of the windows while vendors moved up and down the carriages selling cakes and drinks. One large Russian woman tried to sell us a small hard cake. We gave her a dollar, which was much too much but of course it was *de rigeur* to look affronted, which she did, although she then moved very quickly to change it with the attendant. Miraculously an attendant arrived with a plate of salami sandwiches so we handed over cigarettes and more money, including our last Dutch guilders. This burst of gaiety, however, was short-lived and the train soon settled down to its usual gloomy atmosphere as we moved on.

In any journey the last few miles always seem to be the most trying and this journey was no exception especially as we realised that we would be several hours late and were worried about Adrian, Niall's colleague working in the Irish Embassy in Moscow, who would be waiting for us. The towns were very similar, undistinguished apartment blocks contrasted with industrialised areas and occasionally a single attractive building stood out, a proud reminder of a former era. Lines of military equipment passed by – green painted tanks and trucks, scary symbols of war. Eagerly we scanned the countryside for hints of the Moscow suburbs and anxiously looked at our watches. Finally the suburbs came into view, rows and rows of high rise featureless buildings it could be part of the suburbs of anywhere even Paris. Eventually we slowed down and entered the station. Hundreds of Muscovites rushed onto the train, hugging and helping their friends and relatives. I watched in fascination as parcels, parcels and even more parcels were carried off, all wrapped in brown paper tied with string and loaded onto trolleys.

Niall struggled off the train but could not find either a trolley or Adrian. Meanwhile I was imprisoned in the compartment unable to climb over the luggage piled up on the floor. Niall searched for his colleague while the attendant helped me with the cases as the platform cleared of parcels and travellers. Then Niall suddenly appeared with Adrian who sadly had been on another platform waiting for us for the previous three hours, unable to get any information other than that the train would be half an hour late!

7. RED SQUARE

Apologising profusely for our delay, we all three moved out past queues of Russians who were waiting for a taxi, happily we were approached by a man who offered to take us to Adrian's apartment. It was great to see Niall's colleague with whom we were staying and I could not wait to hear about daily life in Moscow. The view of Moscow so far, was very stark, with endless rows of drab, concrete, utilitarian buildings. Life seemed equally drab for most ordinary Russians under the Soviet regime.

We arrived at a huge crumbling apartment block, which was reminiscent of old university halls of residence for undergraduates in the 1960s. The buildings certainly looked very depressing from the outside but the inside was much better and appeared quite comfortable. Adrian pointed out an important feature which had nothing to do with comfort. The light in the centre of the room flickered when the 'bug' was working. As soon as Adrian acknowledged the presence of the listener by saying 'we're home again, Boris' the flickering was terminated. Fortunately we did not have any important secrets so the Soviet 'bugging' machine went largely unnoticed but I suppose it would only increase the sense of paranoia felt by most visitors from the West. After we freshened up and had a welcome cool drink we went to meet the other colleagues from the embassy before going to a Georgian restaurant for an evening meal. This was another unfortunate experience of Soviet cuisine. On this occasion the *hors d'oeuvres* were reasonably good but the main course was a piece of chicken, all bone and no meat or vegetables. On the plus side, however, there was lots of champagne and vodka to make up for our forthcoming stay in Iran.

Thursday May 28th 1981

'Its commanding situation on the banks of the Moskva river; its high and venerable walls; its numerous battlements, towers and steeples; its magnificent and gorgeous palaces; its cathedrals, churches, monasteries, and belfries, with their gilded, coppered, and tin-plated domes…'
This was a description of the Kremlin at the time of the Czars, by traveller J.L. Stephens in the 1830s. Our visit was, one hundred and fifty years later, at a much different time of Marxist socialism but the former glory was still there for all to see.

It was beautiful weather as we set off full of anticipation to see the famous Red Square. The metro, itself, was a living museum piece. It consisted of marble and gilded art works dominated by huge escalators, which were lit up by beautiful antique lamps. The escalators were also very steep and the possibility of 'pile ups' as we tried to get off them was terrifying. We emerged unscathed and took a boat across the river. In the distance the gilded domes of the Kremlin seemed part of a magical fairy tale as we approached the square from the back of St Basil's Cathedral with its amazing coloured domes. A moat ran along the Kremlin wall separating the Kremlin from Red Square where many commemorations and military parades have taken place over the centuries. In the centre of the square was Lenin's Mausoleum where the body of Vladimir Lenin, who died in 1924, lay in state in a crystal sarcophagus. A guard of honour stood at the entrance of the Mausoleum but unfortunately the queue to view the body wound halfway around the square so we decided if we had to queue all day we were not that interested in Lenin's body after all. We waited with crowds of Russians for the changing of the guard at Lenin's tomb. The two guards moved out, strutting alongside the crowd and standing before the tomb as the clock struck. They then moved into place and the change-over was completed. Niall held his camera aloft as, without blinking, the returning guards passed in front.

We moved on to see Saint Basil's Cathedral, which was truly a masterpiece of Russian architecture. It was built in the middle of the seventeenth century by order of Czar Ivan the Terrible. An amazing piece of craftsmanship both inside and out, it consisted of nine elongated-shaped chapels all unique in appearance with a central taller one shaped like a spire and a tenth chapel erected beside the cathedral a few years later. Although the chapels are all different in appearance they blend together perfectly to make a remarkable artistic design. Inside the chapels were magnificent frescoes and icons. Legends suggest that so beautiful was the Cathedral that when Ivan the Terrible heard that the creators of this artwork said they could build an equal or even finer piece of art he blinded them to prevent this from happening.

The next venue was GUM, the large store by the Red Square where Russians gathered to eat ice cream. I risked a glass of some kind of a sweet sticky drink and a rock-hard cake. There were long queues for ice cream but no form of mechanisation in the shop, which meant that unappetising, big, white pools of melting ice cream sat forlornly in large containers.

The metro was more crowded than ever when we returned to Adrian's flat. I tried to flatten myself against the door, hoping I would not be catapulted out onto the platform as burly Russians jostled against each other.

After a meal we set off for the Bolshoi by taxi. It was a beautiful grand theatre with boxes at the back and at the sides fringed with sweeping red and gold curtains. That night there was a sense of anticipation in the air as everyone was expecting King Hussein of Jordan but apparently he did not show up. The first piece of music was an 'avant-garde' work with amazing lighting effects and giant cobwebs draped across the stage. A huge squid hung for some unknown reason from the ceiling. I wondered was the music a symbolic piece emphasising the triumph of good over evil but I really did not have a clue whether there was any significance at all.

All around, members of the audience were holding flowers which they threw at the end of the last piece of music and everyone charged up the aisle at the interval to shout bravo. We were not that enthused about the music so we quickly ran in the opposite direction to join the queue for champagne. The second half was more lively and involved a selection of different colourful dances, traditional and folk. On all sides enthusiastic groups were again calling bravo. The TV cameras were there and Adrian felt that the enthusiasm of the audience was staged, probably because King Hussein was supposed to attend the event.

8. LUBIANKA PRISON

At the end of the performance we walked back past the Lubianka prison and the KGB headquarters. Looking down into the basement I saw two Soviet officers playing chess through barely parted curtains. I shivered slightly as we discussed the Swedish diplomat Raoul Wallenberg who saved so many Jews during the war and was thought to have been imprisoned in the dreaded Lubianka Prison when he disappeared and was never seen again. It was really depressing to think about the fate of a person who had done so much good and I could only wonder what else he would have achieved if he had lived. Maybe he would have gone on to be an advocate for the Palestinians, who also had no state.

Finally we called in to a colleague's apartment and embarked on a discussion about the relative merits of hardship posts. We were interested to work out whether Tehran was a more difficult posting than Moscow. The general consensus finally seemed to be that both were difficult postings but the potential for violence was more likely in Iran than Russia.

Friday May 29th 1981
Slept well but I was getting more tired each day maybe because of stress over our impending journey to Iran or maybe just that the weather was very warm and I do not cope too well with hot weather. Went to various museums but the most interesting was the State Tretyakov Art Gallery. The paintings were housed in an impressive nineteen-century building, which was completed in 1904 in the style of a mini Kremlin. It contained an amazing collection of paintings but for me the most impressive exhibits were the jewel-coloured Russian religious icons. (We would see more of these exquisite icons in a shop in Bethlehem many years later when Russian émigrés smuggled their valuables out of the country and sold them in order to survive.) Old fat baboushkas sat in every room, wearing little ankle socks and headscarves while they guarded the pictures, casting fiercely baleful looks at anyone who passed by. Obviously they would much prefer to have no museum visitors at all!

Lunch consisted of a cup of sickly sweet coffee, a salami sandwich and cake in the museum café. At one point Niall and Adrian moved to examine a functioning barometer and a well-built baboushka hurled her substantial self into view, her hand raised to prevent them from getting too close. They are by far more formidable than any of the male guardians of western museums. After our wonderful cultural experience we headed to a bread shop to buy some chocolates to fortify ourselves for anything else that might happen. That was another big mistake, the chocolates were totally tasteless and seemed to be made of mashed cardboard rather than cocoa.

In the evening we went to the Kremlin Palace to see the Barber of Seville. It was a great experience, of course, but it was never my favourite opera at the best of times and in Russian it was pretty terrible. The audience, however, seemed to love it and once again rushed down the centre aisle waving enthusiastically. Maybe they were paid to be enthusiastic, certainly I would need to be paid in order to look that excited. Meanwhile we were ignoring the rush and moving in the opposite direction to look for ice cream or champagne, or preferably both. Back in Adrian's flat we bid goodnight to the flickering light and 'Boris the bugger' and fell asleep after our exciting but tiring day.

Although there was so much architectural and artistic beauty in Russia from previous eras, at the time of our visit under communist rule, Moscow seemed a very dull, automated place that lacked a feeling of originality and creativity. This left us with the question as to whether the tyranny of Ivan the Terrible was better or worse than the brutal influence of Lenin and Stalin.

9. SOFT CLASS

Saturday May 30th

On our last day it was raining heavily as we went to shop in the 'Gastronome', the diplomatic shop that sold western goods for hard currency. On the way we saw hordes of Russians oblivious to the rain, holding empty bags in case they could find food anywhere in Moscow. Only one man, carrying two large bags of oranges, seemed to have been successful. Inside the shop the array of food items that greeted us was not good at all but it was still a far cry from the meagre selection of jars of pickled fish and vegetables that we saw in the other food shops. For us it was particularly helpful because we could stock up with food for our journey to Tehran. There was, apparently a dining car on the train but for a four-day journey it was important to get some extra provisions.

As a chocolate addict, my great delight was finding a huge pile of

Cadbury's fruit and nut bars, which I realised, could be the last proper chocolate I might see for at least a year. I also picked up a box of 'Gastronome Fancies' which were exotic-looking tiny cakes, French in appearance but unfortunately not in taste. Of course this shop could only be used by diplomats and privileged local officials. A very common sight in Moscow in those days was fleets of black limousines with darkened windows behind which reclined the communist elite. Ordinary Russian citizens suffered badly from food shortages. Soviet Russia seemed to be yet another failure of a political system.

At 8.30 in the evening Adrian's colleague, Andrew, came to the apartment and we all left together for the train station. I was quite upset to leave this final 'bastion of civilisation' and our sombre mood was reflected in the dank, murky night. We decided to park outside the station and drop off the bags. The Russian police arrived and an argument ensued. We dropped the bags anyway, all ten of them and got into a conversation with a drunk who did not seem any more impressed with the police than we were. No one could find any train information, which was anxiety-provoking because the time was moving on and we could not even find a porter. Finally we came across Platform 1 (9.12pm at this point), the notice board says Baku. It is the same number as that on the ticket but we were not meant to go through Baku. We were meant to go through Tbilisi and Yerevan but not Baku. Anyway the time was nearly 9.30pm so we rushed to Platform 1 although by this time we had already lost Adrian who was searching for a porter in the crowded station.

At last Adrian came back with a porter just as the train was pulling into the platform. Our next problem was to find compartment 17, which was not after 16 and we realised that the compartments were definitely not in the correct sequence. The porter was getting very worried about the imminent departure of the train and told us to board immediately and he would pass the suitcases through the window. We squeezed onto the crowded train and tried to edge down the corridor to where the porter was standing with Adrian and Andrew. Desperation set in as we wondered would we get the luggage through the window on time. Finally we squeezed to the window outside our compartment and heaved in the bags. We were now on a train to Baku, which we hoped would be the correct one.

Two attendants appeared at the compartment door and the burly, dark-haired man started to fix the bunks while the slim blonde Russian pulled up the windows. Standing in the corridor we leaned out of the train windows, waving goodbye as light rain washed over us. Feeling the damp evening air on our faces, we watched the waiting Russians on the crowded platform until we left the station behind us. Reluctantly we sat down in our 'soft class' compartment. The words 'soft class' meant that we had a compartment for two with dark brown upholstery on the lower seats and a wash hand basin. We could store our luggage under the seats and could pull down the upper bunk at night. This touch of 'luxury' enabled us to rest rather than to sit upright in seats for the four-day journey. The slim Russian waiter dressed in an immaculate brass-buttoned white jacket appeared again at the door. He had brought us tea in the usual silver holders with a small wafer biscuit and two sugar cubes in the saucer and informed us with a proud smile that he spoke German so at least we could have some sort of communication during the following days.

We were much more organised and prepared for this part of the journey than on the previous train trip and everyone seemed friendlier; so we began to feel a bit optimistic and hoped that everything would go smoothly. We stowed away our luggage a little more tidily because there was much more room in the carriage and the bathrooms were in a better state than the last train. So far, so good but we wondered how long this would last.

Sunday May 31st
During the night the train occasionally stopped at local stations but there was not much to see: just the usual small groups of Russians standing in front of a large picture of a stern-faced Lenin.

In the morning, after a night of fitful sleep, we awoke to the welcome sight of our attendant bringing more tea. The corridor was already smelling of smoke as we joined our friendly, fellow Russian travellers. We did not smoke ourselves but were happy standing there watching the scenery unfold through a smoky haze of endless cigarettes, the butts scattering all over the floor. The scenery that was not obscured by swirls of cigarette smoke did not initially appear to be too exciting, as it mainly consisted of small patches of vegetable gardens springing up at intervals along the track.

Occasionally a scarecrow was seen or a dead crow hung up to scare the birds. These small scrubby patches of growth possibly explained the lack of vegetables in Moscow. Occasionally a goat was seen tied up and sometimes an odd cow appeared. This was definitely a far cry from the farms of Western Europe. Finally we moved back into our compartment to get away from the smoky atmosphere and to eat some of our food from Moscow while reading guidebooks on Iran. The books, unfortunately, were from the time of the Shah, so although we could learn about the cities and countryside we were still not sure about what to do in an Islamic Revolution.

The vegetable patches were getting bigger and becoming more like fields and we could even see a tractor in the distance along with cows and sheep. Every now and then I spotted an old man in an Astrakhan fur hat trotting along with a walking stick. The countryside was finally beginning to come alive as we left behind the environs of the robot-like capital city. There were beautiful brightly coloured birds perched on the telegraph wires and small parrots decorated the pale blue sky with orange smudges as we passed by an area of flooded land and what looked like little paddy fields. Although whether the fields were flooded by accident or design was difficult to ascertain.

A small child appeared out of the next compartment and stood gazing at us with great interest. We offered him some sweets, which he accepted and some chocolate which he refused, probably because his mother, looking very embarrassed, had suddenly come to get him. Perhaps, the stories we had been told by Adrian were true - that the schools taught children not to accept sweets from foreigners because they might be poisoned. Or maybe this was just another example of Western propaganda rather than Soviet paranoia.

Soon, although we were still several hours from Baku, we could see the Caspian sea, long stretches of golden sand glinted in the sunlight beside the deep blue water. Encouraged by this beautiful sight we decided to try Russian train dining in the hope that it would be better than the food in Moscow. The dining car was crowded with Soviet soldiers who looked more Iranian than Russian with their dark skin and heavy mustaches, we guessed they were probably Azerbaijani. A guitar was passed around and they all took it in turns to play and sing folk songs. At this point a lovely warm atmosphere filled the dining car and everyone seemed happy and relaxed. A waiter came back over to our table and burst into laughter as we tried to explain that we wanted to order dinner. In the end, it did not seem to matter whether we were understood or not because there was no choice and everyone was eating the same food.

Dinner arrived finally – a metal bowl of soup. We wondered could this have been the labour camp food that Ivan Denisovich was served in Alexsandr Solzhenitsyn's description of life in the Gulag Archipelago. Very possibly. It appeared to be water filled with scraps of carrot and tiny slivers of onions and one small piece of unidentifiable meat. This 'beef steak' was a relatively raw meat ball topped with a flattened hard fried egg, a few mashed potatoes and a spoonful of vegetables. Maybe it was a little more substantial than the Russian political prisoners would have been given in the Gulag prison camps but it was perhaps sufficiently tasteless to be used as an instrument of torture.

The meal (which was cold) was served with a glass of red wine (which was warm). The food and the wine, tasting like a very sickly sherry, may have been dreadful but the atmosphere and service were charming. The meal came to seven and a half roubles and the waiter seemed amazed when we gave him ten roubles and told him to keep the change. Obviously tips were not expected in a communist society as people were meant to be equal; although, as we had seen, some people in their fancy limousines were definitely more equal than others.

We walked back through the swaying carriages which were all, with the exception of ours, serviced by baboushkas or old Russian ladies sitting in the corner of these carriages beside a giant brass samovar doling out glasses of hot steaming tea. The living conditions in these carriages were very cramped and the smell was not so good. There seemed clearly to be a much bigger difference between hard and soft class in the USSR than between first and second-class in Western Europe.

Our dark-haired attendant greeted us sympathetically as he re-opened the compartment and brought us tea while telling us - alas too late - that the dining car was not too good. Anyway, despite the food, the visit to the dining car had been an eye-opening and very pleasant experience.

Monday June 1st

The following morning when the train stopped at one of the stations, local vendors rushed forward with bunches of beautifully coloured peonies and buckets containing cones of newspaper full of cherries. Our windows unfortunately did not open so we could only sit and watch as life in the Soviet Republic unfolded before our eyes.

The train arrived in Baku, the capital of Azerbaijan, at seven o'clock in the evening. It was nearly dark as we walked down the platform and we saw that some of the now empty 'hard' carriages had little bunches of flowers in their windows to brighten up the bleak conditions. Trying to find a stall that might sell food was my first priority but only the usual textiles, sweets and bread products were available. To my horror, I found that even the stalls containing chocolate were closed.

Soon an announcement came over the speakers saying that in one hour the Baku carriages would be removed and a new engine would arrive. As we rushed back down the platform the dining car attendant gave us a big smile and wave. Further up the train in the carriage that stores the bedding, some policemen were examining the storage area. Maybe they were searching for more 'escapees', which seemed to be the main pastime of the Russian and East German authorities. We passed a tourist shop, which was full of souvenirs from Azerbaijan, shiny tinsel material, gaudy colours and poor quality. I decided to buy an Azerbaijani shawl, which was a black-fringed piece of material covered in brightly coloured peonies. I was not really too keen on the colours but thought it might be useful in Iran. In fact, as I soon found out, the colour proved to be much too bright for the strict newly established Islamic Republic.

Passing the queue at the sugary coffee stall, we headed for the restaurant which turned out to be a large room full of small tables where a handful of people were sitting. We were led to a table in the corner just below the 'band' of Azerbaijani musicians making what could only be described as a dreadful racket. Or maybe I was just feeling grumpy and sleep-deprived but, regrettably, their enthusiasm appeared much greater than their musical talent. Ordering soup and salad we pointed to our watches trying to explain that we were in a hurry.

Immediately a steaming plate of red spicy beetroot soup appeared accompanied by a plate of celery leaves, spring onions, radishes and tomatoes. The borscht was excellent and bore no comparison to the soup on the train. When we had finished we headed back and joined the attendant on the platform outside our carriage who wanted to have a discussion in all the languages he knew, French, German and Polish. He had learned these languages because he used to work on the Moscow to Vienna train and had recently been transferred to the Tehran route. At this point in the conversation he started to sound a little nervous as he explained that he had never really left the train to see Tehran city and - sensibly enough - was very wary of the new Iranian authorities. He was not too nervous, however, about expounding his strong views on other Soviet cities but did not seem to know all that much about them, even those cities with truly great historical pasts.

Tbilisi, the capital of Georgia, he thought was interesting but when pressed for information he did not seem to know why. The Armenian capital Yerevan had 'prima' restaurants, he explained, but despite this city being a historical centre, he thought it was an uninteresting place because, as far as he was concerned, there was nothing there. The latest Soviet guidebook reiterated his point of view to some extent and only mentioned recent Soviet-style monuments rather than the ancient past glories.

An engineer from a mining area in the North of Russia joined us. He told us that he was going to Isfahan for two years to work on a mining job there; although he had heard it was a wonderful city, he was a little nervous at the thought of entering Iran. We laughed and told him he was not the only one. Our carriage seemed quite a mixture of nationalities, which was great and the attendant informed us proudly that we were being accompanied by Iranians, Russians and Estonians.

Refreshed after our break on the platform, we climbed back onto the train, somewhat apprehensively at the thought of the next part of our journey. In the corridor everyone was smiling and greeting us as we passed by - although this may have been a way of relieving their own anxiety over the customs checks that would await us the following morning.

The attendant offered to hide our beer and ham in ice in his compartment. It was becoming exhausting trying to work out and fit in with the particular requirements of various governments. As we were not all sure exactly what was in store for us the following day, our sleep was a little fretful that night.

Tuesday June 2nd

The countryside was getting more beautiful and interesting as each hour went by. On one side of the train were weird and wonderful rock formations and on the other, groups of people were standing watching the train as it sped by. We seemed to be passing along the Iranian border all morning. In front of an electrified fence was a neatly raked border of earth and every now and then a Soviet soldier was seen raking the soil or working on the fence. From time to time a lookout post on stilts, reminiscent of those along the Berlin wall, appeared and a second fence seemed to be protecting the initial one. The attendant brought the ham and we ate some with a chunk of bread and packed the rest back into the bag with the beer, keeping our fingers crossed as we returned the bag to the attendant.

Sometimes the border was fortified with as many as four fences, then a river and the Iranian mountains. When I was saw all of this I really was quite fearful about the fortified prison we were about to enter. My apprehension subsided a little, however, when occasionally we glimpsed a small Iranian town built of mud and stone high up on the side of a hill. The sight of the little houses made everything seem normal again.

The attendant managed to put the window down and we heard a strange noise, which sounded a little like an army of cicadas, but it turned out to be the hum of the electric fence, not the exotic sound of insects. Finally, we passed under a tunnel, chiselled deep under the mountain and emerged to a spectacular view of the Araxes River. We had arrived at the border. Suddenly there was a mad rush for the bathrooms as everyone realised the length of time the next stop was likely to take. The train slowed down to a halt and the bathrooms were locked.

A surly taciturn individual, the Russian 'boss man' entered the train, took the passports, said nothing and walked off. At this point the customs arrived, and when we said 'diplomatic,' the custom official checked us off against a list asking how many bags we were carrying and whether we had any roubles. Meanwhile we could see that every item was being examined in all the other compartments. Every book was taken out of cases and carefully scrutinised. From time to time books were handed over to receive an even more thorough check from the 'boss man.'

Soviet soldiers started tapping the wheels and checking under the train and a final inspection involved checking compartments in the ceiling of the corridor. The thought of a tiny Russian hiding in the small space above our heads, trying to smuggle himself into a war-torn Islamic Republic was really too much for me. I tried to look serious and stifle a smile. The Soviet guard gave me a suspicious look. Maybe he too thought it was all rather ridiculous or more likely he dare not think at all in case he thought himself out of the system. No one or no thing was found so the passports were returned but there was a final flurry of activity when one passenger discovered he had no stamp and rushed off the train to show this to the guards.

10. REVOLUTIONARY GUARDS

It was getting hotter all the time and flies were beginning to swarm around. Backing out of the station the train started to cross the bridge spanning the river, which was, in fact the border. A Soviet jeep followed the train down under the bridge to the riverbed, it then reversed quickly and drove back. An empty Russian champagne bottle was thrown out of the window followed by an assortment of wine bottles. I checked my clothes were covering me in a suitably Islamic fashion and sat and waited in trepidation for my first live encounter with a Revolutionary Guard. The train stopped and the custom men and army arrived. They were very polite with big smiles. 'Irlanda' seemed to be the magic word.

Unfortunately nothing could be taken for granted in the new Iranian Republic and the next encounter was far less cheerful. The revolutionaries burst in, one man in ordinary clothes and one large unfriendly looking man in khaki fatigues with a black moustache, a jagged scar across his cheek and an AK47 slung over his shoulder. They exuded the rough, emotionally charged arrogance of new boys in the power game, which contrasted with the ice-cold mechanised confidence of the Soviet guards. I was not quite sure which demeanour was more frightening, although probably the unpredictability of the new Iranian elite was more dangerous. Our passports were taken from us and Niall and I tried to practice a few words of Farsi from our phrase book but there was no joy there either.

It was getting hotter and hotter. In each compartment the baggage was being examined and everyone looked very nervous, much more so than they had seemed in Russia. Scarface came back with another equally unfriendly, older man and Niall handed over his diplomatic card. The man asked where mine was but did not understand when I tried to explain that I had a diplomatic passport but I did not have a card because I was the wife, not the diplomat.

Nervously I rushed through the phrase book to find the necessary words but no luck because, of course the usual phrases in these books consisted of questions like 'can I have a cup of tea?' and 'where is the museum?' and neither of these phrases were going to be of much use in this situation. Suddenly the leader of the local Revolutionary Guards appeared. He was a young, eager-looking man who seemed extremely friendly although unfortunately he did not speak any English, which made our attempts at communication much more difficult. He moved on up the corridor quickly but despite this we still felt more hopeful.

Scarface arrived back. Watching me desperately leafing through the book he wanted to know if I spoke Persian. I shook my head and he moved off again looking totally disgruntled at the fact that he had actually acknowledged my existence. He returned shortly with the pleasant young Revolutionary Guard. They cleared part of the bunk and sat down squashing in beside Niall. The friendly guard started to fill in forms while Scarface tried to show Niall how to write in Persian. When the formalities were finished, they gathered up their papers and with a cheery wave left the compartment. We had been officially allowed into the new Islamic Republic of Iran!

The train began to move into the station past a couple of petrol dispensers and a few old tanks and then we shunted on into the siding once again to change the gauge, which is broader in Russia than in other countries. Two army men laughed and joked outside the window and I moved my seat away from view. One of them got up on top of the goods train and peered in. Foreigners were obviously a novelty after the revolution and this game of hide and seek continued for over an hour as the carriage was being gently raised.

The new undercarriage was fitted in and then the carriage was gently lowered again. The temperature was getting hotter, the flies were getting more numerous and our tempers were getting ever more frayed. We shunted back to the station and waited for the new Iranian carriages to join us. We had spent from 11 a.m. in the border town of Jolfa. Finally at 5 p.m. after six hours in the suffocating heat we set off. At this point to our great relief some cool air started blowing into the compartment.

The Iranian countryside looked amazingly beautiful. Exotic mountain formations were shadowed with a range of ever changing colours - red, green, mauve and brown. We passed close by the mud villages which we had seen from the Russian side as the train moved around in a huge loop. Everywhere appeared breathtaking in the silvery evening light. Close by Jolfa station, Iranian women in long pale grey chadors entered their houses, flashing coy smiles at the foreigners who were watching everything eagerly through the dusty windows in the corridors.

The countryside was quite wild and rugged like Afghanistan and every now and then people standing beside the train line waved a greeting. In the fields the shepherds tending their flocks of sheep also waved their arms and sticks (hopefully as a greeting rather than in anger).

Niall, meanwhile, was settling down to finish his ham and bread with a cup of tea. I noticed that there was a policeman and several guards on board who were walking up and down the train. I went to tell him to shut the compartment door.

There was a knock at the door. I stood in front of Niall to shield him (because of the ham) and whirled around to say 'salaam aleikum'. The guard looked suspiciously at Niall's tea and left. Niall hastily finished his meal. The two attendants by now had disappeared from view and their place had been taken by two old grey-haired 'Zam Zam' men.

11. ZAM ZAM MEN

The two men moved noisily and cheerfully up and down the corridor, dispensing a truly dreadful post-revolutionary drink 'Zam Zam' which tasted a little like a very sweet version of Pepsi Cola. Meanwhile the overweight dark-haired attendant, who was perspiring heavily, reappeared sullenly arguing with a passenger. When he had finished this heated discussion he ran petulantly down the corridor and could be heard locking himself into his compartment. Obviously we were all going to be looked after very well for the rest of this trip!

We had, of course, forgotten about the 'Zam Zam' man who suddenly entered the compartment to seek recompense for the bottles he had given to us earlier. He would not take money but seemed to be asking for something else. After several minutes of persistent gesture, we realised he wanted some perfume. The only perfume I had was the unopened bottle of French perfume I had bought on the boat. He accepted this with great thanks and expressions of devotion. That was definitely my most expensive fizzy drink ever and I did not even like the stuff!

To our horror, the Zam Zam man returned five minutes later with yet another bottle of the awful 'Zam Zam.' He then re-appeared with plates of chicken and steak for the Revolutionary Guards in the next compartment. Oh, to be a Revolutionary Guard! It certainly looked and smelled like the best food we had seen since we left Moscow four days earlier.

There were no more pictures of Lenin in the stations, now small pictures of Ayatollah Khomeini were printed onto the walls. During the night there was not too much activity but I was still relieved to see the policeman and guards all leave the train at the northern Iranian city of Tabriz.

Wednesday June 3rd

By morning the Zam Zam men thankfully had also disappeared and our attendant returned to bring us tea, which we drank with the last pieces of our fruit and nut chocolate from Moscow. The countryside was becoming more desert-like. The odd sheep led along by small children and groups of mud houses, screened by poplar trees, appeared every now and then as the railway line ran through the brown and ochre, rocky Elborz mountains which in winter would be covered with gleaming white snow. I changed out of my jeans and tee shirt back into my pale-pink cotton dress in an attempt to look more respectable and sat back to take in the final stretch of our journey.

We were five hours late, which I suppose was not too bad for a four-day journey. Soon the outskirts of Tehran were reached. Elegant houses came into view. They were surrounded by large verdant gardens filled with trees, colourful flowering bushes and swimming pools. Then a few minutes later the burst of colour changed to grey as we passed dreary unfinished apartment blocks, cranes still in position, girders rusting. A city stuck in time!

As we started to slow down coming into the station, young boys ran alongside the train shouting slogans and throwing stones at the window. It seemed that the Soviet Union was no more popular in Iran than America, the 'Great Satan'. This was not a reassuring start to the idea of home for the next few years and I started to feel a little tearful as the strain of the long journey finally got to me. We gathered all our luggage and stepped down onto the platform. All around us were families waiting to meet passengers off the train but we could see no one waiting to meet us. The platform cleared and we were on our own.

After another period of time, which seemed like hours, Niall recognised a straight-backed grey-haired man walking towards us. He introduced himself as Archie, the Armenian driver at the Irish Embassy. Niall had met him on his previous visit to Tehran a few months earlier and was quite amused when Archie's first and only comment was that the train was five hours late. Maybe the delay explained his morose expression or alternatively, as he didn't look too happy to see me, maybe he just felt he was too important to drive women. In fact, Archie turned out to be both work-shy and fairly hot-tempered and - as for driving wives - well, that too was way down his list of favourite occupations.

12. MURDER MYSTERY

Wednesday June 3rd 1981

We arrived in Tehran on Niall's thirty second birthday. Getting into the car outside the railway station we embarked on a silent journey back to the embassy. The journey was a blur of revolutionary slogans and wall painting; even the walls of the magnificent mosques were disfigured with graffiti. This was so different to our stay in Tehran several years previously and it all reminded me of my time in Belfast at the beginning of the seventies. It seemed to be a way of expressing a sense of both frustration and victory for a group who had earlier felt they had no real voice in society.

In the North of Ireland I had always marvelled at the creativity and talent of the artists and I would feel the same way about the talent of the artists in Iran. The content of the pictures, however, although equally disturbing, did not seem quite so original or creative maybe because they were inspired more by governmental pressure than by individual passion or ideals.

The streets of Tehran seemed less clean and orderly than three years earlier when we had last been here on our way home from Japan - but I suppose that was to be expected after several years of violent revolution and war. Huge pictures of the Shah had obviously been replaced by those of a new leader, Ayatollah Ruhollah Khomeini, whose steely eyes seemed to bore into one's soul. This replacement of dominant personalities was beginning to seem similar to the story of the Soviet Union where decades previously the Czar had been replaced by Lenin. Very soon the communist idealists had turned into a communist elite, becoming even more autocratic than the Czar. Only time would tell if the same would happen here but already the signs were beginning to appear.

Unlike before on my previous visit, I could see very few women in Western clothes nor could I see too many men in business suits. The new uniform appeared to be jeans, open-necked shirts and unkempt beards for men, and black dusty chadors or long grey or black coats, trousers and headscarves for women. In previous times Iranian women had been among the most beautiful, elegant and glamorous in the world; now they were still very beautiful but seemed, at least on the streets, to have completely changed from glamorous to dowdy.

It was, of course, only the wealthy who had spent their money on haute couture in Paris and it was the wealthy that had lived well under the Shah, not the majority of the people. For this reason, therefore the revolution had enjoyed a great deal of support among students, poorer people and some intellectuals – the basic mainstay of many a revolution. Sadly, however, I felt that once again many of the poor people would gain very little from the revolution. In the short term there could be an increase in self-esteem in line with the vilification of the upper classes but it was difficult to see how ordinary people would benefit materially, especially when there were such food shortages.

We soon arrived at the Irish Embassy. It was a small villa in Razaneh Shomali, a side street in the quiet district of Mirdamad. The chancery was downstairs and the residence upstairs but it could only be reached by an external staircase behind iron railings. Archie let us in the main door of the embassy and went to get our bags. We stood there in the foyer, feeling a little shell-shocked after our long journey. We were joined by the two remaining members of staff, Latif and Esther. It began to feel like a scene from a murder mystery. Here we were, thousands of miles from home in the midst of a revolution. We had very primitive communication links to the wider world and we were about to attempt to manage an embassy on our own for the next few years with only a skeleton team of local staff.

I had run the psychology department of a big psychiatric hospital in Dublin before my previous posting to Japan but I was not sure that was going to help. I would probably have been more suited to this current post if I had been the hospital chef rather than the psychologist. Although when I saw the embassy staff I began to revise my opinion and think that my psychological training might be very useful after all. The three members of staff on whom we would have to rely for everything, including our personal safety until we began know the system, stared at us with blank faces and a semblance of wary smiles.

The embassy had been without any diplomatic personnel for nearly two years and the local staff had become accustomed to doing very little work. It was, of course, difficult for them to meet their new boss but I still got the distinct impression that we were in the way and spoiling their daily routine. Latif, the Pakistani man who looked after the residence, stood there smiling. He seemed very obsequious but I noticed that although his mouth was smiling his eyes were not and appeared quite dark and sinister, as if he was hiding some terrible secret. Years later he was to be found dead in his room from a drug overdose.

Esther, the secretary, was an Armenian born-again Christian. Very prim, she was dressed in a full skirt, cardigan and demure high-necked blouse. In her hand she held a bible, which she played with as if it would ward off any evil the newcomers had brought with them. When she later learned of my interest in Zen Buddhism because of my time in Japan, she was convinced that she had been right all along – I was a child of Satan. Even worse she felt she had to save me; but sadly for her I was a lost cause.

That first day she couldn't stand still but kept hopping nervously from foot to foot. Her sweet voice belied an iron will, which I would soon realise when she was trying to get us all to read the bible. Archie the misogynist driver soon gave up attempting to smile and began glowering as he moved over to sit behind his desk, no doubt plotting his revenge on any women he might have to drive. The three members of staff just stared at us. It was starting to feel very weird and all the murder mysteries I had read were beginning to look very tame when I compared them with our situation in Tehran.

The final straw was when Esther let out a high-pitched scream and dropped her bible. Three huge, shiny, black cockroaches were scampering happily across the carpet to meet us. My immediate thought was that at least some members of the embassy appeared pleased to see us. Whatever the reason for their sudden appearance, however, it caused quite a stir. Latif picked up a large shovel from under Archie's desk – this was obviously an on-going occurrence - and ran in all directions making wild ineffectual swipes which missed their target completely. At this point, not sure whether to laugh or cry, we politely declined a cup of tea and left the office in a hurry to go upstairs to the residence in the vain hope that huge cockroaches had not made their home there as well.

Happy birthday Niall! Hopefully tomorrow will to be a new day.

13. BODIES IN THE TEAPOT

June 1981

The embassy, at that time, was a villa close to a wide leafy avenue leading to the cool, shaded northern suburbs of Tehran. The foyer opened onto offices which led out into the small garden where colourful flowering bushes surrounded a small blue-tiled swimming pool. In the foyer a cactus garden flourished behind a glass shaft, which led up to the upper floor. Beside this area was the telex room. In those days there was no internet or mobile phone and the local radio stations were of little value. As a result of this, Niall would spend a lot of his time attempting to tune into the BBC World Service which could only be accessed occasionally.

Most normal people would be horrified by this situation where they were cut off from the rest of the world but obviously, not being normal, I loved it. It was like being on a desert island. Niall had to take responsibility for the embassy and its occupants so he was a little more circumspect about the situation but I was in my element. We had to wait until the following morning to get the news from the previous day, which in a dangerous revolution is not ideal but we soon learned how to break into the local rumour mill.

The telephone system worked spasmodically and was undoubtedly listened to by the Iranian security services. Any confidential messages were sent in the Irish language which was deemed to be the safest form of information transmission (although the Israelis were believed to be capable of translating it!). So the communication system was not great but the condition of the downstairs kitchen was even worse.

A corridor led to the kitchen, which had been requisitioned by a small army of cockroaches, some of whom we had become acquainted with on our first day. Others just pushed their antennae through the small metal grills covering the drains on the kitchen floor, waving them with great enthusiasm as if defiantly letting us know of their presence. It was a constant battle trying to rid the kitchen of these persistent creatures but every few weeks a cockroach elimination process was put into action. Fortunately, the kitchen was only used for making tea and coffee for the office.

The next few days after our arrival were quite uneventful almost feeling like the calm before the storm. Niall started to organise the chancery - not an easy task after nearly two years without any diplomatic staff - while I checked the residence. This too was not in a great state because it had not been looked after for several years. The cream wool curtains had been newly cleaned before our arrival and were now at half-mast and the inner voile curtains were hanging forlornly six inches below them. The once-lovely cream sofas and armchairs were streaked with dust and sand marks and there would be no replacements in the middle of a war-torn revolution. The next task, therefore, would be to rectify the situation as quickly and easily as possible by the use of colourful throws and any other techniques that might come to mind.

It was slowly dawning on me that I would also have to get used to the cooking and kitchen arrangements. The kitchen upstairs was a large open space, thankfully as yet with no apparent residents from the cockroach community. The cooking implements, however, were not great and the cooker only worked when it felt like it, which like the embassy staff, was not too often. On top of that there were at times several power cuts a day, not to mention the many stoppages in the water supply. The most alarming of which was not the water shortages but was when there had been a landslide into the reservoir, which had taken a whole army camp with it. The radio warned us that until the dead bodies of the soldiers had been removed we should not drink the tap water, which normally was fine to drink. I was standing in the kitchen about to make tea, when that news came through. In horror I stared at the dripping taps. Water shortages were one thing but dead bodies in the teapot were quite another!

Tehran is at quite a high altitude, which altered the cooking time for various dishes, especially baked dishes; also it was difficult to find ingredients. Consequently my home-made bread was as hard as a rock and my quiches, which had been quite acceptable in other countries, turned into a soggy mess in Iran. Cooking, however, has never been my strong point so maybe I was just looking for an excuse to explain my culinary disasters.

In the first few days, Niall met up with other European chargés, to try to get some understanding of what was really happening. The message seemed to be that everything was improving, everyone was more relaxed and there were fewer religious restrictions. In the northern areas of Tehran I could walk in the street in a short-sleeved shirt and midi-skirt.

We learned a few weeks later how wrong this original analysis of the situation would prove to be. I very soon met some women from the Irish community whose knowledge of the situation and advice on the local shops would be invaluable, especially as there were very few diplomatic wives at that time. Initially Niall made contact with the British and Belgian Embassies and I met Maureen, a Belgian national, who worked at the Belgian Embassy. There were already some Irish businessmen in Tehran who were either trying to get new business or to be paid for previous deals. When they heard the embassy had been reopened they immediately came around to see if they could get some assistance in their dealings with the many very difficult government offices.

14. HEADSCARF IN THE SOUP

Sunday June 7th
Went to 11 o'clock mass in the lovely chapel at the Italian Embassy and got some food at the local supermarket, which was not at all well stocked and reminded me of the shops in Russia. I rang Maureen who said her husband had broken his toe and she has been very busy and will meet up as soon as she can. After an afternoon swimming, I watched a sad pre-revolutionary video of famous Iranian singers who had either left or been executed. After a long history of fine Persian music, there is no longer any music played in public as it is not regarded as Islamic.

A Belgian journalist dropped in for coffee and told us that journalists are not allowed to talk to anyone in the government any more. Things were really starting to get bad.

Monday June 8th
I went to the zoo with Archie. It was rather run-down but quite interesting to see the typical Iranian respect - or lack of it - for animals as a child stoned a zebra without any reprimand from his parents. All the women were wearing chadors, which was a little worrying in regard to reports that the situation was becoming more liberal. Suddenly a cheeky little goat with long ears, much bigger than himself squeezed through the bars. To my amazement, Archie showed a softer side to his personality as he picked him up and gently pushed him back through the bars. Very, very hot in the midday sun. I probably will not be going there again as the animals are not really being properly looked after. Unfortunately, neither are the visitors.

In the evening, I felt a craving for chocolate and meat. As usual anything that is not readily available is always more attractive. Set off for the Hilton hotel. Man on the door says I have to wear a scarf. This is definitely a new approach. I am already wearing a long sleeved cardigan, no make-up and feeling very warm even though the sun has gone down. Niall calls for the manager who insists that I may offend the Iranian women. Meanwhile, a group of Iranian women who are standing behind us, all of them covered in make-up and none of them wearing headscarves hastily put on their scarves. We decide any pleasure we might get from the meal would be ruined by the headscarf trailing into the soup so we set off for the Sheraton.

No one on guard at the entrance to the hotel and it appears to be full for the first time, mostly with lots of Iranian women who are wearing very little and looking with amusement at my long cardigan. They have obviously also decided that the Hilton is not the place to be. A few western businessmen are dotted around the place looking quite bemused at the whole situation. We try a beef teriyaki which is disappointing but satisfied my need for a substantial meal.

Tuesday June 9th

Niall goes to a meeting at the Belgian Embassy. In the afternoon he plays tennis with Jan the chargé d'affaires in the luxuriant gardens of the Belgian residence, which is a magnificent house in the North of Tehran. I go swimming in our garden. The electricity as usual goes off 2 or 3 times in the day. We are getting used to this daily occurrence but it really is quite uncomfortable in the heat when the fans don't work, not to mention the fridge and cooker!

Wednesday June 10th

I go with Archie to shop in Naft street. The first time I've seen meat in the shops. I get some T-bone steak and a piece of beef fillet. The electricity has gone off of course and all the food will soon be slowly defrosting in the freezer. We go down town to get a paper shredder; and a manual typewriter because of electricity cuts. Today the vegetables look fresh rather than shrivelled which is a lovely change. We see men lying exhausted in the heat of Ramadan under the bridge. It is particularly difficult for them in this heat, as they cannot even drink water until the sun goes down.

The diplomatic bag is finally collected from the airport. There is a letter from Niall's friend saying he's not coming over because of the political situation and a letter from Professor William Johnson with whom I lectured in Sophia University in Tokyo. He wants to know how we are getting on. After a week we do not even know ourselves how we are getting on!

Cook the steak, it tastes like reconstituted meat but we are grateful for any food at the moment, we sit out on the balcony looking across to the trees, which are covered with clouds of bright green parakeets all the way to the British Embassy grounds at Golhak. A very pleasant Iranian family are eating opposite and wave at us across the street. When we go to bed the electricity goes off again but the mosquitoes are still biting and we cannot plug in our electric 'Pif Paf' pads to zap the mozzies. The mosquitoes come out every night to feast on our flesh, so any loss of electricity is difficult. Apparently there is no risk of malaria, nevertheless I'm afraid we are becoming addicted to our killer Pif Paf pads and I am not sure what the chemical vapours might be doing to us.

Friday June 12th

The weekend in Iran is Friday and Saturday so we can rest in the morning after our nightly battle with the mosquitoes and a leisurely breakfast followed by a swim. Go to the New Zealand Embassy for a reading of a New Zealand play, sit out on the grass. A Swiss diplomat who, because there are no longer any American diplomats in Tehran, is looking after the American interests section and his Australian wife come back for drinks. Some bottles of whiskey have been left behind in the storeroom so I make my first Irish coffees since arriving in Iran. The cream is not so rich and swirls to the bottom of the glass: it's not a great success but once again any gesture is appreciated in Iran.

15. DEATH ON A SUMMER AFTERNOON
Saturday June 13th

Early in the morning I try to make a quiche for our picnic but the oven is not very effective, The quiche is not a great success and my attempt at a cake is only fit for the bin. Meet Don and Pat at British embassy and pile into their Land Rover with their nanny and baby. Niall is navigating and we get lost heading out of town, past Niavaron Palace. See the usual beautiful mountain formations, not a cloud in the sky and then notice the highly suspicious looks as we pass through the villages. This is probably because since the revolution the local Iranians have not seen many foreigners. Try to find somewhere to eat our food surreptitiously (Ramadan has started). We find a little tree by a stream where a stone pen and signs of a fire suggest that this is a favourite local picnic spot. Pat feeds the baby and we wander off but too hot to go far. Every now and again lines of donkeys, led by women, pass by and we make sure that we hide our pieces of melon and sandwiches and of course our soggy quiche. Heading off for the dam, we ask directions from an old man. 'Why do you want water'? the old man asks suspiciously. (Ramadan again). When told we only wanted to see the dam not drink it, he told us the way but the road was blocked. So we set off back to Tehran.

In the evening we go to a party to say goodbye to a French diplomat that we did not know. Meeting people from the Lebanese Embassy we plan a holiday through Cyprus and Beirut. This does not happen because in the eighties Beirut becomes very dangerous and the hostage-taking begins. Wild dancing (I don't have the energy for that) to Brazilian music.

Set off at 2a.m. on the expressway and run into five groups of Pasdaran and Hezbollah with guns, searching every car. Quite frightening, we wonder what has happened.

Sunday June 14th

BBC says mass executions and arrests yesterday, which would explain the late-night activity. Go to Italian church at 11, very depressed at the news. In the early evening go for a concert in the British Embassy, which at least means we can have a break from the constant discussions about the terrible situation. On our way we heard lots of shooting in the centre of the city, while on our way back we came across a car in the middle of a crossroads. The doors were flung wide open and the car stretched right across the road holding up all the traffic. Then a man appeared holding an ice cream in his hand. laughing at all the irate drivers he got into his car and drove away with a gleeful wave. It was probably his way of dealing with stress but he certainly managed to induce tension in a lot of other people.

Today would be the start of violent, open conflict between the Islamic fundamentalists and the leftist activists aligned with the Mujahideen-e-Khalq and the communist Tudeh party. This violence would spread and intensify.

Thursday June 18th
Niall is sick all night with terrible stomach pains. In the morning, I hear a loud bang coming from the bathroom and find Niall lying on the bathroom floor. His stoical explanation so as not to worry me, was that he was lying down on the cool tiles to rest. In fact he had fainted from dehydration. As soon as she heard about this, Esther informed us how the locals dealt with stomach problems. The first step, she explained, is to cut out all food and open a sugary fizzy drink to let out the fizz. That will help the patient regain energy and hydration. Next the Iranians boil some dried limes and rock sugar in water and drink that delicious concoction. Finally when there is some improvement, boiled rice and natural yoghurt are introduced. (I have continued to use this method over the years and it has never failed and seems much superior to a diet of dry toast.)

A businessman rings from the airport to tell Niall that the authorities will not let him change his money or take it out of the airport. Gerry who works with Bord Bainne, the Irish Dairy Board, comes round waiting for a phone call all day. Niall is still in bed feeling terrible and trying to drink his glass of lime and sugar. Maybe it is a change of food and water or more infections around after the revolution or just the heat but Niall is frequently getting sick since his arrival in Iran.

In the evening a 'mini hurricane' blows up and the area is battered with heavy rain and strong winds. The electricity goes off three times, no coffee, no lunch and no dinner. I eat bread and cheese and Niall drinks more lime juice.

Gerry phoned from the hotel for the telephone number of one of the Irish businessmen. Reluctantly, feeling rather scared, I go down the external stairs to the chancery armed with torches to search for the number in the dark. Finally I find the book of telephone numbers in Esther's desk, lock the door and run up the outer stairs as fast as I can, nearly squashing a stray cat on the way. I'm really fed up and I think next time Gerry needs a telephone number in the dark he can come over and find it himself.

At last Niall is starting to feel a little better. The lime 'cure' is working.

Saturday June 20th

I swim early in the morning. Maureen rings to say her Armenian hairdresser could come to the embassy any time I want. That's good because it might improve my 'dragged through a hedge' look. Went to Naft to get some food and buy an iron and found a great flower shop. At least there was no flower shortage in Tehran. The shop overflowed with bursts of colour. Lemon roses won the prize for best scent and stately white lilies for beauty. The flowers were wrapped in tissue paper with lots of multi-coloured satin ribbons. Standing in the calm atmosphere, enveloped by the exotic scents, I could not have imagined the carnage that would follow in the late afternoon when we set off for the lecture on Ferdowsi at the French Cultural Institute.

Ferdowsi was a renowned master of the epic poem and wrote 'The Epic of Kings' or 'Shah Nameh' which told the stories and exploits of the great mythological kings, such as Jamshid, who founded Iran. It was my first real trip to the centre of the city and I was very keen to see this historic part of town and to get some insight into the Persian culture of previous centuries. Instead we ran foul of the previously mentioned violence (described in the first chapter), trapping us in our car. Now, however, surrounded by chaos, there no longer seemed much point in trying to reach the French Cultural Institute in the middle of a deadly feud. The peace of a sunlit afternoon had been shattered.

That night we were both feeling subdued as we entered the embassy and an all too familiar sinking feeling began in the pit of my stomach. Niall and I had met at Queen's University in Belfast in the early seventies were Niall was completing his Ph.D. in biochemistry and I was working on a fellowship on schizophrenia. Sadly, both of us were used to violence; although being familiar is one thing, feeling comfortable with violence is quite another. The nightmare, however, appeared to be over as we swung through the embassy gates and went upstairs to the residence to make a comforting cup of tea. Nevertheless, we had a strong feeling that this particular incident was just temporarily on hold and it would need more than warm tea to wipe it out next time.

We had arrived in Tehran only three weeks before this afternoon of violence and had been assured by everyone we met that this was a good time to come to Iran because the situation was finally changing for the better. The new government was settling in, women were coming out of their chadors and the American hostages had been released. In fact, after two years of executions and terrible violence, the revolution was appearing to be a success. Then to everyone's dismay, sporadic shooting attacks started in the daytime, like the one we had just witnessed and Ramadan heralded a round of new clampdowns, particularly in regard to women. Within a few days, women were ordered to wear chadors and were not allowed to show even a strand of hair in public. The Revolutionary Guards sniffed under women's armpits to check that they were not using deodorant and roughly wiped their victims' faces clean of any make-up. Finally they resorted to harassing women at gunpoint.

Unaware then of the massive consequences of the day's events - yet still with some feelings of trepidation - we quickly changed and once again set off in the car, this time for dinner at Golhak, the Summer Residence of the British Embassy. I was really quite scared and shaken by the day's events but maybe as a psychologist I always try not to show my distress. I knew from my experience in various violent incidents in Belfast, however, that it would take some time to come to terms with the day's events.

16. TOAD ALERT

In June 1892 Gertrude Bell wrote from Golhak (Gula Hek):
'This also is pleasant: to come in at 7 o' clock in the morning after a two hours' ride, hot and dusty, and find one's cold bath waiting for one scented with delicious rose water, and after it an excellent and longed for breakfast spread in a tent in the garden.'

The grounds of the British Embassy Summer Residence at Golhak were very beautiful although there were no lights and at night it looked quite eerie. Glimpses of pale forms appeared to float between the trees in the moonlight as if the ghosts of previous centuries might be making their way to a summer ball.

On this evening, however, the only occupants of the embassy grounds appeared to be huge fleshy toads slumped lazily on the road through the grounds of the residence. Their eyes glowed malevolently, illuminated in the headlamps of our car. Seemingly glued to the road in a trance, they flopped down apparently unaware of danger as we carefully tried to drive through this badly lit obstacle course.

Don, the commercial attaché, and his wife Pat had invited the Swiss chargé d'affaires to join us for dinner so we engaged in a sombre discussion about the tragic events of the day. Our main question was how many people had been killed in the demonstration and what its repercussions would be for Iran and the world. We soon found an answer, although maybe not the complete answer, to our first question. As we talked, the Swiss Embassy duty officer rang the Swiss chargé d'affaires to say that twenty bodies were lying outside the Swiss Embassy. The French Institute was very close to the Swiss Embassy and it was only at this point that we realised how very lucky we had been to survive that day.

This latest information led on to discussions about the role of the BBC and whether or not they were really impartial – a question that for many years has been levelled at news agencies reporting from conflict areas. Many Iranians already believed that Britain had been behind the Ayatollah Khomeini's return and the downfall of the Shah. Although some government changes in different countries could definitely be attributed to the British and Americans, including the overthrow of

Iran's first democratic prime minister Mohammed Mossadegh in 1953, this could hardly be the case in relation to Khomeini. Nevertheless conspiracy theories have always abounded in Iran and Britain and America were usually at the heart of them. Both countries remained very unpopular with some groups in Iran - although ironically huge numbers still wanted to obtain British or American visas. This antipathy really only affected the lives of British diplomatic staff as of course the American Embassy in Tehran had ceased to function since the infamous storming of the embassy in 1979 when fifty of its staff were held hostage for 444 days before being released.

Pat explained to us how they still had not managed to get their personal effects out of Iranian customs. Apparently the truck carrying their container had been held up at gunpoint several times on its route through Iran. On one occasion their goods had been unloaded and thrown down a green verge with cries of 'we hate the British'. Freezer, dishwasher and washing machine all toppled into a deep gully. That had been two weeks previously and they were still attempting to negotiate the container's release from customs. Pat intimated she was not in fact too worried about the electrical gadgets but she was upset about the missing cot and other items for Stephen, her baby son.

Niall and I looked at each other in horror. If they tipped our 'furniture' out on a grass verge, they would find more than they bargained for - in the shape of a large wooden box marked 'furniture and books' which actually contained bottles of Irish whiskey. In those days, before the advent of sophisticated German scanning machines, most diplomats brought their alcohol supplies into the country by such subterfuges. Happily most local officials ignored this – unless of course they had a specific reason to make problems for the country in question.

As we made our way back through the embassy gates, we saw several squashed toads flattened on the pathway in front of us. That was the sum total of casualties in the British embassy that day. Sadly, I knew that there would be a much larger toll of crushed and dying bodies in the city that night.

17. CANADIAN HOSTAGES

Sunday June 21st

Stories came in fast and furious the following morning as the magnitude of Saturday's events became clear. Typically in conflict situations there would always be different strands of information from various sectors of local society which were often more reliable than the official line. The first piece of information that Sunday morning was from what was to be one of our prime sources of information: the secretarial rumour machine. Esther, Niall's Armenian secretary, told us that a local employee of the Australian Embassy was checking to see if his brother was among the 20 unidentified bodies lying on the floor of the mosque. She went on to describe how her own brother had seen fifty bodies outside the Armenian church and estimated that as many as three hundred protesters could have been killed. The official toll according to the BBC was thirty dead, although official numbers were often underestimated; trying to get accurate information was to become very much a guessing game.

Niall had a frustrating early morning meeting with the Iranian Tobacco Company. He had taken some samples of Irish cigarettes and was trying to get some business for Carroll's cigarettes who were producing a much higher quality product than the Iranian group. The Irish technology in the manufacture of cigarettes was superior to that of Iran as was the tobacco quality. Niall's efforts did not seem to be working but he decided he would try again at a later date.

In the office there was a continuing saga of the diplomatic bag. it had either not arrived at the airport or there was a conspiracy and the officials were refusing to hand it over. Archie, our Armenian driver, was not too pleased at these continual visits to the airport, preferring to sit at his desk, drinking tea and looking important. That particular evening, Archie was in a better mood because he was taking us to a piano recital in the Canadian Embassy.

Archie was not too keen on work outside office hours but he liked to meet his fellow drivers at embassy functions. The recital was given by the Danish Ambassador who was an accomplished pianist and the concert was held in the Canadian Embassy because Canadian interests were being looked after by Denmark after all the Canadian diplomats had left the country.

The reason for the Canadian departure was that during the American hostage crisis two years previously six members of the consular section had left the US embassy by the side door as the students broke through the main entrance. They were sheltered by the Canadians and a complex plan was organised by the CIA in which the hostages managed to escape as part of a Canadian 'film crew'. (This escape was documented decades later in the film Argo and was probably the only impressive part of the CIA's operations during the hostage crisis. Certainly the US military's brave but shambolic attempt to free the hostages by helicopter proved to be a disaster, leading to the death of eight Americans.)

After the concert we were shown the hiding place of the American consular officials, in a room under the stairs. We did not hear too many details about the escape which was kept secret for some time but we did learn that the hero of the situation was the unassuming first secretary not, as the film implied, the Canadian Ambassador.

Much of the discussions during that first summer were about hostages because everyone was keenly aware that, in view of the unpredictable situation in Tehran, being taken as a hostage could happen again to anyone. It was a short time since the release of the American hostages and many of the diplomats knew Bruce Langan the former American Chargé. He had been in the Foreign Ministry at the time of the takeover and had remained there until the rest of the embassy staff were released after four hundred and forty four days. This was several months before our arrival but the hostage crisis was still an important topic of conversation.

It was this backdrop of violence and uncertainty that would make so-called 'normal' diplomatic life seem so strange. Several days after the unnerving afternoon in downtown Tehran, we began the diplomatic merry-go-round when we attended a reception at the Italian Embassy. After our previous experience it seemed quite a surreal event. We stood with a group of other diplomats upstairs on the balcony overlooking the beautiful garden, as men in formal suits and women wearing pale pastel-coloured dresses drifted across the manicured lawns. Waiters walked around with silver trays of wine and champagne and the dignified Italian Ambassador Francisco Mezzalama and his wife welcomed the guests.

This glamour and formality was reminiscent of our previous posting in Japan but here it was slightly different. It was more like Germany in the 1930s where some people lived in denial of the appalling political reality. Scenes of desperate violence and scenes of opulent denial - I suddenly realised - were to be my life for the next several years.

18. WHERE IS PRESIDENT BANISADR?

Monday June 22nd

The Ayatollah Khomeini dismissed President Abolhassan Banisadr (the first Iranian President following the revolution) after he had been impeached in the Majlis the previous day. Exiled by the Shah, Banisadr had returned to Iran with the Ayatollah but seems to have been more of a socialist than an Islamist. Although his name was on everyone's lips, Banisadr had not been seen for nearly two weeks. Another game of hide and seek was evolving and rumours about his disappearance seemed to be the most important topic of conversation.

As the day cooled we decided to go for a walk in the local area. Just around the corner an Iranian woman quietly asked did we have any dollars. She was an educated woman, not asking for charity but wanting to buy dollars in order to leave the country. There were a lot of foreign exchange restrictions so it was a difficult time for the Iranians who were used to international travel. A little further on we heard shooting and saw motorbikes and truckloads of revolutionary militia who were driving around the square shooting in the air. It was a little frightening because the men looked far too young and enthusiastic to be trusted with such dangerous weapons.

In this part of Tehran there were many shops filled with fancy clothes, jewellery and cosmetics and several places still looked just like Paris or London. It certainly did not look as if this area was in the throes of a revolution. This was old stock, however, and probably would not be renewed with any more foreign items. A little farther on was a less cosmopolitan area, open - fronted food shops sat beside hardware and Islamic clothes shops. Aware of the dark stares we were getting we quickly decided it was not too safe to hang around.

Niall went back to set up the coding machine so that he could start sending coded messages to the Department of Foreign Affairs in the hope that his secret reports of meetings with Iranian ministers, European Heads of Mission and descriptions of the political situation would remain secret.

Archie returned from the airport looking very disgruntled to explain that once again he had been sent on an impossible mission. He had been searching for a apparently non-existent diplomatic bag, which was meant to arrive every week but had either been mislaid at the airport or not sent at all. Either way it gave Archie an excuse to complain.

During the night another bad storm broke the stifling heat as the streaks of lightning lit up the surrounding gardens. Crashes of thunder disturbed our sleep all night long.

Tuesday June 23rd

We are all still reeling from the downtown massacre on Saturday but we have to get on with the mundane task of fixing the embassy. The old-fashioned oven was still not working so Archie and I dropped Niall off at a Heads of Mission meeting and continued on to deliver a letter to the foreign ministry. Our plan was to look for a new cooker and dishwasher. We got caught in a traffic jam on the bridge, which was quite close to the shooting incident of the previous Saturday. Below the bridge there were more demonstrators chanting slogans and we tried to double back but after leaving the bridge we ran into more traffic jams from an accident. This was, definitely, getting to be a case of '*déja vu*'.

Two truckloads of Hezbollah suddenly drove up, shouting and shooting. I sat in the car outside the foreign ministry feeling a little vulnerable until I saw the army headquarters on the other side. Somehow the official army seemed a much safer proposition than the rag-tag bunch of revolutionaries who were driving around, shouting and shooting.

Archie returned to the car and by now it was too late to go to look for a cooker. It seemed that I was never able to get the items I was looking for but at least I was getting involved in a sociological study of a city in the midst of revolution. We drove back to collect Niall at the Italian Embassy and I sat in the car writing my diary. As we arrived the different drivers were waiting outside the embassy lounging against their cars or standing chatting and smoking. Maybe that's why embassy drivers seem to know so much about what is going on. One rather disinterested policeman, who was meant to be guarding the embassy building, seemed more keen to prop up the wall and play with his gun than to involve himself in guard duty. In the street there was a more inspiring scene where a bird was singing beautifully in a cage high up on a balcony. The Iranians were very fond of their birds and it was a delight to hear birds singing even if only in cages.

All around the old houses look like those in any sleepy provincial French town apart from the occasional sight of a woman in a black chador. I was watching from the car as the British chargé d'affaires set off accompanied by an armed guard. It always seemed to me that armed guards point people out as targets, rather than protect them.

Niall finally came out and we at last were able to check out equipment for the kitchen. The cookers were not great, so we would have to try other places; unfortunately everything was very expensive because they were the last foreign items in stock. We ended up getting some emergency lights for the frequent electricity breakdowns and some black lacquered Japanese trays.

In the afternoon I sat in the sun, reading and swimming in the small pool, which cooled me down after the frazzled morning. A telex arrived to say our belongings had arrived in Rotterdam. It would be great to get our things but we still probably had some time to wait until they arrived; even then we would have to deal with Iranian bureaucracy.

In the late afternoon I set off to meet the Irish wives in one of their houses. The walls outside the apartment were covered in revolutionary slogans. It was across the road from a boys school run by the Christian Brothers so maybe that accounted for the extra graffiti. Once again the main topic of conversation was the political situation. The expatriate wives were very worried but also quite resilient. Some were newly married like Lorraine and others like Jacqui had been settled there for many years. Ali, Jacqui's husband, was an interesting Professor of Linguistics at Tehran University who felt that the Iranians would have to suffer for many years. Sadly he did not realise how true his prophecy would be.

That day there had been a lot of trouble although I had not been aware of anything. The previous day eight people had been executed including a journalist and a poet who had been a friend of Ali. All of these men had spent most of their lives in the dreaded Evin Prison, persecuted by the Shah and now they had finally been killed by the opponents of th e Shah. It seemed very ironic and very sad. The day before that, sixteen people had been executed in Evin. It was all so arbitrary that the guards did not even know their names and had to ask their parents to bring along identity. Sometimes they would throw the dead body outside the gates of the home of the executed individual with a note attached to the body asking for the price of the bullets used to kill them. These young people were suspected of being leftist or belonging to the communist Tudeh party. The Americans and British did not want the communists to take over, thinking that Iran would become a client state of the Soviet Union but what they failed to recognise was that the threat from the mullahs could ultimately be even more damaging to their interests.

Everyone was very upset that afternoon. It was horrible to hear about the executions in Evin, the Kafkaesque prison in the foothills of the mountains north of Tehran. The group of Irish women were also afraid for their own safety and that of their children as another story described how an English girl, on stepping out of a taxi, was chased by pro-regime militants. She escaped into a shop where the owner hid her and another foreign woman. Stories of corruption also abounded, a great deal of money was being paid by Iranians to bribe some of the mullahs to reduce extortionate government fines.

On a lighter note we all had a great discussion with Ali about the similarities between Buddhism and Sufism and especially the wonderful Sufi poets such as Rumi and Omar Khayyam. The children were singing some lovely Persian songs when suddenly the mood was shattered as a clash of thunder obliterated the children's voices and an electrical storm flashed across the darkening sky. A strong wind began to whip through the trees, all of which was apparently very unusual at this time of year. We were all a little unsettled by the violence of the storm and the news that the Pasdaran would be out this evening - so the party broke up quickly and we set off down the motorway as fast as we could. The whole landscape was illuminated by lightning and the car was battered by the strong wind and rain.

There were more rumours this afternoon that one man who stood up for Banisadr had been stabbed, which is very possible as people are divided and both sides are very passionate about this case. Archie tells me that the Iranian news says Banisadr is in Cairo, West Germany or France. It now looks as if the central government has lost control of the country. That is very dangerous and Esther suggests that we should not put up the Embassy sign for protection.

More shooting at night. Esther is probably correct in her assessment of the situation.

19. BROWN SUGAR

Wednesday June 24th

The radio says there was a bombing at the station in the holy city of Qom.

'A bomb explosion in Qom railway station resulted in the martyrdom of 6 and the injury of more than 50.'

(This attack was listed in a book 'FELONIES OF THE MKO (Mujahideen-e-Khalq) TERRORISTS IN IRAN' which was sent out the following year to embassies.)

Several are dead and many injured. Unusual to hear of an attack on the holy city. To get a feeling of normality I watch a man in a nearby apartment block as he calls in his pigeons. It really feels reassuring to get involved in everyday activities in the middle of such turmoil.

Once again Archie sets of to retrieve the diplomatic bag and to try to get money belonging to one of the Irish businessmen. He achieves neither objective, which gives him extra reasons to grumble. It is very difficult to get business contracts in Iran and even more difficult to get paid for the work. Get a phone call to say one of the Irish community that I met yesterday is coming to the residence. I put down my book and go to prepare a tray of tea and biscuits. She breezes in, full of life and chatter. When I meet someone who is very chatty, I always seem to go very quiet. Still, at least she does not notice and carries on chatting away regardless. It seems her main purpose for being here is to get some Irish newspapers, which are sent out every week in the diplomatic bag. When we can find the bag that is.

I hand over all the papers we have and her next question is whether I want to teach English. I decline because I just want to steep myself in the culture as much as I can and maybe carry out some work in my own area of psychology. She tells me that would be impossible because there are too many Iranians out of work. She is right of course but still an English-speaking psychologist is always useful in a very stressful situation and I do have five years experience dealing with violence in Belfast. I offer her some tea and biscuits but she turns them down because she is into health food. Oh well, I did my best. Sitting down again with my book I eat the biscuits myself.

Thursday June 25th

There is a lot more shooting during the night and news of more executions. Archie says Banisadr is now with the Turks. Esther and I walk down to the local shops in Zafar to see what we can find. We find some glass tea cups edged in gold and a bag of brown sugar, hard as a rock, probably pre-revolution. Esther complains to the shopkeeper, as only she can, and we get a softer packet of sugar. She screams with delight when she discovers a packet of paper tissues and the shopkeeper cannot wait to get us both out of the shop.

Our next port of call is the chemist across the road and as nothing is simple when with Esther, we both fell into a djube (this is a kind of large gutter filled with rain and sometimes waste water). On this occasion it was deep and flowing with dirty water. My knee was scraped and Esther's thigh was bruised. She was very upset but the injuries were superficial and the disinfectant we got in the chemist should sort it. My leg is aching by the time we get back to the embassy so I washed and disinfected it but there was no real risk of infection because it was only superficial scraping.

In the evening we try to find the house of a British businessman. We get lost and a group of teenagers in a car try to help us but they take us round in a circle until we are back at Ali Shariati. At this point we give up and go back home. The Iranians try to be helpful but they do not want to let you know they really don't have a clue so they send everyone off in the wrong direction.

Friday June 26th
Go to meet the other diplomats at the Intercontinental Hotel because we are going for a tour to the Lar dam, which is under construction in the mountains. I'm worried because I forgot my suntan lotion. What a joke, by the end of the afternoon we will have been subjected to hailstones and freezing rain rather than burning sun. The trip to the mountains was very interesting because the mountains are a beautiful patchwork quilt of multicolours and half moon earth patterns. The old casino standing forlornly on the hill was pointed out and the odd green bush stood out on the mountains and in the valley.

Along the road, mangled remains of the metal safety fence and crashed cars are reminders to drive carefully. Scores of black sheep gather on the hillside like tiny ants as the bus climbs up and up. Passing through a pretty village we cross the river and drive up to the dam check point which is guarded by armed guards, only letting in authorised people.

We get out of the bus at a site surrounded by huts and enter a building. Along the gravel path and up the walls are lots of beautiful, immobile moths, many of these fragile creatures were soon trampled in the rush for coffee by the foreigners. Shown into what is probably the dining area for the Italian management team who are constructing the dam, we queue for a cup of cappuccino served by a pair of surly Iranians who make us wait an interminable length of time. We then enter the reading room to flick through the newspapers which date back to

February and March. Piling back into the buses and a couple of Land Rovers and we set off to view the site. By now it is extremely cold and the missing sun tan lotion would have been no use whatsoever in the rain.

On both sides of the road stunning deep red poppies brighten up our spirits although we almost miss the dam, so keen are we to discuss food shortages and especially the availability of chickens with others on the bus. Stopping to view the construction work we walk in the mud to peer at a group of Iranian nomads sitting in patched tents and surrounded by animals. We then start to return and the bus gets stuck in the mud as we go up the hill. One abandoned bus is already off the road.

The Norwegian Ambassador dressed in a chic safari suit tries to push our bus out of the mud. We all watch him out of the back window terrified he might slide under the wheels. Giant hailstones start to fall like golf balls, banging off the roof. The bus moves perilously close to the edge of the road while the Land Rover backs out of sight. We remain stuck for fifteen minutes until finally the driver frees the bus. The frozen ambassador returns to the bus to huge cheers, his beige safari suit splattered with mud. I felt we should have helped but it would really have been a pretty futile gesture.

We go back to the camp for a superb Italian lunch and play-reading. Outside there is more rain as lightning flashes across the darkening sky. The Iranian waiters stand listening to the play and the laughter of the audience with a look of total bewilderment on their faces. A boisterous singsong takes over the bus on the way back to the Intercontinental Hotel showing how everyone enjoyed themselves.

When we get back to the embassy we hear the news of a huge explosion that afternoon at a Friday prayer service. This was supposedly set off by the Mujahideen-e-Khalq using a tape recorder and that Hojatolislam Khamenei (eight years later he became the Supreme Leader) was seriously injured in this attack.[1]

---

[1] An official publication declared: The hypocrites attempted an assassiantion on the life of Tehran;s Friday Prayer Leader, Mr Khamenei, in the Bazaar Mosque after noon rtual prayers that resulted in the paralysis of his right hand.

20. TEA ON THE EMBASSY STEPS
Saturday June 27th

On the way to Biblos book shop I stop at a big supermarket. It looks like a large tent moedeled on an old traditional Iranian building. There are no foreigners to be seen, only women in long dust-edged, black chadors and I feel a bit self-conscious although I am wearing a long-sleeved cardigan. At the door I am searched but everyone appears to be quite friendly. There are huge piles of minced meat at the meat counter which the locals are buying up at a great rate but when I reached the end of the queue I was told I needed coupons.

Archie was smirking as he watched me leave the shop empty-handed because he obviously knew that the coupons were only for the families of martyrs, killed at the war front. It's a very sad situation and certainly no one would begrudge them their food coupons but it is very difficult finding any meat in this situation and soon I will have to start cooking diplomatic dinners.

Biblos is a fantastic book shop and I bumped into the Swiss diplomat from the American Interests Section, who was checking what books are still left as obviously no new books are being imported. Go to the Hilton for a coffee and cake overlooking the 'men only' swimming pool. A few small boys are splashing around supervised by a bored attendant. In the cafe there are three foreign businessmen and three Iranian girls whose choice of thick make up is a bit risky if the Pasdaran come in.

The radio blares out with the usual sermons and prayers. The fancy cakes look lovely but are totally tasteless especially when I compare them to the desserts at the Italian camp yesterday. Around me my hotel companions seem more dead than alive. The foreign businessmen stare gloomily at the cigarette-smoke rising from their ashtrays while the blank-eyed girls contemplate their brightly painted fingernails. Obviously revolutionary fervour is dying in some quarters – especially the Hilton. I decide to leave the hotel before I also succumb to the ennui of most people there.

It's time to look at the shops in Jordan Street. Pictures of the Irish hunger striker Bobby Sands are everywhere on the walls. The Iranians really like the idea of political martyrs. I am looking for a long-sleeved blouse but cannot find anything suitable and it is very hot so I go back closer to home. Zafar is alive with the beautiful sound of songbirds in cages hanging outside many of the shops. I go to the glass shop but the owner tells me that all the foreign goods are nearly finished. The table is covered with revolutionary pictures. Even in our short time here, things are definitely changing, Zafar was probably one of the least revolutionary streets in the area.

That night the street guards come to talk to us but we do not understand what they are trying to say. We have been taking lessons in Farsi but the only useful word we can remember is tomorrow - *fardah* - so hopefully they will return during office hours and we can have a proper discussion.

The prosecutor Ladjevardi announced that even young girls of nine years old would be arrested and thrown into Evin Prison if they spoke out against the regime. This is quite barbaric. The Iranian news says there have been 70 executions this week. This terrible blood lust never seems to stop.

Sunday June 28th
Niall goes to the Netherlands Embassy and I go to look for meat but again nothing in the shops.

Esther works late to get the letters ready for the diplomatic bag and the embassy goldfish dies and is buried under a rose bush. Esther comes out with some biblical interpretation about the death of the goldfish, the meaning of which totally escapes me so I go for a walk in Tajrish up near the mountains, to clear my head. It really is a lovely fresh day. The guards return to the embassy and Esther tells Niall they want to move in with us! Even for me that's a step too far! There is an old man, wrapped in a blanket with a big gnarled stick and a young man by his side. Eventually we work out that as a form of neighbourhood watch they need somewhere to sit and make tea. Unfortunately, much as we would love to help, the doorstep of the Irish Embassy is not exactly an appropriate place to camp out with a teapot.

Monday June 29th

Hear on news big explosion at IRP (Islamic Republican Party) meeting at the Majlis (parliament) yesterday- 32 dead or probably more, several days of mourning. No sign of Chief Justice Beheshti who was the second most influential person in the political hierarchy after Khomeini. When Archie arrives he has heard the latest news that Beheshti is dead. Rafsanjani left five minutes before the bomb, whatever that means.

Later the official statement says: 'The explosion of a bomb planted by the hypocrites in the Central Headquarters in the Islamic Republican Party in Tehran which resulted in the martyrdom of more than 72 of the Imam's best aides, including the Chief Justice of the Supreme Court, Dr Beheshti, ministers and representatives of the Islamic Consultative Assembly.'[2]

I go with Archie to do the shopping and to deliver the diplomatic bag to the airport but they refuse to take it because of the bomb the previous day. There is now extremely strict security at the airport and we are told that even the bag from the Iranian Department of Foreign Affairs has been returned.

On our return we try to get petrol but there is a huge queue so Archie tells a policeman that he has to go to the airport with the bag and he is allowed to jump the queue. Our next mistake is running into a procession of Hezbollah on motorbikes who are all flying black flags. It seems that all the shops are closed so we cannot even get a newspaper to see what is happening. Officials from the Agriculture Ministry come to get visas but they seem to know no more than we do except that everyone is extremely nervous. During the night there is a lot of shouting and noise on Mirdamad.

Tuesday June 30th

Hear on the news 72 dead or maybe 74. Everyone is shocked. Niall goes to the Netherlands Embassy for a meeting. The whole city seems

---

[2] In 2023 an article in the Sunday Times offered evidence that Mohammad Reza Kolahi Samadi, murdered in 2015, had planted the bomb. (page 364)

very quiet. The funeral leaves from the Majlis at 8 a.m. so there could be trouble this afternoon. The Australian chargé d'affaires rings Niall to invite him to lunch. He says he is reeling from the news but the lunch is going ahead. Niall has to go to the Netherlands Embassy for lunch because it is the end of the Dutch Presidency but he drops into the Australian Embassy for a drink. The British are next in line for the presidency but because of the situation - the Swedes are looking after British interests - the Belgians will do the presidency instead. At the Dutch lunch I discuss survival in Tehran with the wife of the Spanish Ambassador. She tells me how long it took her to settle in and how they were very afraid at the start of their posting. It is reassuring to hear her story. We have been here less than a month but so much has happened it seems as if we have been here for years.

There are rumours of infiltration in the government by the Pasdaran and of an army coup. Everyone is a little apprehensive.

Wednesday June 31st

News of more executions. 40 or 50 Mujahideen were rounded up yesterday. Not sure where it is going to end. See horrific commemorative journal of the Tehran Times with pictures of mangled bodies and weeping crowds, not to mention congratulations to the martyrs. The Governor of Tehran has also been killed in a mutiny in Evin prison. Once again the whole city seems out of control.

Archie finally gets the diplomatic bag but only one personal letter from a friend and lots more work for Niall. In 1926 the post arrived in the British legation in the South of Tehran in a much more reliable way. Vita Sackville-West describes how the Diplomatic bag arrives every fortnight. It is "corded on to the splash boards of a muddy motor, and Indian soldier on the box, the headlights stream down the road, lighting the white trunks of the plane trees, and then there is a scramble to sort the letters out on to the table.."

As the weeks go by we hear more and more rumours about the whereabouts of former President Banisadr - including one that suggested he had escaped on a plane to France dressed as a woman. No one knew which of the rumours was true but soon they all stopped.

There were too many other important issues to worry about than that of a missing president. (Banisadr survived and continued to live in Paris until his death in 2021).

21 CAVIAR FOR BREAKFAST (lunch and dinner)
August 1981

After a few months, Niall joined the other diplomats in the competition to produce the best wine. Well, actually, at the beginning the aim was to produce any wine at all - although after a couple of years he was regarded as an excellent wine producer, second only to the Spanish Ambassador. Of course Esther did not approve of this evil carry-on and attempted to change our sinful ways with more prayers. Once again, these did not work and fermentation vats were soon installed in the embassy kitchen.

Like many of the other diplomats, Niall started to enjoy his new hobby. At the beginning of this new venture I was afraid that I would have to trample grapes barefoot in the bath and was relieved to discover that imported grape juice was going to be the main ingredient. As well as wine, non-alcoholic beer was transformed into excellent real beer with the addition of yeast and sugar. This activity took a lot of work because the proportions of these ingredients had to be exact and some of the early productions were pretty awful. Niall did not give up, however, and continued to attack this problem with his usual scientific precision. The initial batches were more like cheap vinegar than wine and definitely did nothing to enhance any meals they accompanied. At least the bad white wine could be turned into a rather inferior sherry.

After work there was nothing to do, we could not even listen to the news. So until the wine-making process was perfected, Niall spent most of his free time in the office kitchen with the cockroaches as loyal companions. It was encouraging to know that his doctorate in biochemistry and his long scientific training were at last proving to be of some real practical value in diplomacy!

From time to time quite an interesting scent wafted into the foyer from the kitchen and visitors from the Foreign Ministry looked a little bemused as they sniffed the air, their noses twitching like mice discovering a piece of cheese. Immediately, however, a delicious competing aroma of coffee and freshly baked cakes would take over and the officials would begin to relax.

During that first summer we began to realise that the embassy staff were entrenched in their ways and whatever we did would not change them. Archie would always rather do anything other than drive me to an appointment and Esther would never give up trying to make us born-again Christians.

Niall always believed in the carrot rather than the stick approach and usually accomplished better work and relationships with this method. I on the other hand had perfected a look that could kill at ten metres. Neither of these approaches worked with Archie and Esther although we were getting used to coping with their behaviour and actually beginning to quite like them. Latif however was a completely different story, as he seemed to be a very troubled young man. At times a dark look would appear across his face and we were afraid he might attack us at some point. Although we did not realise he was probably on drugs, he certainly seemed to have pent up anger issues and we knew that sooner or later we would have to get rid of him.

At the end of July there was a flurry of activity in the summer residence of the British Embassy. A reception was planned to celebrate the wedding of Prince Charles and Diana. On the day of the reception I had spent the afternoon taking a stray kitten to the vet to see if there would be any treatment for his infected eye. The vet had a very good sense of humour and after treatment he fixed a tiny eye-patch over the small cat's eye and, with a big grin, named him Moshe Dayan. The vet was smiling because no one in Iran would dare to talk openly about the Israelis and, of course, Moshe Dayan was a cavalier Israeli general in the Six Day War of June 1967. His trademark was an eye-patch whereas the trademark of educated Iranians was to make fun of the revolution. From that day on, the kitten was called MoshKat and - as his eye did not recover - he was looked after in the embassy until sadly, to my great distress, he was attacked and killed by a pack of wild dogs a year later.

That evening I was so happy thinking that we may have saved the kitten's eye. When talking to the British chargé d'affaires I joked that I had taken a one-eyed cat to the vet and returned with a two-eyed cat. He rolled his eyes while suggesting to the group that I was 'sweet but unbalanced'. For me that was going too far and for him, it was good his bodyguards were on hand. Being called unbalanced, especially by a boring bureaucrat, actually seemed a rather interesting label but sweet was a step too far. That was my only memory of that evening, as I do not remember anything at all about the royal wedding. In fact after that inauspicious beginning we all got on quite well and Niall and I went on some interesting trips around Iran with him.

During the month of August trade began to pick up and we had a fairly steady stream of visitors as Irish beef and dairy products were vying with produce from other countries for a place in the newly opened Iranian market. Gerry from Bord Bainne (the Irish Dairy Board) was probably our most frequent visitor as Ireland was selling a lot of butter and milk powder to the Iranian market.

Violence was rife on the streets especially near government offices and trips down town to the Foreign and Agricultural Ministries could be quite risky and I was always very relieved when Niall returned safely from his official trips to ministry buildings. On one occasion Niall went with the entire diplomatic corps to meet the Supreme Leader Ayatollah Ruhollah Khomeini who was presiding at a local Mosque. Niall said he did not address the diplomats directly and appeared to be detached and disinterested and lacking any semblance of emotional empathy. He and his colleagues found it hard to understand how this individual could have had such an impact on a great and civilised nation like Iran.

Meanwhile I was getting used to Archie's grumpy behaviour and was becoming quite expert at dodging Esther's bible attacks; nevertheless I was trying to keep busy as I really missed my work in the hospital in Dublin. Maybe I was busier than I thought because, with the food shortages, even trying to find food could take up a lot of time. The Iranians had been refusing to accept foreign imports of basic foods so the shops were quite empty when we arrived - apart from tea, eggs, yoghurt and rice. There were also lots of jars of pickled gherkins and other unknown pickled substances, which would not have looked out of place in the pathology lab of any hospital.

Some foods could be imported through the Danish diplomatic suppliers but this could take several months and we were never sure if the order would get through Iranian customs. When the order finally did arrive, there would be great excitement all around. Boxes of biscuits and chocolates were scattered over the floor as we dug deep in the cartons to retrieve jars of coffee, tins of meat and fish and washing powder. On our arrival in Iran It was very difficult to find meat for several weeks and I was worried as to how I was going to produce diplomatic dinners with such little food available. I thought we had solved our problem when we were invited to dinner by Maureen, who worked in the Belgian Embassy. A very tasty stew was produced and I immediately forked a piece of tender-looking meat only to leap out of my chair as a bitterly sour taste seared through my mouth. I had bitten through a dried lime which is a wonderful way of adding flavour but not great if eaten. After that incident I was more careful but still could find no meat in the shops.

Finally after a summer of food shortages, the Iranians announced that diplomats could buy a limited amount of food every week from the government shop. This was great news and we eagerly awaited Archie's return from the first shopping adventure. Archie arrived into the residence kitchen with two plastic bags and, with his usual charm, dumped them down on the counter. I tentatively opened the bags and found a very scraggy chicken, one bottle of milk, one bucket of the most delicious creamy natural yoghurt, one small packet of butter, a bag of rice and two flat, green tins.

I looked at the two tins puzzled, as I had no idea what might be inside. The tins had no labels, were scratched and scuffed and obviously had been made locally. Slowly pulling the piece of tape which was keeping the lid in place, I opened the tin. To my amazement the tin was filled with big, glistening, grey balls of the best caviar in the world, Beluga caviar from the Persian side of the Caspian Sea. I was stunned that this luxury commodity should be lumped together with the other mundane items on the list. So started our love affair with Iranian caviar. With very little meat or fish for several months we began to regard our exotic supply of 'fish balls' as normal. It really was a case of caviar for breakfast, lunch and dinner!

The other diplomats were as surprised and delighted as we were when they received their caviar 'rations' and immediately began to hold caviar parties. Huge silver bowls of caviar were served with chopped boiled eggs, shreds of raw onions and strips of toast, washed down with vodka if it was available. It was all beginning to feel a bit like the French revolution but in this case it was not cake that was being suggested by Marie-Antoinette when ordinary fare wasn't available; on this occasion, it was the best caviar offered by the revolutionaries themselves.

We soon started to make friends partly because most of the ambassadors had been recalled and the embassies left in the hands of younger chargés d'affaires; but mostly because we all had to work together to overcome the daily difficulties. It was almost impossible to get family or friends into the country even if they wanted to come, which was probably unlikely. This sort of 'hardship' posting is particularly rewarding because you are reliant on a small group of people who often become life-long friends.

In Iran at that time there was no form of public entertainment. Theatres, cinemas and musical concerts had all been closed down at the beginning of the revolution so we had to make our own entertainment. This return to the 'good old days' was actually very enjoyable. Niall began playing his guitar again and I started writing. The weekend in Iran was Friday and Saturday so on a Thursday evening we would all meet together for play-readings followed by a meal. This was great fun, whether it consisted of sketches about the current situation, which were written specially for the evening, or plays written by modern playwrights. We usually chose comedies which contrasted greatly with our everyday situation.

Sometimes we had musical concerts in the embassies but apart from that there was little to do. We could not get a good radio connection and television only showed scenes from the Iran/Iraq war and pictures of dead 'martyrs', which were both very sad and very depressing. It would have been easier if there had been videos but at that time they had not yet become available.

On a Friday we would travel to see archaeological sites and on Saturdays we would ski in the Elborz Mountains in winter and swim in summer in the embassy pools. Not exactly a 'hardship post' at times. Because of the violence and lack of the usual entertainment opportunities, everyone was forced to be creative and interact more with other people. Consequently it seemed that many people really enjoyed their stay in Iran. It is ironic that these posts are called 'hardship posts' because, if approached with the right attitude, they can be the most interesting and rewarding of all. For me personally, one of the popular postings such as Paris, London or Washington would have been far less enjoyable and certainly much less interesting or exciting.

22. THE BIG COVER UP

September 1981

At the end of summer we were all preparing for a major trade fair in Tehran in September. This was the first business fair since the start of the revolution and was a great opportunity to break into the emerging Iranian market. Niall made many trips to the government offices and collaborated very closely with the Irish Trade Board to make the necessary arrangements. Lists of businessmen brave enough to risk the dangerous situation were drawn up. Plans were made for embassy receptions and food rations were put aside. In September the carpentry team came out to set up the Irish stand. The Trade Fair went well and lots of smoked salmon and chocolates were kindly brought out for the reception by the businessmen themselves. Of course we also had our caviar.

It was great fun to meet everyone. Visitors were always welcome in Tehran as there were so few people who could get into the country. There were a couple of extra bedrooms in the embassy and the hotels were pretty dreadful: empty, not too clean, no good food and an overdose of Pepsi or Zam Zam at every turn. We really enjoyed having people to stay and felt quite sad when everyone returned home.

Meanwhile on the streets of Tehran every day the situation was getting more difficult. The Pasdaran were becoming more confident and more intrusive in everyone's life especially in regard to women. I had a lovely group of friends, many of whom I have maintained contact with after all those years. Among the wives in the diplomatic corps there was a group of seven or eight who refused to put on a headscarf in the street; they saw it as a strong-arm tactic against women, which had been recently introduced, as part of a general 'crackdown'. All of us dressed modestly to show our respect for the culture. We all wore long coats and trousers even in 40 or 50 degrees heat and if we had seen the oppression as a sign of religion we would also have complied with the head-covering rule. When most of us had arrived in Tehran, however, it had not been necessary for women to cover up and a few weeks or months later we watched women's freedom being eroded step by step as they were forced to cover up at gun point. There had been a gradual change since that afternoon of protest and shooting soon after we arrived. Many Iranian women stopped us in the street and begged us not to cover our hair for their sake but obviously it had to be our protest not theirs.

Jennifer and her husband Roger, the new Belgian Ambassador, had just arrived in Tehran. Very practical and full of life, she soon became a close friend. She had been a student at Manchester University where I also had studied, although as we studied different subjects we never met. A brilliant linguist, Jennifer had just come with her husband from Ethiopia. The Belgian Embassy was uptown in a beautiful setting and, as there were no coffee shops in the area, it was lovely to go and meet her there. Her constant supply of Leonidas chocolates via the diplomatic bag was another obvious attraction. She was quite happy to join us in our charity work and in our protests if it helped the morale of the Iranian women. In the whole scheme of things, we all realised it was really only a case of raising their morale. Our actions, of course, did not have any real effect and one by one the diplomatic wives left the country and were posted elsewhere.

The new wives saw everyone covered and wanted to fit in, so they felt less inclined to protest. In the end I was practically the only diplomatic wife left still making my ineffectual little protest. My Irish connection was a great help because Ireland continued to be seen as a revolutionary country who had taken on Britain (known locally as the 'little Satan') and if any of the Pasdars were in doubt about that I would remind them very quickly. What I would not tell them was that I was in fact English but had taken an Irish passport when I married my husband a mere six years earlier. At that time, people were not allowed to have two passports and if I did not have an Irish diplomatic passport I would have had to leave Japan every few months (Niall's first posting was in Japan).

The new regime had great difficulties with the British and American Governments for many reasons and not least because of the lasting legacy of the coup in 1953 engineered by both the CIA and MI6. In '*Lords Of The Desert*', James Barr describes the events leading up to the coup which through the usual dubious methods of lies and 'rent a mob' demonstrations led to the removal of Prime Minister Mohammed Mossaddegh and re-instated the young Shah - who from then on was always seen as a puppet of the West. The reasons for this ousting were the usual ones, with which we are now familiar - oil, of course, together with the fear that Mossaddegh was too close to the Tudeh Party and the Soviet Union. The actions of some Western countries never cease to amaze me; they don't seem to learn that such behaviour is ultimately self- defeating.

Indeed, after the revolution, anyone who was seen to have taken on the forces of imperialism was greatly admired by the Revolutionary Guards. To make that point, the street behind the British Embassy was changed from Churchill Street to Bobby Sands Street. Around the city there were many signs proclaiming that 'Bobby Sands is not dead' as the fate of the Irish hunger striker appealed to the 'martyrdom' complex of the Iranian Shia mentality. At that time I only had to say the word Ireland or Bobby Sands and even my lack of a headscarf was often forgiven.

23. AK-47

Things did not always go well, of course. One Sunday we were getting ready to drive up to the Church of St Abraham in Ali Shariati. The Iranians had traditionally been tolerant of other religions and Christians and Jews both coexisted quite well although after the revolution the situation became a lot more delicate. That day I was quite late - as usual. Archie, Niall and an Indian friend were already sitting in the car waiting for me, so by the time I got into the back seat there was quite a tense atmosphere. We turned into Ali Shariati and stopped dead in the traffic jam on the big avenue going up to the church. Two lines of traffic were stationary on both sides of the road. Suddenly there was a commotion in the middle of the road. A Pasdar was running down, pointing his AK-47 directly at my head and screaming at me to cover my hair.

I was wearing a coat buttoned up to the neck, the windows of the car were shaded and the Revolutionary Guard was quite far from the car when he pointed his gun at me. He really must have been wearing heat-seeking binoculars to see me. His next stage would have been to bang on the car window and force me to put on my headscarf at gunpoint.

This time, however, I had had enough. The guard had attacked me on the wrong day. I opened the car door and jumped out into the middle of the road shouting back at him in my few words of Farsi telling him to go away and leave me alone. Women on the pavement were very alarmed and shouted to warn me that I had to be careful because he was a Pasdar. I shouted back that I did not care who he was. At this point the Pasdar looked at the fury on my face and skidded to a halt, sparks literally radiating from the heels of his boots. He quickly turned around and disappeared. Obviously my face was so frightening that even his old ally the AK 47 was not enough. I waved at the women and got back into the car without a word.

The atmosphere inside the car was electric. No one was yet ready to point out that I had just done a very stupid and dangerous thing. I burst into fits of laughter, partly because of the atmosphere in the car and partly because the sight of this bully with his gun - backing off and running away had just been too ridiculous. This broke the tension and everyone in the car began to see the funny side of the situation. On this occasion even Archie managed a smile because like so many others he had suffered at the hands of the Pasdaran. I did not learn my lesson, I'm afraid, and twenty years later I again jumped out of the embassy car, this time with my daughter, Clare, when we saw Israeli soldiers abusing blind-folded, crouching Palestinians in Hebron and Gaza.

After that episode we carried on up Ali Shariati Avenue past the British Embassy residence at Golhak and parked outside the gates which led to the church. Suddenly a black car pulled up and a group of Revolutionary Guards tumbled out and hit Niall on the face. They did not hit me because they were not allowed to touch women, only shoot or threaten to shoot them.

Fortunately Niall was not hurt and it was more a gesture of defiance after the Pasdaran had lost face over my actions but of course it did not improve any one's general mood. Archie was let go and after church Niall drove back to the embassy. In silence he parked the car outside the gate because he was going out later. I was worried, however, that after what had just happened someone might put a bomb under the car. I was not the best driver in the world and Niall had banned me from driving the embassy car, nevertheless I decided to bring the car in through the fairly narrow, heavy wrought-iron gates. I was still on a bit of an emotional high so I swept in at a wrong angle, almost trying to squeeze between the concrete pillars. I heard the crunch of the side mirror along with scraping and denting of the side of the door.

Niall did not speak to me for three days, so I never got the opportunity to tell him that at least I had not taken the door off completely. He did, however, speak to the Indian cook, who worked with us several days a week and had been guiding me in, asking how on earth he had allowed me to do such a stupid thing. Devji explained 'Oh sir, I am so sorry. Madam was driving so fast that I was 'fraid for my life because I thought she was going to knock me into the swimming pool'.

Niall was not impressed with either of us and the atmosphere was pretty chilly in the Irish Embassy for a few days. Eventually, however, everyone began to laugh at the happenings of that eventful Sunday. The importance of a sense of humour for life in the Islamic Republic was becoming more obvious by the day. Many diplomats and wives who took themselves too seriously did not stay very long. Maybe my years working in psychiatric hospitals helped more than I realised. At times, I definitely felt that the psychiatric patients whom I had previously treated were much more sane than many of the people I was dealing with in Iran.

24. ALADDIN'S CAVE

We soon had further proof that the Iranians were monitoring our phone calls when, on the day after the 'incident', I phoned Pat at the British Embassy to tell her of my encounter with the Pasdaran. We were laughing away at the thought of the look on the face of the Pasdar when our phone call was abruptly cut off. At first, thinking it was the usual fault in the line I phoned back and again when I reached an 'interesting' part, the phone call was terminated. Obviously humour was not a part of the new regime.

My minor protest on behalf of the 'freedom for hair movement' continued until one Friday afternoon two years later when I walked with a friend across Pasdaran Avenue off Ali Shariati to an antique shop. If I had a free afternoon on a Friday I would often walk across to this shop to drink tea with Joseph, the Jewish owner. Pre-revolution, Christians, Jews and Muslims had co-existed peacefully, as Joseph would recall, speaking longingly of those times. I would get quite upset at the sight of any new items left in his shop by Iranians leaving the country. Unable to take their belongings with them they were often lucky to escape with their lives.

The contents of the shop seemed like part of a great history lesson. Glowing glass lamps and gleaming silk carpets from the time of previous Shahs sat beside deep blue lapis lazuli boxes from Afghanistan and huge brass antique Russian samovars. Beautifully engraved bowls and serving spoons, many dating back to the era of the Russian Czars, would be jumbled together on top of glass topped trays of priceless antique gold jewellery. It all looked like a rather untidy museum or maybe more like Aladdin's cave.

When we entered the shop Joseph would put on all the lights and make the tea from boiling water in a samovar. We would sit and sip tea through sugar cubes and discuss the political situation while looking through the boxes of tribal jewellery, which was more reasonable in price than the rest of the antiques.

On this occasion Joseph greeted us at door of the shop, he was looking very apprehensive and questioned my lack of headscarf. Apparently that day the Governor of Tehran had issued a pronouncement that all women had to wear hejab or they would be beaten or imprisoned. So ended my protest. From then on, as it was for many Iranian women, it became a mini covert protest; it was a case of allowing as many strands of hair as possible to escape to freedom and visibility while still retaining a headscarf. Unfortunately, in my case it was more often that my hair refused to follow any rules rather than an active protest.

25. ARABIAN NIGHTS

October 1981

In the autumn I decided it was time to think about some work in psychology again. I rang up a contact in the German Institute to make an appointment to see what journals might be available although I did not have much hope that anything useful would materialise. I was sitting in the large open dining area and Latif was cleaning the window with big sweeping arm movements. As my conversation progressed I noticed that his movements were getting wider and wider and slower and slower and he was practically falling off the small step-ladder as he bent backwards to hear my conversation. Finally at the end of my call he could contain himself no longer and jumping down from the ladder he ran up to me breathlessly demanding 'Madam, tell me the name of the person you are meeting and the time and the place where you are going to meet him'. I immediately realised why Latif was frequently asking to go down town to a government office to 'sort out his papers.'

Executions were carried out daily at that time and there was a terrible feeling of fear and mistrust among both foreigners and Iranians. There were of course very few foreigners except for diplomats, embassy staff and a small number of businessmen. We were all aware that embassy employees had to provide information to the ministry in order to get their visas renewed but it was a shock to get proof of this in such an unsubtle way. Most employees were either more clever and did not let their employers know what was going on or they were more loyal and gave very little information to the authorities.

When I did go to the German Institute without, I hasten to add, the assistance of Latif, I found that the psychology journals stopped at the beginning of the revolution. As a result, because there were no computer facilities in those days, only journals and books, instead of reading psychology articles I spent my free time in a little bookshop beside the embassy in Zafar street. There sitting on the floor of the dusty and dimly lit shop I found a great selection of all the books I really wanted to read. The Rubaiyat of Omar Khayyam, poetry by Hafez, the Conference of the Birds by Attar - many wonderful books were there. To feel and smell the old books and to know that I might be able to visit the places in which these poets had lived centuries ago was so exciting. The old shopkeeper had not seen any customers for two years and was delighted to see me day after day walking away with books on Iran, Sufism and Zen Buddhism. Back in the embassy Esther was not too pleased when she saw the works on Iranian and Far Eastern mysticism pile up in the room beside her. The dreaded bible was produced once again.

At the beginning of October, representatives from all the embassies were taken down to Ahwaz by plane in order to access the war front. They were to be given the propaganda tour of progress in the Iran/Iraq war although from the accounts of casualties on both sides it seemed as if no side was winning. We had accepted an invitation to dinner that night with our Swiss friends, but as Niall did not return at the appointed time and there was no news whatsoever of the return flight, I had to cancel at the last minute and sit in the embassy waiting for news from the war front. There were no mobile phones in those days, so the only point of contact was the rather unreliable embassy landline.

There was no news during the evening or during my sleepless night and I heard later that one wife had been so worried that she spent the night at Tehran airport. It was certainly very upsetting because the military planes were not very well maintained at that time of war and revolution and the war front itself was obviously also very dangerous. Finally at eight in the morning I heard from the Foreign Ministry that the plane was on its way. Apparently it had broken down the previous evening and there had been no way of contacting any of the wives. The real story probably was that wives were not regarded as very important. For me this was only the start of a series of worrying trips and disappearances by my husband over the years in countries like Yemen, Iraq and Kuwait during the invasion by Iraq.

By October everyone had gone home after the Trade Fair and we could take a short break to see some more of this fascinating country. Every weekend we made day trips to the desert or the mountains. The ruins of ancient caravanserais were probably the most interesting. There in the desert under the star-scattered sky I could imagine caravans of tired camels and traders lodging for the night, returning from the Far East along the fabled Silk Road with their jewel-coloured lengths of delicate silk. The exotic scents of perfumes, precious oils and spices from Yemen and Arabia must have permeated the heady evening air as conversations went on through the night about exciting journeys East and West. The caravanserai really seem to sum up the wonder of Arabian Nights.

Gertrude Bell wrote in 1892:

'Oh the desert round Tehran! miles and miles of it with nothing, nothing growing; ringed in with bleak bare mountains snow crowned and furrowed with the deep courses of torrents.'

Beautiful mosques and ancient archaeological sites stretched out before us throughout the country. In summer we would walk in the sun-bleached Elborz Mountains through the villages of Shemran and Shemshak stopping to trail our hands in the cool mountain streams and sit under the shade of the trees to eat a picnic - all the time trying to seek knowledge and understanding of this enigmatic culture and country.

26. HALF THE WORLD

After a few months the city of Isfahan, which should be ranked as one of the most exotic and interesting cities in the world, beckoned once again. Three years earlier, Niall and I had visited the city when we came to Iran on our way back to Ireland from Japan. On this occasion, however, our friends Don and Pat from the British Embassy decided to join us. Don was a fluent Farsi speaker, which would be helpful as we were taking lessons in the Persian language but our Farsi was still pretty rudimentary. Farsi originates from the Indo-European group of languages so its basic structure is familiar enough for English speakers although the Arabic invasion of the seventh century introduced the Arabic alphabet and many Arabic words.

We packed the bags with everything we thought we might need including a bottle of Polish vodka. We passed the Great Salt Lake, and various groups of camels while continuing in the direction of Qom, the holy city and the religious capital of Iran. A view of minarets and golden domes greeted us as we approached the holy city, a view described by Isabella Bird in her book, which was first published in 1891:

'Situated in a great plain, the gleam of its golden dome and its slender minarets is seen from afar, and the deep green of its orchards, and the bright green of the irrigated and cultivated lands which surround it, are a splash of welcome on the great brown waste.'

We decided to keep going, intending to investigate Qom at a future time. Tired and dusty we arrived in Isfahan – the famous city built by the Safavid ruler Shah Abbas (1589-1627) in the sixteenth century. We had booked into the Shah Abbas Hotel, originally an old caravanserai which had been renovated as a luxurious hotel.

On our last visit we had been invited to the hotel for lunch by a colleague from Tokyo who was staying there on her way back to Japan. It had been quite a different scene then. The magnificent foyer lit up with lights and sparkling chandeliers was alive with guests and sightseers admiring the carved wooden doors, central staircase and priceless Persian carpets. In the huge dining room waiters were dressed impeccably and served the guests the best food and wine with great expertise. The hotel had been used as a setting for the film of Agatha Christie's book 'Ten Little Indians,' although in the film the hotel was portrayed as being in the middle of a desert rather than in a city and flashes of the archaeological site of Persepolis were shown as part of its landscape.

Now, however, the difference was quite shocking. The place was overrun with members of the Pasdaran, although otherwise quite empty. Everywhere looked very different, the hotel appeared quite run down, the lighting was dim, the carpets were dusty and the previously gleaming huge brass and copper urns were tarnished. In the empty dining room the waiters were dressed in the uniform of the revolution – open-necked shirts and dirty jackets. They served the usual rice. kebabs and the ubiquitous Pepsi Cola instead of the finest Persian and international menus and wines of previous times. I didn't mind, it was all an adventure but it was still a little sad to compare the two visits.

The huge square, Meydan-e-Shah (now Meydan-e-Imami), constructed by Shah Abbas was twice as big as the Red Square in Moscow. It was filled with the most magnificent royal buildings and mosques which meant it was always difficult to know where to start. It really was a magical scene of oriental beauty as deep blue tiles contrasted with gilded cupolas while cedar columns were reflected in the mirrored depth of sunlit pools.

On the square were several mosques but the most imposing was the Masjid-e-Shah (now Masjid-e-Imami) with its heavy wooden doors worked in gold and silver, its dome and minarets and tiles depicting calligraphy and pictures of animals and flowers and the wash of subtle, blue colouring that dominates the whole area. Arthur Pope's book *Persian Architecture* tells us that this 'represents the culmination of a thousand years of mosque building in Persia, with a majesty and splendour that places it among the world's greatest buildings.'

The Royal Square also contained the Ali Gapou Palace, the seat of government where Shah Abbas, sitting on the upper level surrounded by slender wooden columns, presided over military parades and games of polo, the Iranian national sport. Now these historical buildings were defaced by revolutionary slogans and posters.

Fifty years earlier, when there were no revolutionary distractions, Robert Byron was also greeted by a magical scene as he drove around Isfahan 'past domes of turquoise and spring yellow in a sky of liquid violet-blue; along the river patched with twisting shoals, catching that blue in its muddy silver and lined with feathery groves where the sap calls…'.

By 1652 the Jesuit Order had established itself in Isfahan with two priests who could speak Persian and four years later two more were sent out to 'win the Shah's favour by offering him presents from the Christian Princes.' Their aim was to open up an overland route to China as the sea route was proving too hazardous. When the two priests arrived in Isfahan they found that: "the Shah was at that very moment arming for war against the Prince of Samarkand. Trade was interrupted. Any further progress along the 'northern route' seemed out of the question."

We did not find any trace of that early expedition but the Armenian Christian community was still thriving in Isfahan and we spent some time walking through the Armenian Quarter and the old cemetery. Shah Abbas, seems to have been a wise ruler under whose leadership international trade was boosted and the country thrived. He, therefore, did not wish to disturb this situation by indulging in religious persecution. Consequently he allowed thousands of Armenian Christians to live beside his new capital Isfahan.

In Iran bazaars are always a major attraction and of course the vendors, anxious to sell regardless of any political dimension, could always be trusted to give a warm welcome to potential buyers. Pat and I wandered through the maze of gold shops. Rope after rope of solid gold was strung across the windows but the most beautiful of all were the famous hand-worked filigree gold pieces from the city of Yazd. When we tired of admiring the gold, we moved on to examine the gleaming silk carpets and next to find the miniaturist we had visited on our previous trip.

He was still there, the official painter of the Iranian Tourist Board, still in the same room with his paint, brushes and pieces of camel bone and ivory laid out on the table in front of him. It was amusing to see that the only change since our last visit was that the large picture of the young Shah which had previously hung on the wall had been replaced by a similarly large photo of the Ayatollah Khomeini; also the name of the shop had been changed from Shahi to Imami. Choice or necessity? We will never know, although I suspect necessity.

The painter looked up from his painstaking work on tiny polo players in front of the Ali Gapou, a familiar theme on the miniature paintings of Iran. He smiled warmly and much to our surprise he seemed to recognise us immediately and stood up to greet us. We soon realised why he recognised us after three years, when he opened the visitor's book. Our signatures, dated the end August 1978 were the final signatures in the book, showing that we were among the last tourists in Iran before the Shah left the country. When we had first been there we had heard rumours of grave discontent and of vicious crackdowns and the diplomatic corps discussed what sort of retribution would occur if there was any dissent, but there were few indications of the coming revolution.

We quietly watched the painter at work, his concentration remarkable as he turned flowing brush strokes into precise polo players. It was a really sobering experience to see such perfection in action. Eventually we had to leave, so we chose some miniatures and with promises to return we went back to the hotel to pack the car. For us, Isfahan would always be a special place. Arthur Upham Pope explains that Isfahan in the seventeenth century had so many bridges, parks, mosques and palaces that European visitors described it as 'half the world' and for us, even in the throes of a revolution, it could never be forgotten. Everywhere was quieter than we remembered probably because there were no tourists but the people were just as kind and friendly as before. Over the next few years we would visit the city many more times.

27. LAND OF SUFI POETS

The nightingale with drops of his heart's blood
Had nourished the red rose, then came a wind,
And catching at the boughs in envious mood,
A hundred thorns about his heart entwined.
                            Hafez (translated by Gertrude Bell)

At last we arrived at Shiraz, the beautiful city of nightingales and roses and home of two of the most famous Persian Sufi poets of the last Millennium. We checked into the Intercontinental Hotel and the cheerful man on the desk was delighted to see guests at last in his empty hotel. The Revolutionary Guards were hovering, although on this occasion quite friendly and wanted to try out their few words of English. We chatted away for a little while and then casually picking up our cases and plastic bags we headed for the lift. Two Pasdaran accompanied us continuing their friendly chat. At the lift we put down our bags as we pressed the button to open the door and then we froze in horror. The plastic bag containing the vodka had fallen on its side and the bottle was rolling as if in slow motion towards the two Revolutionary Guards. Niall jumped into action and scooped up the bottle with a nonchalant smile as Don tried to distract the men by bursting into a stream of Farsi about something or other. We never found out what he said but it seemed to work and we put our bags into the lift without any further incidents. The vodka and orange juice tasted especially good that evening.

Shiraz is the birthplace of two famous Sufi poets, Saadi and Hafez. It was the mausoleum of Hafez in a secluded garden full of cypress trees and roses, that we visited first. The sheltered garden with its faint scent of roses and sweet sound of bird song was the resting place of this most revered of all the Persian poets who wrote his eternal verses in the fourteenth century. Engraved on his tomb were several stanzas of his beautiful poetry:

'Sit near my tomb, and bring wine and music
Feeling thy presence, I shall come out of my sepulchre
Rise, softly moving creature, and let me contemplate thy beauty.'

John Baggot Glubb (Glubb Pasha) tells the story of when Tamerlane or Timur, a cruel Mongol successor of Genghis Khan, took Shiraz, he insisted that he would be served wine by the most beautiful women of the region. He was considered a patron of the arts so literary figures and scientists were sent to Samarkand ' to grace the Conqueror's court'. Hafez wrote:

'If that fair maid of Shiraz would give me love,
I would give Samarkand and Bukhara for the mole upon her cheek.'

Tamerlane, annoyed, informed Hafez that the treasures from all his many world conquests had been sent to Samarkand and Bukhara and he was not impressed with the references in Hafez poem. The reply was, 'Alas, O Prince, it is this prodigality which is the cause of the poverty in which you see me.' Tamerlane, fortunately for Hafez, was pleased with this reply.

Close by was another large garden in which the tomb of Saadi nestled in the midst of stately cypress trees and sweetly scented rose bushes. Treading gently on a soft multi-coloured carpet of rose petals we wandered over to admire the inscription on the tomb of Saadi which read:

'From the tomb of Saadi, son of Shiraz
The perfume of love escapes
Thou shalt smell it still one thousand years after his death.'

Saadi wrote short lyrical love poems called ghazal. He died in 1291, yet centuries later Iranians were coming, just as we did, to pay their respects to these great Sufi poets. In modern times Shiraz has been an amazing cultural city even into the twentieth century; but when we were there it was bereft of any modern festivals or artistic activity and of course the famous Shiraz wine was no more. We decided to visit the mosque containing the mausoleum of Shah Shiragh. A little worried that we would not be allowed in we went to ask permission from the Mullah in charge of the mosque. He was a kindly-faced elderly man who with a pleasant smile allowed us to enter. He did think, however, that my chador was too short so he called for another chador and sitting in a chair he carefully tied the second one around my waist.

Now the new chador was sweeping the dusty ground and everyone was happy. As we started to leave his office he called us back to tell us to leave our shoes on unlike the Muslim pilgrims who had to remove their shoes. We were a little surprised at that because we thought that it would be more respectful to go barefoot, as was the custom in the mosques in Turkey. He insisted, however, so of course we did what he said although we were a little wary as we stomped through the holy shrine in our sturdy desert shoes. We realised only too well what a great privilege it was to be allowed inside this great mosque.

Our final destination in Shiraz was of the bazaar where it is possible to find a real appreciation about the culture and daily lives of the Persian people of the area. Filled with various crafts of the local nomadic tribes especially striking was the sight of the Qashqai women with colourful full-skirted dresses selling their richly coloured kalims and hand-made silver jewellery. All of this was truly fascinating but for me the main interest of this amazing city would always be that it was home to two of the greatest Sufi poets of all time.

28. PERSEPOLIS

Close to Shiraz lies the ancient 'City of the Persians'- Persepolis or Takht-e-Jamshīd (this refers to the throne of Jamshid who was a mythical hero in Ferdowsi's great epic poem). The huge plain, fringed by imposing mauve-shaded cliffs, was chosen by Cyrus the Great for the site of his magnificent structure. He reigned from 559 to 529BC over his empire and appears to have been a fair and wise ruler who unified the different nations. The construction of this city started by Darius, the son in law of Cyrus, was begun around 518 BC and continued for two hundred years before it was destroyed by a great fire after its capture by

Alexander the Great in 330BC. This was thought to be either by accident or out of revenge for the burning of Athens by the Persians many years previously. Professor Lloyd Llewellyn-Jones in his book *'Persians - The Age of The Great Kings'* suggests that it was neither an accident nor revenge but an attempt by Alexander to destroy and put an end to the long-lived successful Achaemenian dynasty of Cyrus and Darius. By doing so, however, he also destroyed his own potential legacy as a great ruler of Persia.

The archaeologist Pope suggests that - contrary to most Western thought the city was not built as a political capital but rather as a 'sacred national shrine, potent setting for the spring festival of Now Ruz.' It was thus a ceremonial setting rather than a place of government; the huge gate to this city, the 'Gate of All Nations', was guarded by human-headed winged bulls.

After the destruction of the city by the great fire, the ruins were undisturbed for two thousand years. In 1971 the Shah held a very lavish commemoration ceremony at Persepolis celebrating 2500 years of the Persian Empire. Some of the special tents were still standing when we arrived there ten years later. Shah Mohammad Reza Pahlavi invited royalty and dignitaries from across the world for his extravagant champagne party and it is not hard to imagine that this wasteful opulence would not have gone down well with the religious establishment or the ordinary people.

The intricate friezes on the walls of the staircases, were carved out two and a half millennia ago by so many generations of dedicated and talented crafts men, who probably never dreamed that their work would still be admired many centuries later. Processions of the Imperial Guard and envoys from the twenty-three countries in the empire carrying gifts of gold, spears, musical instruments and animals moved in a gentle rhythm up the sides of the open staircases. Their procession was only broken every now and then by reliefs of the tree of life, a very important symbol in Persian culture, as was the bull which signifying both strength and fertility, decorated the towering columns.

The writer Robert Byron, however, was not too impressed by the endless lines of sculpted figures moving up the stairs and suggested in his inimitable way: 'they have art, but not spontaneous art, and certainly not great art.' He only really seems to have found some artistic value in the huge doorways; 'They and they alone, boast a gleam of true invention…' Happily I do not pretend to have any artistic expertise and consequently could freely enjoy the sheer magnificence of the ancient archaeological site of Persepolis.

Before the revolution, each evening there was a *'Son et Lumiere'* display to evoke the glory of the ancient history. This had finished, of course by the time we arrived because there were no longer any tourists and probably also because Persepolis was not an Islamic commemoration. We were alone in this great ancient city of the Persians, free to just wander wherever we wanted without interference from the Revolutionary Guards who had no interest in pre-Islamic monuments. One interesting find was a name and date etched onto one of the walls, which said 'Stanley, New York Tribune 1879.' This was the same Henry Morgan Stanley who had uttered the immortal words 'Dr. Livingstone, I presume' when he finally met the famed explorer in the heart of Africa after years of searching. He had been sent by the New York Tribune to cover the opening of the Suez Canal in Egypt and had travelled on to Persepolis. It was thrilling to see a piece of history come to life after reading about his signature in the guidebooks.

The temperature was extremely hot and it was difficult to imagine the men who toiled in the desperate heat, pulling the huge slabs of stone more than two thousand years before. It was equally difficult to imagine the huge battle between Darius and Alexander the Great in 330, which signified the end of Persepolis and the great civilization of the Achaemenian era.

We returned to the hotel and relaxed in the restaurant by drinking an ice-cold glass of Pepsi. Zam Zam and Pepsi were the only drinks available in Iran because Coca Cola had been banned, as it was a product of America, the 'Great Satan.' Under normal circumstances neither of these would have been my favourite drink but in Iran in those days there often was no other choice. Once again we were joined by a group of Revolutionary Guards who wanted to talk to foreigners. It was beginning to seem that the further south we travelled the fewer foreigners were seen and the more interesting we became, even to the Pasdaran.

At that point it was decided it would be safer to admit only to being from Ireland. Britain was definitely not in favour with Iranian officials at that time. There was no British Ambassador and the Swedish were looking after British interests so to admit that Don was an official of Britain or, the 'Little Satan' as it was called, did not seem too sensible. The Pasdaran were very friendly and a pleasure to be with but we decided it might be better not to get involved in too deep a discussion in case we ran into problems. We therefore made a hasty retreat into the empty dining room to face the usual tasteless soup followed by tough, bony chicken or lamb kebab. Persian food is actually excellent – wonderful herb and lamb stews, amazing pomegranate and aubergine dishes, rice layered with pistachios, toasted almonds, dried fruit and saffron. Really delicious cuisine comes from Iran but unfortunately those aromatic dishes were rarely found in hotels even the top hotels in the early days of the revolution.

After dinner Don and Pat came to our room to relax and chat about the wonders of Persepolis. Suddenly there was a loud knock at the door and two members of the Pasdaran entered the room. They sat down and wanted to talk about Ireland as they had heard about the foreigners 'farangi' from the earlier group discussion. This time the Pasdaran wanted more information about this fascinating country that they had never heard about before. A country, which it seemed, had stood up against Britain or the 'little Shaitun' as they liked to call it.

One of the Pasdaran looked at Pat and asked her to describe her country. Once again there was silence as everyone stared at poor Pat who knew nothing at all about Ireland. She appeared very nervous, afraid as were we all, that the wrong answer could put us in an Iranian prison overnight or worse still, taken hostage. This was obviously something it was imperative to avoid and we were all aware that the situation in Iran was so volatile and uncertain that anything was possible. Pat continued to gaze around the room as if desperately searching for divine inspiration. She looked at all of us for help but we all stared back with fixed expressions of horror. Finally she looked up at the ceiling and with great relief appeared to find the answer - 'green' she spluttered 'very green, in fact it's very very green.' The Pasdar gave her an encouraging, slightly confused half smile but Pat had said all she knew about her new country.

At this point everything started to disintegrate. I could feel a bout of revolutionary giggles coming on, which I fortunately was able to control. Niall launched into rich descriptions of all things Irish and Don valiantly started to translate. Another potential disaster was averted but Pat was teased for a long time afterwards about her new nationality and her description of Ireland. Fortunately after an eventful few days we were able to return to Tehran without further drama.

29. LEPROSY CLINIC

The next few months were filled for Niall with visits from different milk men and meat men and many trips to the various Ministries as he and the Irish Trade Board (CTT) tried to get the Iranian Government to purchase Irish agricultural produce. Our local Irish milkman, Gerry, from the Dairy Board seemed to spend more time in Iran than in Ireland and had a semi-permanent room in the embassy. He was doing a really good job and had already organised several business contracts during that first few months. On a personal level he was great fun and his quirky humour was exactly what we needed on some of our darker days in Tehran.

This was my first time of not working since I had qualified eleven years previously and I really missed my work; so I started to see several Westernised Iranians (who spoke English) for psychotherapy sessions. Many of these individuals were quite traumatised by the changes in their lifestyle; their children in particular found life under a strict Islamic regime very difficult and often experienced problems at school. The 'Peak Performance' programme, which I had developed for Olympic athletes, worked very well on improving concentration and dealing with stress; it was interesting to use this programme for such a completely different group of individuals.

I was settling in quite well. There were regular meetings with the few Irish wives who had stayed after the revolution, especially Jacqui and her husband Ali who kept us informed about the happenings and - equally importantly - the rumours in the university and on the streets.

By now diplomatic functions were beginning to occur at a great rate and I was always happy when my Belgian friend Jennifer, or Livleen from the Indian Embassy, were there. Often these diplomatic occasions could be very stilted and not too interesting, especially for the wives, as people often struggled to find something meaningful to say.

On most postings the usual topics would be previous postings if you were new, next postings if you were leaving, problems posed by local maids and, not least, problems with schools/children. As I was not too interested in those topics, I was relieved that conversations in Iran were usually different and were more likely to be about the situation at the war front or the changing political scene and, of course, food shortages. It was on one of these occasions that Jennifer, Pat, Livleen and myself discussed the possibility of trying to raise money for the growing group of people who were unable to buy food and medicines. It was decided that the simplest and quickest idea was a bazaar, which would be held in our embassy. We all returned home relieved that at least one diplomatic function had led to a meaningful outcome.

Two weeks later, a group of wives got together and baked cakes and biscuits, I made loads of pies and quiches (my quiches were improving with the new oven) and the stalls were laden with any delicacies we had ordered from the Danish diplomatic suppliers. Jennifer, of course, had her usual supply of Belgian chocolates - so we were all set!

We never found out what charitable activities had taken place in the Shah's time but certainly nothing had happened since, so there was a wonderful turn out of expats and wives from other embassies. It was a tiring day but very worthwhile as we served tea and coffee and worked until nearly everything was sold. The bazaar was sold out by the early afternoon and all the helpers went upstairs to sit down and discuss the day over cups of tea and coffee and any food that may have been left over. There was so little happening in those early days of the revolution that everyone was delighted to experience a day out once again. It was also good that people could buy foods that were no longer in the shops and of course the best part was that Sister Maryam would be able to get medicines for her leprosy clinic. It was decided that we would repeat this every year and rotate the bazaar to different embassies.

It was now December and the weather was starting to get colder. We looked forward to the start of the skiing season in the Elborz Mountains and planning a Christmas Eve party; but then we got some unexpected news.

Changing of the guard at Lenin's Tomb, Red Square

View of electric fences from train at Soviet-Iranian Border.

An Apprehensive Arrival in Tehran by train from Moscow

Tehran Railway Station

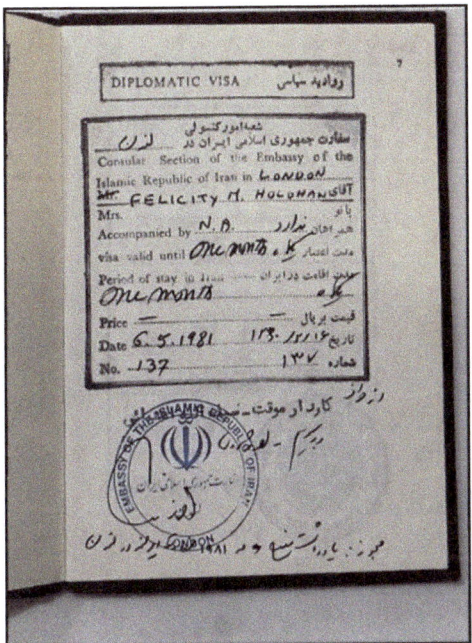

My Iranian Diplomatic Visa 1981

Ruhollah Musavi Khomeini *was the Iranian Islamic revolutionary, Leader of Iran from 1979 until his death in 1989.*

Play-reading at the New Zealand Embassy

MoshKat and half-mast curtains

Niall at his desk

Diplomats visit Ahvas War Front

The Ahvas War Front

Gun-toting militant women wearing chadors

A staged protest at the war front

Diplomats visit the Lar Dam

Lar Dam is located at the foot of Mount Damavand in Amol county, Mazandaran, Iran

Nomad Camp, Lar Dam

Tehran – The Djube into which Esther and I fell

Ali Gapou, Isfahan

Isfahan Mosque Masjid-e Emam (Shah)

Former Caravanserai, Shah Abbas Hotel

Official Minature Artist beside picture of Ayatollah Khomeini 1981

Official Minature Artist beside picture of young Shah – 1978

Armenian Church Isfahan

Sitting beside Tomb of Sufi Poet Hafez (1325 -1390)

View of Persepolis - Remnants of Reza Shah's tents (in the background) for the Anniversary Commemoration (1971)

*Grafitti of Stanley,
New York Tribune, 1879*

*Niall at the Gate of All Nations in
Persepolis*

Apadana Staircase at Persepolis

The double griffin (combination of Lion and Eagle), the Apadana, Persepolis

Ancient Tombs of Achaemenian Kings and Ka'ba-ye Zartosht also called the Cube of Zoroaster at Naqsh-e Rustam

Tomb of Cyrus the Great, who ruled from 559 to 529BC, Pasagardae

PART 2
-1982-

30. SIX – FINGERED YOUSEF

December 1981

Six months after we arrived in Tehran, the Irish government decided to close down the embassy. This was despite that fact that there had already been, in this short time, significant trade negotiations and visits by businessmen. The Iranians were very short of food and Irish agricultural produce had a ready-made market in the Islamic Republic. Meat and dairy products were in high demand. For some unknown reason, however, various officials had decided that the Irish Embassy in Tehran was not a viable option and needed to be closed. (The same scenario happened over thirty years later when the Irish embassy would again be shut down just as negotiations were being undertaken by President Obama to lift international sanctions. While other countries were again queuing up to get a slice of the Iranian economic pie, Ireland was closing down its embassy. By the time President Biden came to power the situation looked brighter and the embassy was once again opened up.)

In 1981, Niall tried to convince the Irish Department of Foreign Affairs that Iran would soon be a lucrative, competitive market and he indicated that it would be counterproductive to close the embassy. Common sense, however, is rarely a major commodity in government circles. Consequently Niall's suggestions (and those of the Irish trade board) were ignored.

We were, it seemed, being brought home. Once again I was full of apparently brilliant but in fact quite reckless ideas which I would start to regret as soon as they came to fruition.

I thought it would be a good idea to travel home through various exotic and - at that time - little known countries. The only way we could accomplish this was to travel overland. I could see Niall's eyes begin to first glaze over and then when he realised I was serious, they started to widen in alarm. I carried on my discussion regardless. This I had learned is the only way to behave when embarking on a series of crackpot ideas. Basically it is a form of assertive training: the secret is I just keep pushing until my poor husband is worn down.

On this occasion we could travel by bus through the mountain passes of northern Iran into Eastern Turkey. As this would be in the month of January, it was probably going to be snowbound but that did not seem to bother me too much at that time. From there we could cross the mountains of Anatolia (also by bus and also probably in the snow). After this we would travel through Syria and Jordan.

Passing close to the Lebanese border and the Golan Heights we would then travel through Palestine. At this stage Niall was either being sarcastic or in favour of the idea, when he suggested entering the Sinai Peninsula and crossing the Suez Canal. Sinai and Suez, closed by Israel for several years, had just been opened up again after the Camp David Accords between Anwar Sadat and Menachem Begin. That was the agreement that had cost President Sadat his life. One evening in October a few months after we arrived in Tehran we had heard noisy, jubilant cheers throughout Tehran. The following morning we got the news that Sadat had been assassinated in Cairo. Now Mubarak was president and a bus route between Israel and Egypt had been opened so it looked as if our final destination by bus might be Cairo.

It was settled, that is what we would do. I began to realise that I was actually a bad influence on my normally sane and rational husband. He should of course, have pulled me back from the brink of madness but he did not. In fact he seems to have encouraged my rash actions. Maybe attempts to make him feel guilty about leaving my job in Ireland were working, or more likely he too loved an adventure.

I had already sounded out our French friends who seemed quite eager to make the journey but, of course, they sensibly backed out several days before the departure date offering to fly to meet us in Damascus. We were on our own at least for the difficult part of the journey.

We were able to go skiing in the mountains for several weeks and were scheduled to depart in the middle of January, which meant that we left the embassy in a snowstorm. Esther and Latif came to the door to see us off. Once again the threat of embassy closure hung over their heads yet they seemed quite happy to resume a period of very little work. The look on their faces, however, showed that they felt we were quite mad to undertake this trip. We asked Esther what present could we bring her back from Ireland when we returned (either to pack up or resume our posting). She clasped my hand and said that the only present we could bring her would be if we became closer to God. So much for an exciting shopping trip buying presents for Esther!

We loaded our bags into the car and Archie, looking a little less grumpy than usual, drove us to the local bus station. By now I was starting to have serious misgivings about the trip as we stood shivering in the rundown station surrounded by piles of dirty snow and slush. The bus station had obviously been a vibrant place during the Shah's time when it was used by many adventurous young backpackers making their way through Iran to Pakistan and India. Now it just seemed sad.

Joining a group of bedraggled travellers, we waited to board the coach to Istanbul. Needless to say we did not look too out of place in our thick coats, woolly hats and scarves. We also had a rucksack containing guidebooks and sunglasses in case we ever saw the sun again. The only things that might stand out in the middle of a pile of assorted well-worn bags were our new leather cases, which had been a present from my father. Inside our cases we had souvenirs for friends and family, including some exquisite miniatures painted on pieces of camel bone bought from the miniaturist in Isfahan. Inside the bags were also several wooden boxes decorated with camel bone mosaic and some lovely trinkets of silver, lapis lazuli and turquoise, which had come from Joseph's shop. Various pieces of light clothing for our stay in Egypt were also packed.

Archie gave us a pitying look of sheer disbelief at our stupidity as he gleefully waved us goodbye and turned to leave the bleak bus station. The floor seemed to glisten with a mixture of melting snow and oil, which shimmered in the form of electric blue and dark green psychedelic patterns. Or maybe I was just feeling light-headed at the thought of driving in a blizzard through the dangerous passes of Northern Iran and Anatolia. It was, however, too late to change our plans.

Some of the passengers smiled as we entered the coach, although a few, perhaps preoccupied with their own fears, looked at us rather suspiciously. As usual, the last in the queue, we walked to the back of the coach and took the two remaining seats. The majority of the passengers seemed to be Turkish or Kurdish migrant workers returning home. There were two single seats at the rear of the coach. I gingerly sat down beside a man in his forties wearing a large anorak and fur lined hat which covered his head and his ears, a sort of all-in-one hat and ear muffs. He removed his hat and I could see a pair of friendly eyes peering from under dark bushy eyebrows. His cheeks and big mustache were frosted with flakes of snow unable to melt in the ice-cold bus. He introduced himself, flashing a wide gold-toothed grin and holding out his right hand uttered the words 'Six-fingered Yousef.' He watched to see my reaction and seemed a little disappointed when I clasped his one thumbed hand with a polite smile and reciprocated with my own name.

Yousef had an air of mystery surrounding him, a touch of the sinister as if nothing about him could be ordinary. He never told the full story of how he lost his four fingers but he implied it was because of some murderous feud, the details of which it would be better if we didn't know. That meant that the rest of our friendly discussions on, this long trip, would have to centre on the beauty of Eastern Turkey as he was also getting off the coach at the largely Kurdish city of Erzurum. That was just fine with me as I didn't really need any more explanations or drama.

Niall was sitting in the seat behind us relieved, no doubt, that his silent companion appeared to speak no known language. The bus, now completely full, pulled out of the station and set off through the snowy streets of downtown Tehran. The heating was turned on and the passengers started to relax, some sleeping and others staring, as if a trance, at the snowflakes sliding down the window like patterns in a giant kaleidoscope. The ice on Yousef's moustache was melting and the drops made damp patches on the sleeve of his anorak.

We moved slowly through the heavy afternoon traffic. Everywhere pictures of mullahs, Ayatollah Montazeri, Khomeini and Rafsanjani looked down at us through a thin veil of falling snow. Slogans were strung across the walls of the American Embassy proclaiming in large letters – 'MARG BAR AMERIKA' or 'DEATH TO AMERICA'. We had seen and heard those slogans many times on the television during the crisis when American diplomats were kept hostage in the embassy for over a year. Seeing them, however, on the actual embassy walls always seemed a little more chilling. I slid down in my seat a bit and surreptitiously watched the women scurry along the snow-swept streets, the ends of their black chadors dragging behind them along the dirty, wet pavements.

Another common sight was jeep loads of camouflage-dressed Revolutionary Guards passing by, shouting slogans, their AK 47 rifles at the ready, their eyes scanning the environment for signs of trouble. Young men were frequently picked up from the street and taken to Evin Prison or the war front. The Pasdaran struck fear into the hearts of many. After six months I had come to respect the Tehranis, their resilience, their combination of simplicity and sophistication and particularly their humour. They were constantly joking about the new regime and passing around secret cartoons at great personal risk. I would never, however, get used to the violence of some of the Revolutionary Guards.

Soon we were driving past the luxurious villas in the northern suburbs of Tehran. After an hour the Elborz mountain range overshadowed the road on the way to the town of Qasvin where years later we would be involved in a deadly car accident. The silvered mountain range looked magnificent, even though the tops of the mountains were covered in cloud. Every Saturday in December since the snow started we had gone to the Elborz Mountains to ski in the resort of Dizin with groups of diplomats and friends. Although the cafes were pretty primitive and the après-ski was non-existent, the skiing conditions were wonderful and it was a great break from the frenetic activity of the city.

Niall produced a flask of coffee and sandwiches; Yousef got out some fruit and biscuits and we shared our food with the passengers at the back of the bus. After this 'picnic' I slept for a little, awaking as the bus pulled off the road into the parking space of a roadside café on the way to the town of Tabriz. The windscreen wipers were making deathly gasping noises as they attempted to scrape through the piles of fresh snow on the window. I hoped against hope as we all piled sleepily off the coach into the freezing night air that the wipers would survive the trip, not to mention the rest of the bus.

A wave of warm air greeted us as we entered the café which consisted of one rather stark room filled with several small square tables covered with oilskin cloths An electrical two-barred unit was attached to the wall its blue light waiting to attract and dispatch any flies who were brave enough to venture out of hiding on such a cold night. It was basically a dismal place like so many small enterprises in Iran but as the men huddled round the kerosene stove warming their hands and chatting happily about returning home to their families it took on a different atmosphere. It really was the warmth of the people we met during our stay in Iran that turned a relatively spartan existence into a truly marvellous experience.

I was no longer hungry so we ordered glasses of tea which we sucked through lumps of sugar. It was wonderful to warm our cold hands on the glasses of steaming liquid. Yousef and some of the passengers tucked into big plates of fluffy rice, lamb, chelo kebab, pieces of crusted rice (tadiq) and large bowls of creamy yogurt, mint and chopped cucumber (maast-khiar) with piles of freshly baked Iranian barbari bread. It all looked and smelled delicious and in the spirit of true Turkish and Iranian kindness and hospitality, everyone tried to share their meal with us but we were too tired to eat anything in the middle of the night.

The snow had stopped when we got back into the coach and the driver had fortunately managed to clean the windscreen. We had several more stops as we passed through Tabriz and Iranian Azerbaijan but I stayed on the bus trying to get some sleep. I was really relieved when finally, after driving through the treacherous mountain passes; we arrived safely at the Turkish border post of Bazargan.

31. MOUNT ARARAT

January 1982

It was minus 14 degrees when the passengers put on their coats and stepped down from the bus into the freezing early morning air at the Turkish border. There had not been an excessive amount of snow that

December so the dangerous passes had caused no major problems. The next winter, however, the high mountain passes through which we had just travelled were completely blocked with snow. A great many of the motorists stranded in their cars or trucks froze to death in the isolated passes before help could arrive. At that time of course, we had no idea how lucky, once again, we had been.

The border post at Bazargan was fairly nondescript and the customs office looked like a makeshift shed. We dragged our cases across the slippery ground into the shed and lifted them up onto the long tables. Maybe it was just too cold or too early but the guards on both sides of the border did not seem very interested. On the Turkish side of the border we ate some hot barbari bread, salty feta cheese and olives and drank our first cup of Turkish coffee, hot, dark and delicious. Happy to be on the road to freedom we all laughed and joked as we got on the bus to Erzurum although we realised that neither snow-bound Eastern Turkey nor Syria (then under the rule of Hafez al-Assad, the brutal father of his equally brutal son, Bashar al-Assad) were going to be easy.

It was exciting to look out of the bus window and see Mount Ararat, which is the mythological site of the landing of Noah's Ark after the biblical flood. My imagination took over as I visualised a scenario from childhood of a large, battered, wooden boat perched precariously on the mountain top, rocking from side to side as exotic animals ran down the mountain, two by two. I was soon brought back to earth by the shouting and laughing inside the bus as the passengers discussed the relative merits of various drinking establishments which they were about to visit. So much for Noah's Ark!

This area of Eastern Turkey was a very impoverished part of the country with poor agricultural land and scraggy animals wandering along the 'main' road. At the small Kurdish border town of Dogubayazit (known colloquially among some Tehran expats as 'doggie buys a biscuit') we saw the imposing view of the ruins of the Pasha's Palace, high on the mountainside. The Ottoman governor Ishak Pasha ruled over one of the most important trading routes between Europe and Asia, including the famed Silk Road. This stunning view of the mountains, however, was definitely not what was contributing to the sense of rising excitement among the passengers, instead it seemed that once again, thoughts were only concentrated on the next stopping place.

The coach drew up outside a dilapidated roadside hostelry where everyone jumped down the steps and rushed inside to drink their first beer or whiskey for a long time. Anyway the verdict of the excited revellers was that Efes beer had not changed over the intervening years and was still excellent!

Finally we reached the city of Erzurum surrounded by snow-covered mountains, where the temperature can sometimes drop to minus 40 degrees. Although Erzurum was an important town over many centuries and even recently was a staging post for thousands of camels making their way along the old caravan route to Persia, when we arrived it appeared to be basically a run-down provincial town. There was a hotel at the bus station, which did not look too salubrious, but there was no other choice. We were hardly in a position to go searching for better accommodation in the freezing cold of the late afternoon. On our arrival at Hotel Ornek, we were shown upstairs where we walked along a small, dingy corridor with torn wallpaper and chipped paintwork, into the tiny room at the end. The dirty windows overlooked the bus station, so at least we did not have far to go in the morning. It was a two-bunk room with a wash hand basin but sadly it was nowhere near as nice or clean as the compartment on the Moscow train six months earlier.

Washing as well as we could we changed our clothes and we were just going to see if there was anywhere we could eat, when there was a knock on the door and Six-fingered Yousef popped his head around it to ask if we wanted to join him and his Kurdish friends for a meal in a nearby café. We were delighted to see them and we all trooped across the snowy street, past the handful of buses standing in the bus station and into a café which was similar to the one we had been in earlier on our bus trip. This time we were hungry and we enjoyed helping ourselves to the big plates of rice, lamb and chicken kebab.

Yousef was in great form and he was really happy to be drinking whiskey and good Turkish beer. The pale moon was peeping over the snowy mountains turning the white peaks into silver. It was a magical scene. We were all too tired and cold, however, to stand around too long so went back to the hotel where we said goodbye to Yousef, He had started to explain the reason for his missing fingers but seemed to think better of it.

There was a large Kurdish population in this area and it might have been that Yousef was a Kurdish activist or maybe was involved in rebel activities in Iran. We never found out but we certainly did not believe that he had lost his finger in a mundane machinery accident. Although we still thought there was something quite sinister about his life, we had become fond of him on this short trip because he really seemed to be a true original, able to be himself and to be totally happy with that self. We would never forget him or his six fingers.

32. NIGHT CALLER

The room in the hotel was not very clean; neither were the sheets so I lay down on my coat and wrapped it around me. That was not too much of a problem because I had learnt years ago that if you embark on unusual journeys you have to put up with the consequences.

I was just starting to sleep when there was a loud knock at the door. Startled I held my breath until I heard heavy footsteps retreating down the corridor. Niall was already fast asleep in the top bunk so he was completely unaware of the night caller. The following morning we went for breakfast in one of the small rooms downstairs. We hoped to discover the identity of our mystery caller thinking that the most likely explanation was that Yousef and his friends from the bus wanted Niall to join them in late night carousing. Everyone, however, had already left the hotel and possibly they never even went to bed on their first night of freedom. Years previously on her amazing trip by bicycle to India, Irish writer Dervla Murphy described a much more terrifying experience. Down the road from Erzurum in the nearby village of Dogubayazit on awakening she saw a local Kurd bending over her. That night visit ended very quickly when she fired a gun at the ceiling!

As our bus would not be leaving for another hour, we had time to eat breakfast. The meal was very similar to breakfast in Iran and consisted of delicious hot flat bread, olives, honey, jam and yogurt. Unfortunately there was no caviar.

The sun was warm and starting to turn the icy road into a dirty layer of slush as we crossed over to get to the bus station. The bus had a sign for Antakya on the front; it was quite old and I hoped the tyres were in better condition than the bus itself for our long journey across the high snowy peaks of Anatolia. The tyres proved to be fine but the journey itself turned out to be quite nerve racking as we hurtled at top speed down the narrow, slippery road overlooking the deep valleys.

The view was spectacular as the hot sun shot rays of sparkling light through the crystal-covered mountains. Three years earlier we had experienced a similarly breath-taking journey when we had travelled by bus from the frontier town of Peshawar down the magnificent Khyber Pass to Kabul in Afghanistan. On that occasion, however, the trip was at the end of summer and the winter snow had not arrived. Consequently the painted brown and ochre mountain slopes did not seem quite so magical as the snow-covered slopes of Anatolia.

Once again the bus was very full and all the passengers greeted us with warm smiles. When we stopped on the way for coffee and kebabs they seemed very anxious to tell their story. One of the passengers, a little out of place in his smart business suit, was Haji the Greek, a member of the small Greek Orthodox community permitted to stay in Constantinople after the Treaty of Lausanne in 1923.

We were passing through Eastern Anatolia, where a large Kurdish population lives. Indeed the Kurdish passengers on the bus appeared openly hostile to any Turkish troops they passed on the road. They took great delight in using their few words of English to explain how badly the soldiers treated the Kurds. Unfortunately, years later, nothing much seems to have changed. The Turkish government is still persecuting the Kurdish population and the Kurds are still perpetrating acts of violence against the Turks.

It was fascinating to read how in 1929 Arnold Toynbee took the train from Constantinople to Aleppo across Anatolia. He describes the breath-taking view of the mountains and deep gorge we passed on our bus journey to Syria.

'Here it comes, a sheer wall of limestone on either hand, scaling the sky in fantastic pinnacles. And here, at last, are the Cilician Gates, through which Cyrus the Younger threaded his way with the Ten Thousand, and after him Alexander, and after Alexander the Arabs and the Crusaders.'

Apart from the sheer beauty of the path through Eastern Anatolia, the list of ancient heroes, such as Alexander the Great, who passed through the Cilician plains offers an interesting history lesson. As the night darkened, Toynbee watched the landscape and felt that 'Turkey is slipping away. Already I am almost in the 'Island of the Arabs,' whose coasts are the Mediterranean and the rivers of Mesopotamia.'

After a day's journey through this amazing scenery on our way to Toynbee's "island of the Arabs", we reached the town of ancient Antioch, locally called Antakya. There we drank some hot Turkish coffee and ate some delicious honey-drenched baklava. Strolling around the market area at the bus station, we were happy to stretch our legs after the long journey. We dragged our cases with us and bought some fresh figs, bread, feta cheese and Turkish delight for the next part of our trip to Syria by bus.

33. BUS TO ALEPPO

As we passed through the border post we were a little apprehensive because Syria was a bit like Iran in those days, it was definitely the unknown part of the equation. We did not need to worry, however, as the Syrian border guards welcomed us profusely and seemed very pleased that anyone would want to come to Syria. This time the bus was going to take us to the town of Aleppo, which tragically has been destroyed over the last few years since the disastrous civil war initiated by the Arab Spring.

Gertrude Bell described Aleppo in her letters dated 1905:

'It had been a great great Arab town. An endless barren world stretches round, uninterrupted by hill or tree – you can see the Euphrates from the castle in clear weather.'

Now, the great Arab town Aleppo has become one of the largest humanitarian disasters of this century as various factions from both within and outside Syria, tore the historic city apart and an impotent world stood by and watched the death and destruction.

In 1982 I was very excited at the thought of encountering this ancient culture and our only regret was that we did not have the time to go to the world-renowned archaeological site of Palmyra. In his book *Persian Architecture*, Pope quotes the description of Palmyra by Philostratus, a Greek sophist from the 3rd century AD;

'... a room roofed with a sapphire vault, gleaming with heavenly light. Against the blue ground the stones ... were like stars in the sky. Here sat the King when he meted out justice.'

We hoped we would return to see this magical archaeological site at a future time. Unfortunately we never made that journey and Palmyra has now also been partially destroyed (by ISIS).

When we arrived in Aleppo that evening in 1981 we found a small hotel near the bus station that had aspirations to grandeur but in reality resembled a rather run-down boarding house. Exhausted, we checked in and went straight up to the room and fell sleep. In the middle of the night we were again disturbed by an uninvited guest. This time the knocks were very loud and very insistent as the intruder tried to force the lock. We lay there barely breathing until whoever it was gave up and went away. Fortunately that was the last time that we had a night visitor during our journey.

The next morning we walked around Aleppo with Haji the Greek, who showed us the imposing Citadel and famous bazaar - now both badly damaged by Russian bombing and the government troops of Bashar al-Assad. The beautifully decorated windows and doorways and huge brass and carved wood doors of the houses were also quite lovely and it is extremely upsetting forty years on to hear of the utter destruction and devastation in this beautiful city. Even more distressing, of course, are the killing and bombing of thousands of people, including patients and medical staff in hospitals.

Gertrude Bell's 'great, great Arab town' of Aleppo is no more. No longer either is Lawrence of Arabia's city where 'the races, creeds, and tongues of the Ottoman Empire met and knew one another in a spirit of compromise.'

Aleppo is now little more than a pile of ruined buildings. Syria was in a politically tense situation even when we passed through that winter of 1981/82. A short time later the then President, Hafez al-Assad reacted to a revolt by the Muslim Brotherhood with a massacre in Hama that was believed to have killed tens of thousands. Over thirty years later, his son Bashar al-Assad has been accused of war crimes and has greatly contributed to the destruction of his country. (He finally fled the country to exile in Russia in December 2024.)

After lunch with our new Greek friend we set off to Damascus. We had agreed to meet our two colleagues from Tehran there, so we had to leave Aleppo in order to reach the capital city in time. Another bus had to be found and our luggage stowed aboard. Our friends from Tehran were a French businessman and his young wife who was a member of the Cambodian royal family. He had managed to get her on the last plane out of Cambodia before Pol Pot's genocide got underway, which probably saved her life. It was truly an inspirational story but I was a little unsure how a Cambodian princess or, indeed any princess, was going to cope with the unpredictability of the journey ahead of us which I would find so interesting and enjoyable.

At least we could finally find a good hotel, which hopefully would be a start. We moved into the Meridien Hotel as soon as we arrived in Damascus. Two years earlier Niall had stayed there when he had attended a Euro-Arab Dialogue Conference. Our friends joined us and we spent two interesting days seeing the sights. In those days Syria was quite secular which was a pleasant change from Iran. We were allowed to enter the great Omayyad Mosque which had originally been the basilica of St John the Baptist. Close to the mosque, we found the tomb of Saladin, the great leader who defeated the Crusaders at the Horns of Hattin overlooking the Sea of Galilee in 1187 and drove them out of Jerusalem forever.

This fascinating city is described in 1905 by Gertrude Bell:

'The great splendid city of Damascus with its gardens and its domes and its minarets, lies spread out before you, and beyond it the desert – the desert almost up to its gates, and the breath of it blowing in with every wind, and the spirit of it passing in through the city gates with every Arab camel driver.'

In her description it is easy to see her admiration for the powerful spirit and lure of the timeless desert that surrounds these Middle Eastern cities. It is also easy to understand how so many adventurous travellers of previous centuries fell under the spell of the desert culture.

It was interesting to see the 'Street called Straight' in which, the story goes, Saint Paul had his revelation on the road to Damascus, where according to the scriptures the 'scales fell from his eyes'. This was a long street, now surrounded by the bazaar. Another story of interest about the city walls was described by Viennese writer Ida Pfeiffer in 1842, as 'the place where the apostle is said to have leaped from the wall on horseback, reaching the ground in safety, and taking refuge from his enemies in the neighbourhood grotto which is said to have closed behind him by miracle and not to have opened again until his persecutors had ceased their pursuit'. The only sign of this grotto that Ida Pfeiffer could find was a small stone archway. More than one hundred years later we heard stories of St. Paul escaping from the wall; but no stories of any grotto.

On her arrival in Damascus, Ida Pfeiffer had found the houses very disappointing, just built of mud and clay. She arranged to visit the French and English consuls in order to view the interior of these outwardly unprepossessing dwellings. This time she was not disappointed as "swelling divans, covered with the richest stuffs, lined the walls, which, tastefully ornamented with mirrors and painted and sculptured arabesques, and further decked with mosaic and gilding, displayed a magnificence of which I could not have formed a conception". On our visit we did not visit any consulates but the interior of the hotels and other buildings were also bedecked with drapes woven with threads of gold, with mosaic walls and gilded mirrors. That part of the world is still celebrated for its exquisite and elaborate design.

Bazaars are always fascinating in the Middle East and the bazaars in Damascus were no exception. All of our senses seemed to come to life, seduced by the vibrant colours and scents of the spices. Women were gathered round boxes and sacks of deep red dried chillies, rust coloured saffron, cumin and golden turmeric. Mounds of green pistachios spilled over onto piles of cashew nuts, almonds and walnuts as customers dug metal spoons into the nuts to taste them before buying. The aroma of coffee and exotic spices filled the air as we sat down at tiny tables to drink the rich, black, sweetened coffee and eat the Arabic honeyed pastries.

Mark Twain said of Damascus: "She measures time not by days and months and years, but by the empires she has seen rise and crumble to ruin. She is a type of immortality. Damascus has seen all that ever occurred on Earth and still she lives. She has looked upon the dry bones of a thousand empires, and will see the tombs of a thousand more before she dies."

I had always wanted to see Damascus and I found the city was just as fascinating as ancient travellers had pointed out. Lawrence of Arabia entered the city in the final days of the First World War as the Ottoman control of the city collapsed and described his impressions:

"When dawn came we drove to the head of the ridge, which stood over the oasis of the city, the silent gardens stood blurred green with river mist, in whose setting shimmered the city, beautiful as ever, like a pearl in the morning sun."

Time was running out so we had to leave this fascinating city after two days because Niall was due back in Dublin for discussions on the practicalities of closing down the embassy and we had many miles to cover before we arrived back in Ireland. Consequently we had to set off immediately by bus for Jordan, our next destination on the road to Cairo. We ran into a delay in Amman because there were special requirements imposed by the Israelis for crossing the Allenby Bridge into Israel. Niall and I had no problems with our papers but it took us three days of visits to the Jordanian Ministry in order to solve the problems encountered by our friends. Every day we thought things would be sorted and everyday Jordanian bureaucracy won out.

Finally the problem was solved and we were all free to travel. As a result of this visa problem we had not seen as much of Jordan as we would have liked - apart from its imposing Roman theatre in Amman and, of course, the inside of many different ministry offices. (Twenty years later, however, we would be posted to Palestine and would travel again across the renamed King Hussein Bridge many times. I am not sure that the bureaucracy was any less chaotic but certainly we had some wonderful holidays in Petra and on the Dead Sea coast.)

After the Jordanian customs we had to walk across the Allenby bridge, once again dragging our cases behind us. In the early eighties border posts on both sides of the River Jordan were fairly primitive. The bridge itself was a rickety wooden and iron structure and it was possible to see the famous river through the wooden planks and metal railings as we crossed. It had originally been named after Edmund Allenby, the British general who seized control of Jerusalem from the Ottoman Turks in 1917.

34. HUMAN RIGHTS
January 1982

Having crossed the Allenby bridge, the Israeli custom area was in an open-fronted hut where we placed our bags on wooden tables. Everyone was fairly officious and our luggage was thoroughly searched. I suppose coming from Iran with Iranian stamps on our passports did not help much, although the Israelis were well known for their tough bureaucracy anyway. What really upset me most at that time, however, was that one of the customs men confiscated the little stash of chocolates that I had just bought in Jordan that very day. He was quite humorous about it but still had no intentions of returning my chocolate. Maybe he was just hungry or wanted to share it with his colleagues but whatever the reason I was very indignant at this breach of my human rights!

Thirty years on, Rania, the wife of the Palestinian Ambassador in Saudi Arabia told me of her experiences passing from Jordan to Palestine. All foods, medicines and make-up, not just chocolate, were taken from her. Even though the wife of a top Palestinian official, she was humiliated and strip-searched. Journalist John Lyons also witnessed distressing scenes when he crossed the Allenby bridge with his family in 2010. He described in his fascinating memoir, 'Balcony Over Jerusalem', how an Israeli security guard passing an elderly Palestinian woman kicked over her laden trolley. When the young son of John Lyons helped her to pick it up and reload it, the security guard did the same again.

Years later in 2002 when Niall was posted to Palestine I had less trivial considerations than the loss of a few chocolate bars when I passed through Israeli checkpoints and observed for myself the inhumane treatment of the Palestinians. On that trip, however, after six months in the chocolate-free zone of Tehran, I am ashamed to say that chocolate bars were uppermost in my mind.

When we arrived in Jerusalem we stayed at the famous American Colony, a magnificent hotel with an amazing history. In earlier times during the Ottoman period, the hotel had been a Pasha's Palace. Later it was turned into a hospital run by a group of American Evangelical Christians, and finally it became a hotel. Twenty-five years after our visit, Tony Blair and his band of henchmen stayed there when he was appointed to the post of UN Middle East Envoy. This post seemed entirely inappropriate for him as he was one of the main instigators of the disastrous invasion of Iraq in 2003. Not surprisingly, as Middle East Envoy, he failed to achieve any of his stated objectives. In 2007 when R.T.E. (Irish Television) took me back to Palestine to make a documentary on my book *"The Resting Place of the Moon"* we frequently saw the arrogant Blair entourage lounging around the hotel's garden café.

During Niall's posting in Palestine, I too would go back to the hotel to talk in the garden with Mordechai Vanunu after his release from an eighteen year stint in solitary confinement in Ashkelon Prison on a charge of releasing information about Israel's secret nuclear programme. Profoundly shocked and distressed by the descriptions of his imprisonment and the fact that he was still not a free man, I went on to write a play called '*The Man with no Secrets*' a dialogue which would examine aspects of justice, silence and revenge in relation to prisoners of conscience. All that, however, would be in the future and during our first visit to Jerusalem we were just happy to live in the present, fascinated by the old city of Jerusalem, sacred to the followers of Judaism, Islam and Christianity.

The Dome on the Rock with its world famous gilded dome dominating the skyline of Jerusalem was our first point of call. A few years later the dome would be re-gilded by a firm from Belfast who carried out such a good job of brightening the gold that it affected people's eyesight and had to be dulled down again. Tradition had it, that on the rock inside the golden dome Abraham was told to offer to God a sacrificial ram instead of his son Isaac. It is also believed by many Jews to be the location of the ancient temple of King Solomon, which contained the Ark of the Covenant. This site, therefore, is of great importance to both Muslims and Jews.

Beside the Dome on the Rock sits the Al Aqsa Mosque, one of the great centres of Islam because of the reputed night time visitation to the site by the Prophet Mohammed. The mosque was built in the early eighth century and has been destroyed on several occasions by earthquakes. Professor Jerome Murphy-O'Connor told us that the decoration of the *mihrab* was commissioned by Saladin as was a magnificently carved wooden pulpit that unfortunately was destroyed in the fire of 1969 (started by an insane Christian tourist who believed that the Messiah would not come back until abominations had been cleared from the Temple Mount!). It was also at this site that the second Intifada started in 2001 when Ariel Sharon, who went on to become Israel's prime minister, made an unwelcomed visit there.

Walking through the Damascus Gate into the old city we stopped to chat and to drink sweetened tea with some of the traders. In the nut and spice markets, we bought some pistachios, cloves and cinnamon and then moved through the stalls piled high with brass pots and colourful Arab dresses to visit the Jewish and Muslim quarters. It was quite difficult in this cluttered maze of Hebron pottery and religious objects all lumped together on small stalls, to find the Church of the Holy Sepulchre, which is thought by many to be the burial place of Christ. Eventually, as we turned a corner there it was. Descending the stone steps and entering through the large wooden doors I was quite disappointed. I felt that this church was quite dark both in a physical and a spiritual sense. The actual tiny place of the stone slab, thought to be the burial place of Christ also left me feeling spiritually empty. Maybe it had all become too commercialised or maybe the people who were trying to show us around were just too bad-tempered. I was not quite sure of the reason for my reaction but it didn't change years later when we came to live in Jerusalem on a more permanent basis.

In fact what we did discover then was that different parts of the church were under the control of six different Christian denominations who squabbled jealously to guard their own jurisdictions. Even in the 1930s this church did not seem to be a happy place. Byron pointed out the tension between the Franciscans and Greek Orthodox clergy, describing the Holy Sepulchre as the 'meanest of churches'. The Church of Saint Anne at the Lion's Gate in the old city and the Church of All Nations in the Garden of Gethsemane, on the other hand, had a much more peaceful and spiritual feeling about them.

One of my most enduring memories of that time, is of walking to the end of the famous Saladin Street just outside the walls of old Jerusalem and gazing across to the beautiful Mount of Olives and Garden of Gethsemane with its ancient olive trees. What we did not know was that twenty years later, when Niall was posted to Ramallah as Irish Representative, we would live for four years on that very hillside.

The Church of the Nativity in Bethlehem was another enduring memory. There was a peaceful feeling as we wandered around the old church and then descended with a stream of other visitors into the crypt, which was said to cover the original cave where Jesus Christ was reputed to have been born. The church became famous for a different reason in 2002 when it was used to shelter Palestinian activists in what became known as the Bethlehem siege. After that, visitors would be shown the bullet holes in the church walls and we would give them the political tour as well as the religious one. At that time, however, everything was relatively quiet and outside the church in Manger Square, Palestinian vendors were selling attractive religious carvings made from olive wood. Swinging from their arms were necklaces of semi-precious stones such as onyx, agate, turquoise and amethyst which sparkled in the watery sunlight.

We hired a car and decided to drive around Palestine and Israel. The situation for us was changing by the day because Garret Fitzgerald's government in Ireland had just fallen and Niall suggested that we no longer needed to speed up our journey. He knew it would take time to get a new government together and any new government might possibly reverse the decision on the Tehran embassy taken by the previous government.

At that time there was not much overt trouble in Palestine. Obviously people were upset about the occupation but on a daily level many Palestinian and Jewish people were coexisting very well. There would be more tension several months later when nearly two thousand Palestinians would be massacred in the refugee camps of Sabra and Shatila in Lebanon by the Lebanese Phalangists. The Israelis had already laid siege to Sabra and Shatila and while not actively involved in the killing they deliberately turned a blind eye to the actions of the Christian militia and the subsequent massacre. Seán MacBride, Chairman of the International Commission set up by the UN found that the Israeli government acted contrary to international law and - as the camp's occupying power - bore responsibility for the massacre.

The Israeli government's inquiry into the events, called the Kahan Commission, found that the then Israeli Defence Minister, Ariel Sharon, bore personal responsibility for the massacre and he was eventually forced to resign. He later became Prime Minister of Israel from 2001 to 2006.

Driving through the West Bank we went on to Galilee. Travelling round the Sea of Galilee we stayed the night in the quiet town of Tiberius, which was established around 20 A.D. by the son of Herod the Great. It got its name from the Roman Emperor Tiberius and, although not a pretty town, sitting in a restaurant overlooking Lake Tiberius while eating a plate of St Peter's fish was quite a special experience. In 1877 Selah Merrill, who was an archaeologist with the American Palestinian Exploration Society described the Sea of Galilee as "more like a work of art than like a natural formation…The silent hills about it clad now with verdure, the shadows moving over its surface, the numerous flocks on plain and mountain side, the water-fowl sporting in bay and inlet..."

As we continued alongside the Lebanese border all we could see were barbed wire fences, lookout posts and raked ground to deter intruders. Gazing across the Golan Heights we contemplated the problems associated with the whole area especially, as the PLO had been forced out of Amman and had moved to Beirut. Fortunately everything was very quiet at that time; we felt we had experienced enough excitement in our previous six months in Tehran.

Moving on to the coastal town of Nahariya, we ate lobster overlooking the glittering Mediterranean, as the full moon cast a glowing light on the calm water. Well, I did not really like lobster so I was not interested in the food but I do remember the astounding beauty of the sea and the moon.

Our next stop was Haifa where we walked in the garden of the Bahai Temple. A few years later we would pass the grim prison clinging onto the craggy cliff face above the village of Maku in Northern Iran. It was here that the Bab, the founder of the tolerant Bahai faith was imprisoned in the mid 1800s before his execution in Tabriz (1850).

A visit to the Dead Sea was another unforgettable experience. A vast salt lake stretched out, a silent sheet of silvery water in which nothing could survive. In the Middle Ages terrible stories abounded about the region. It was thought that the vapours arising from the lake were poisonous and killed any birds that flew over it. Valentine in 1897 suggests that Henry Maundrell was one of the first to contradict these claims. In *'Journey from Aleppo to Jerusalem'*, Maundrell in 1697 discusses this claim saying that 'it is a common tradition that birds attempting to fly over this sea drop dead into it, and that no fish nor other sort of animal can endure these deadly waters.' He goes on to say he has seen birds flying over the sea without their coming to any harm, and he has found oyster or similar shells on the seashore. By the year 1897 more exploration had been carried out and it was found that the harmless vapours were probably caused by evaporation but - because of the salt content - there was no life at all in the sea. Valentine explained that Maundrell, was correct about the birds but not the fish as 'shell-fish could not have come from the sea itself, as no fish will live in it; those brought down by the Jordan (River) dying the moment they enter the lake.'

By the time of our visit, this region of the Dead Sea was much diminished due to evaporation but nevertheless bathing in salt-laden water was another unforgettable experience. In those days the whole area was relatively underdeveloped and the bathing facilities consisted simply of a small tank inside a wooden structure. It was a great feeling to float unaided in the salty water imagining all signs of stress drifting away. Afterwards I felt really invigorated, my skin was much softer and it was easy to see how individuals with medical disorders could reap the benefit of such a wonderful experience. Twenty years later when we were living in Jerusalem, the Dead Sea had become a massive industry with resorts, spas and factories for beauty products, built on the edge of the salt sea. Sadly, however, although at least half of the Dead Sea lies in the Occupied West Bank, local Palestinians were not and still are not allowed to travel there.

At that time in 1982 we moved on to stay in a hotel in Tel Aviv and it was interesting to experience the hotel procedures on the Sabbath. The lifts were on automatic and stopped on every floor so that no one had to touch any electrical switch to enter or exit. Full flasks of hot coffee and hot water were also placed on every floor so that people could just pour out their drinks without turning on any electrical devices. We did not know it then, but in twenty years time we would start another fascinating journey in this part of the world.

35. VALLEY OF THE KINGS

The following morning, we caught a bus in West Jerusalem, which would take us into the newly re-opened Sinai Peninsular at the Israeli crossing that was close to Rafah in Gaza. At the border we had to change into an Egyptian bus. As we were dragging our luggage across from one bus to another I wished that we had taken a plane, although that was the only time in the whole journey that I felt that way. Our friends were once again beginning to complain that this was torture, not a holiday; it was too hot, too cold and we should have gone by plane. Niall as usual was uncomplaining and fascinated by everywhere we went. Although in general I usually preferred being challenged and uncomfortable to being too comfortable, I have to admit that at this point I was about to agree with the miserable pair. That was, until we got our first view of the Sinai Desert.

The old bus drove, or rather rattled, down the deserted sandy road and after several hours the deep blue Suez Canal came into view. No plane trip could, for me, evoke such a unique feeling of history. I remembered hearing on the news about the Suez Canal and President Nasser when I was a child and always dreamed of crossing this hugely important waterway. To my disappointment the bus went through the tunnel beneath the canal but I had in part achieved my dream. The Ahmed Hamdi Tunnel had just been opened the previous year because the Israelis had only recently returned the Sinai Peninsula to the Egyptians as part of the Camp David Accords of 1978. One hundred and fifty years earlier, writer and adventurer J.L. Stephens wished to travel in the opposite direction, by camel not bus, to the Holy Land from Suez, an arduous trip across the endless desert to El Arish and Gaza. He changed his route because he would 'be subjected to a quarantine of fourteen days on account of the plague in Egypt' at that time.

The Suez Canal took ten years to complete and was finished in 1859. consequently at the time of the travels of both J.L. Stephens and Ida Pfeiffer two decades earlier, Suez was an unimportant little town with no sign of trees or gardens in the vicinity. (In 2021 the Suez Canal was again in the news when a huge ship flipped right across the canal blocking the entire shipping lane for a week and causing major delays in freight traffic around the world.)

After crossing the Suez Canal the bus drove along the sludge-green river Nile, a crowded road running beside a crowded river. Donkeys and carts, bicycles, cars and trucks tried to overtake each other as they made as much noise as they could shouting and honking their horns. There was little difference between the riverbank and the road and we saw at least one car that had ended upside down in the Nile, killing all on board.

We had been invited by the Head of Mission, Ambassador Brian

O'Ceallaigh, to stay at the Irish Embassy in Cairo. A wonderful man, who looked after us all so well, he was also a very knowledgeable individual from whom we learnt so much about Egyptian politics. Brian was able to give us firsthand information about the assassination of President Anwar Sadat a few months earlier because he had been there at the time. Sitting very close to Sadat on the viewing platform, when the assassins fired on the president, Brian himself although not injured was sprayed with blood. The assassins were members of an extreme Islamist group who were outraged at both the peace deal with Israel and the modernist tendencies of Sadat.

That incident had occurred several months earlier on October 6 and that was when we had heard the shouts of joy and triumph in Tehran that night. Ayatollah Khomeini was particularly incensed by Sadat's regime. It always seemed sad to think of people taking delight in a tragic killing even if that individual was not greatly liked.

The overnight train was the quickest way to Luxor to see Karnak and the Valley of the Kings and we went directly from the station to the Winter Palace Hotel. This was a lovely old hotel on the edge of the river Nile, where Agatha Christie wrote much of her book *'Death on the Nile'*. Forty years after our visit Monica Chambers told me that the rooms where Agatha Christie had written her book had been opened for visitors. In 1982 although the hotel belonged to another era and was somewhat rundown, it was full of character and it was wonderful to wander through the lavishly decorated reception rooms. We were looked after well by the friendly staff who were very elegant in their long white Egyptian robes. The fact that these robes were always in the same pristine condition was to me an absolute miracle. Apart from ourselves the hotel was totally empty. There were, in fact, very few tourists around following the death of President Sadat so once again we were almost on our own exploring all the fascinating archaeological sites.

The Karnak complex covered a huge area north of Luxor and contained a vast array of temples, obelisks and statues. We walked up the entrance road lined on both sides with sphinx statues. At the centre of this massive complex was the magnificent Temple of Amun dedicated to the King of the Gods. Totally entranced, we wandered around Karnak for hours in the heat but at last I was able to wear some light summer clothes rather than a chador or thick winter jacket. Our royal friend, of course, found looking at 'a pile of old stones' too tiring and too hot. She was ignored, except by her solicitous, long-suffering husband.

The next day we went to visit the remote Valley of the Kings. Ancient Egyptians believed in life after death and thought that the body should be preserved so that a life force could re-enter it in the afterlife. It was for this reason that food, drink and every earthly comfort was placed in the various tomb chambers which were also filled with great treasures of gold and silver. The necropolis of the Pharaohs was hidden deep in the limestone hills away from robbers and raiders. Despite this, most of the burial sites were eventually raided and lost their priceless treasures except for that of King Tutankhamun which was discovered with all its magnificent treasures intact by Howard Carter in 1922. This was one of the highlights of the tour. The tomb, deep underground, had to be approached by a steep stone staircase. Inside the small, dark burial chamber I started to shiver, maybe it was just the cold or maybe it was my overactive imagination as I remembered the curse of Tutankhamun and how Lord Caernarvon, who had funded the archaeological dig, died shortly after the excavation of the tomb.

The walls were covered with newly restored paintings of the body's preparation for death while the gilded sarcophagus sat in the middle of a small chamber. A few days later we would need to go to the Egyptian museum in Cairo's Tahrir Square in order to see some of the precious original artifacts. This square since became famous for the demonstrations during the Arab Spring which overthrew President Mubarak.

On our last day in Luxor we hired bicycles and cycled to the temple of the female Pharaoh Queen Hatshepsut. This was another stunning sight, an impressive funerary temple, carved into the sheer limestone cliff. We felt quite safe at that time and enjoyed being independent and seeing all the archaeological sites on our own. Fifteen years later, it was at this same temple that a large group of tourists was massacred by

Islamists in 1997.

On our return to Cairo we went straight to the museum, which contained amazing exhibits including the stunning, iconic, golden death masque of Tutankhamun. The museum was quite disorganised with priceless exhibits all over the place although I believe that since then it has undergone renovations.

There were still two major archaeological sites to see before we flew out of Cairo. One of these was the most famous site in Egypt, namely the magnificent Pyramids of Giza. These were built nearly five thousand years ago on this royal burial ground or necropolis, a testament to the talent and ingenuity of the early Egyptians. The other site was the ancient capital city of Memphis and royal necropolis of Saqqara, which were constructed even earlier.

The three large pyramids of Giza stood alone in the desert. It was an inspiring sight to see them in the open desert guarded by the giant Sphinx. In 1835 J.L.Stephens found the sphinx 'so covered with sand that it is difficult to realise the bulk of this gigantic monument. Its head, neck, shoulders and breast are still uncovered.' He did not mention that several decades before his trip the soldiers of Napoleon's invading army had used this precious relic of an ancient civilization for target practice. Three decades after our visit, the pyramids would be surrounded by buildings and hotels which might make a less stunning setting - but nothing can detract from these wonderful ancient structures.

We entered inside the Great Pyramid, which was the burial place of King Khufu. Once inside the huge dark tomb we all walked up the steep slope to the top where it opened into a chamber containing an empty sarcophagus. This was the burial chamber of the king and was probably robbed of its treasure several hundred years after his death. In 1842 Viennese writer Ida Pfeiffer described how 'the walls of the chambers and of the passages are covered with large and beautifully polished slabs of granite and marble.' We appeared to be all alone inside the darkened pyramid beside the last resting-place of the king whose bones had been scattered to the wind. It all began to seem a little eerie as we cautiously descended the slope and stumbled out into the bright sunlight.

The sense of silence was broken by the shrill chatter of camel men who gathered around trying to persuade us to go for a ride on the camels. This was an offer which was not too difficult to decline after the steep climb inside the pyramid.

Not far south of Giza was the old city of Memphis. There was not much left to see of this ruined, ancient city which once had ruled a united Egypt and which in the 1800s Stephens described as a 'miserable village'. A short distance away was Saqqara, a great necropolis covered with tombs, pyramids and monuments of which the Step Pyramid of King Djoser is the oldest and most important. In the mid-1930s, Professor W.B. Emery started excavating tombs at the site in Saqqara which was established more than 5000 years ago in the first dynasty. During the reign of King Hor-aha, unification of Lower and Upper Egypt came about and the new capitol was originally called White Wall although the name was later changed to Memphis.

The tombs of the ancient kings contained food, drink, furniture and anything else they might need for their journey in the afterlife, including grain in case the dead needed to make more bread. The large tombs of the kings were surrounded by small tombs of servants who were buried with the ruler to serve him after death. Whether this was a voluntary sacrifice or a forced one is not known!

Stephens found this site fascinating and suggested that 'if it were not for their mightier neighbours (the pyramids of Giza) these pyramids, which are comparatively seldom honoured with a visit, would alone be deemed worthy of a pilgrimage to Egypt.' He was right.

On our last day, before we flew back to Ireland, we went shopping in the centre of Cairo for Egyptian cotton items such as long kaftans glowing with a beautiful sheen and soft, luxurious towels. Once again it was a lovely ending to an interesting journey.

What was surprising, however, in the centre of cosmopolitan Cairo was the amount of young female students around the famous American University who were covered up and wearing hejab. Uppermost in our mind was the thought that maybe another Islamic Revolution was on the way there. It would, however, be another thirty years before the Muslim brotherhood came to power following the Arab Spring uprising in 2011, and Sadat's successor, Hosni Mubarak, would be replaced by Morsi of the Muslim Brotherhood - to be followed shortly afterwards by an army coup and the installation of the General Al-Sisi. My Egyptian Coptic friend Irena believed that this would be only a transition period but I was less optimistic. Military coups in Egypt and elsewhere seem rarely to hand over power. So far, after more than ten years there is no sign whatsoever of Al-Sisi handing back power in a democratic fashion.

On our eventual return to Tehran the relationship with our French friends, to put it mildly, was not quite as close as it had been before our holiday. Although to be fair to them, I did remember that not many people ever wanted to get involved in the challenging holidays that I love. As a student in the late sixties, my holidays were spent getting lost in the Arctic Circle and wandering around Iceland, just because I had heard Iceland was the closest landscape to that of the moon. None of my friends from university ever went away with me a second time.

36. WHITE HANDKERCHIEF
April 1982

Due to the fall of Garret Fitzgerald's coalition government in Dublin, we had to stay in Ireland for several months. As we had thought might happen, the new government led by Charles Haughey reversed the decision of the previous one and finally we were told to return to Tehran. Plus ça change!

Returning in the spring we found a profusion of wild flowers in the mountain villages, which had previously been covered in snow and ice. The overflowing streams tumbled down the mountains with great force, ice cold, filled with the last remnants of the winter freeze. The men who had worked on the ski slopes now tended their sheep on the rocky mountainside. This once again was a picture of rural contentment.

We settled in quite happily. The staff were not too pleased to see us back but at least their jobs were secure, for the moment. Unfortunately that was not the case for Latif, whom we found had stolen quite a lot of valuable items when he was looking after the residence while we were away. These items included a beautiful silver-backed mirror and hairbrush set that had belonged to my mother. Stealing and spying! Latif had to go. Years later we were informed that he had been re-employed in the embassy after we left and had died of a drug overdose. In the Department of Foreign Affairs, some individuals never take the advice of previous diplomats about embassy staff so there is often much sacking and re-employing going on!

Our friend Livleen, from the Indian Embassy suggested that maybe Devji who worked with us from time to time could come to work for us full-time. This turned out to be a marvellous idea. Devji had travelled around the world with various Indian ambassadors and could cook an amazing array of dishes from different countries although his speciality was authentic Chinese food as he had lived in the Indian Embassy in China for many years. Even more importantly, he was an extremely nice and helpful person who could get along well with everyone.

The Iranians were very attached to various forms of bird life, especially songbirds. I decided it was time to find some canaries whose singing might liven up the residence so a trip was arranged to the local bird shop. The old shop was filled with birds of every colour and size. Cages containing parakeets and exotic parrots filled every spare inch. The decision was made to buy a red-beaked, green parakeet, a relation of the birds filling the sky of the British summer residence at Golhak.

The deep gold-coloured canaries were also lovely and I was about to purchase a lively pair who were twittering away, when I noticed a cage at the back of the shop containing a quiet pair of birds on the floor of their cage. Out of curiosity I went over to investigate. The birds were not on perches like all the other birds and I realised that their claws had not properly developed and that they could not hold on to anything. As they bobbed around on little claw balls they made nervous squeaking sounds and it did not seem right to take the perfectly formed canaries and leave the frightened birds behind in the back of the shop.

Archie and I left the shop carrying two cages: one held Squeaky and Tweaky and the other larger one contained a rather sullen parakeet. The two cages were carefully placed beside the window in a large airy room in the residence.

The political scene in Tehran was getting worse. Young school girls were dragged from the homes, arrested and put into Evin prison where they were tortured and executed. Although the terrifying physical and psychological presence of Evin loomed over the north of Tehran it was surrounded by secrecy. Diplomats, therefore, were unable to find out any information about what was actually happening. In 2007 Marina Nemet published her shocking memoir of here time in Evin as a sixteen year old showing that even young girls were often treated as brutally as men.[3]

Meanwhile the Mujahideen issued threats of attacks on foreign embassies which led to the Foreign Ministry assigning a police guard to every embassy. Niall, feeling that this would cause more trouble and confusion, informed the ministry that this was not necessary. The ministry insisted that they remain but Niall was right - they were very intrusive and actually drew attention to our presence. Having wall-to-wall revolutionary police protection outside the front door of the residence was not exactly my idea of fun.

The police seemed to have lost any discipline they might have had before the new regime came in. Every night we could hear the bored 'guards' constantly playing with their guns and at every change-over, we would have to produce huge flasks of tea and piles of biscuits, cakes and cigarettes. We were happy to comply with these constant requests partly because we felt sorry for these men who were standing all day or night in the freezing cold of winter and the searing heat of summer. We also felt, however, that they needed something or rather anything to keep them from causing us more trouble.

On many occasions when we returned to the house in the evening, I had to lower the car window and wave a large white handkerchief to identify ourselves to our over-zealous police protectors who were happy to shoot at anything that moved. At another time one of the policemen threatened to kill our neighbour. Now this man could be very annoying at times, maybe even brutal as he had been accused of killing at least two stray cats in his boiler and he constantly complained about

---

[3] Prisoner of Tehran by Marina Nemat (John Murray, 2007)

everything and everyone but a threat of murder was probably over-doing it a little. So another trip to the Foreign Ministry to ask for the removal of our protectors was instigated and again our request was refused.

Things came to a head after two years when we heard a loud noise, which sounded like a single gunshot, outside the main door of the residence. By this time we were so resigned to the police playing games with their guns every night that we did not even bother going to open the door to find out what was happening. The following morning we were told that the police guard had literally shot himself in the foot the previous evening. This was the excuse Niall had been waiting for. He went straight down to the Foreign Ministry to demand the immediate removal of all police protection, as we felt safer with potential terrorists than with the police guards. In fact the police had already disappeared and were never seen again. Mission accomplished! We would now be left alone.

37. OMAR KHAYYAM

By the end of April, however, the city of Tehran was starting to get hot and dusty. My escape from the heat and dust but mostly from the revolutionary fervour was a quiet house in a walled garden in the north of Tehran where I studied Persian calligraphy with a famous Sufi artist. Don and Pat introduced us to Soleiman whose father Ustad Abdol Rasouli had been a high-ranking official in the oil ministry at the time of the Shah and the most famous living calligrapher during the Shah's reign. At the start of the revolution, his calligraphy has been removed from the museum in Tehran. He was also a famous Persian musician who combined all these different aspects of his life with his Sufi philosophy. I had been interested in Sufism for many years and had read quite a lot about it but it was not an intellectual pursuit and unfortunately unlike Zen Buddhism, at that time, it was almost impossible to study Sufism as a Westerner. When, therefore, he accepted me as a pupil to study calligraphy I saw this as an opportunity of entering into the way of Sufi philosophy instead of just reading about it in a book.

Every week I would go to study calligraphy in the peaceful atmosphere of his lovely house and on several occasions he came to the Irish Embassy to teach some of wives of the local diplomats. Sometimes I would meet his daughter-in-law, Farimah, an artist working in the Iranian Television Studios and his young grandson Ali Reza. Mostly I was there on my own, quietly observing his pen moving swiftly across the page, producing the beautiful smooth curves of Persian writing, a single line formed in perfection of action. I also studied the sehtar, a small stringed, long-stemmed Persian musical instrument that looked a little like a spring onion. This sweet-toned instrument was taught by Jamal, one of the calligrapher's music students.

These lessons were very special, although I am afraid I rarely approached a state of perfection in either of these cultural activities. The delicate wooden pen just could not seem to take on a life of its own. Rather, to my embarrassment, it mostly scratched and wobbled its obstinate way across the shiny paper. However much I tried, my moments of flow were very fleeting and my frustration was very obvious. I attempted to imitate the Master but of course I knew from my work with Olympic athletes that the way to success in everything was not by imitation but by letting go of the need to succeed and concentrating purely on the task in hand.

One of the best examples of this was described by Professor Herigel in his book '*Zen in the Art of Archery*'. He spent a long time desperately trying to achieve a state of perfection in archery and it was only when he concentrated on the here and now, thinking only of that one shot that he achieved success. He was finally able to let go of the self and look at his archery in terms of 'it shot, not I shot.' With an empty mind he concentrated on the shot, no longer aware of success or failure. I was very aware of Herigel's realisation that Kyudo, the Japanese martial art of archery, was a spiritual journey rather than a sport but it was still very hard to practice day after day without seeing much improvement. The musical practice was easier because I had studied other musical instruments in the past, but even there I found any improvement very slow. Probably the only reason the Master allowed me to continue for four years was because my delight and interest in being in this amazing cultural and inspirational environment was so evident.

The calligrapher had a great sense of both joy and calm, which reminded me of the Zen Masters I had met in Japan. His work was so beautiful and had pride of place in the museum before the revolution. Most of his writings consisted of lines from the Koran or those of his favourite Sufi poet Hafez of Shiraz. My favourite was the poetry of the famous scientist and astrologer, Omar Khayyam. The mausoleum of Omar Khayyam in Nishapur was decorated with the calligraphy of Master Abdol Rasouli. I was able to see this mausoleum when we travelled there on several occasions. One of the pupils of Omar Khayyam related how he wished his tomb to be "in a spot where the north wind may scatter roses over it". His tomb is in a flower garden in Nishapur. Constructed in the 1930s it is a huge structure made up of eight diamond shaped panels engraved with the poetry of Omar Khayyam from the calligraphy and templates of Professor Abdol Rasouli. At my first lesson, he had given me a piece of his calligraphy which was decorated with the templates from this mausoleum. As a student I had always loved the *Rubaiyat of Omar Khayyam* translated in such a special way by Edward Fitzgerald. He produced many different versions of the poem but I always preferred this verse from his first edition of 1859:

AWAKE! For Morning in the Bowl of Night
Has flung the Stone that puts the Stars to Flight:
And LO! The Hunter of the East has caught
The Sultan's Turret in a Noose of Light.

Even before I arrived in Iran I had decided to study calligraphy because I saw it as a way of achieving a deep state of peace of mind similar to that which I had experienced in my time in Japan. In the Far East calligraphy is regarded as a meditative process and perfection is only achieved when the ego is let go and the calligrapher is lost in the piece of art in a state of flow. My experience with the Sufi Master has lived with me forever.

In May we decided to travel with the Australian and British chargés to see Omar Khayyam's tomb in Nishapur. For me this trip was undertaken in memory of the great poet and of my teacher Abdol Rasouli. We travelled on to Damghan where we entered the magnificent eighth century mosque, the Tarik Khana. Sylvia Matheson says the mosque was damaged in the twelfth century and was rebuilt by the Seljuqs. Outside the town we visited the Pir-i-Alamdar, dating from 1021. Very impressive Kufic inscriptions surround the base of the flat dome. An archaeological treasure still lay in store. The huge tomb tower of Gonbad-e-Qabus (1006 AD) could be seen on the horizon like a huge pointed pencil reaching into the blue sky. This was the tomb tower of Shams el Ma'ali Qabus, whose body is said to have been suspended in a glass coffin high up in the hundred and sixty foot tower. Writer Robert Byron regards it as one of the greatest buildings of the world. "a tapering cylinder of café au lait brick springs from a round plinth to a pointed grey-green roof, which swallows it up like a candle extinguisher."

38. RABIES SCARE

A more mundane pastime which sounds a bit strange but which I also found very satisfying in my unusual world was feeding the local camels. These noble, haughty animals had always fascinated me as a child, conjuring up a fabulous world of endless desert sands and exotic Arabian nights. Twice a month a bell would ring out in the street and I would rush out to meet the camel man and feed his camels. He was not selling anything special, in fact rather the opposite: he was selling camel dung for the garden. I did not need any of this as the garden was very small but I really enjoyed meeting the camels and practising my Farsi with their owner. Camels have a very long memory or so people say. Apparently they remember for years any individuals who have mistreated them and their revenge can be very painful.

We must have looked a strange group: myself, the camel man plus camels and the *ashrali* man who cleaned the streets. Standing in the street drinking cups of tea we used to have great chats in broken English and my limited Farsi about what was happening between the Mujahiddeen and the Pasdaran, the amount of gunfire in the area and of course news of the war front. The camels would stand solemnly their heads in the air with a noble, distant look on their faces as if they were above such petty conversations. Years later, when posted to Saudi Arabia, we would be amused by the idea of 'pretty camel' competitions and the even funnier accusations that some camels were illegally treated with botox to give them an unfair advantage. In Iran at that time, however, the beauty or otherwise of the camel did not seem to be an important issue.

After a discussion about politics, the *ashrali* man would turn his attention to the local stray cat population. Everyone in the street fed the cats and I would take them to the vet if any medical help was needed. On one occasion I was bitten by a cat that was found dead on the embassy steps the following day. The fear was rabies, which was common in Iran at that time and fatal, so I took the dead cat to be checked out in the Pasteur Institute. This sounded very professional but in fact at that time, was just two small rooms with a table and two broken-down chairs in a rather grim building. I hoped that they would examine the cat and diagnose the reason for its death before treating me but I was told that it would take some time to ascertain that information and by then it would be too late for me if the cat did have rabies. The doctor, therefore, moved over to the tiny cabinet on the wall and approached me with a threatening smile and a large syringe. Despite protestations, I had to have my painful rabies injection there and then I had a feeling that the clinic did not have many patients and treating a possible rabies case made the doctor's day. In fact, the medical results showed that the cat did not die of rabies. This was a relief all round, especially for me. Meanwhile none of my friends were too sympathetic and actually thought that it was hilarious - the cat dying because it bit me.

Apart from our sporting activities and archaeological desert trips our social life centred mainly around the embassies. Seeing the same people day after day could have been boring but in fact the majority of diplomats in Iran were very interesting. They were, as we were, fascinated by the culture and happy to be there. Of course the odd few would say with their noses in the air that they did not like Iran at all but it was good for their career. Sadly they would probably realise too late what a wonderful experience it had been. We made some really good Iranian friends who have remained life long friends. One of our favourites was Kian who was the personal assistant to the Danish Ambassador. The daughter of a famous carpet merchant, she had been educated at school in Denmark and at Berkeley University in California. She taught me so much about Persian culture.

On one occasion in 1985, I went with Kian to an exhibition of a famous Iranian painter, Hossein Mahjubi. He was well known for his paintings of horses and of snow-covered valleys in the Elborz Mountains surrounding Tehran. The horses were quite special, a mass of glowing, vibrant colours - green, blue and gold drifting across the canvas. Although full of vitality, the paintings appeared to have an ethereal quality about them.

Kian's friends Agor Teherantchi and his Russian wife had been antique dealers when they were younger. They had specialized in Russian silver and porcelain and to visit their apartment was like a visit to a room in the Hermitage museum. Precious objects and priceless silk carpets filled the room. Fabergé eggs and silver bowls graced the tops of antique furniture. Being with them, drinking tea from delicate gold-frosted Russian glasses and listening to their stories was indeed being in another world of culture and history.

Through Kian, we also got to know Doctor Kamran Fatehi and his wife Kristie who became close friends and were both invaluable when we had several medical emergencies. Kamran was a leading Iranian neuro-surgeon and during the Iran/Iraq war he performed as many serious operations in a week as his American colleagues performed in a year. On one occasion in 1983 he was assigned for a two-month stint in Abadan, the oil centre at the top of the Persian Gulf, which at that time was the principal site of military activity. The city with its huge oil refinery was largely destroyed and Kamran was there the night the Iranians broke through the Iraqi lines to relieve the lengthy siege. One cannot begin to imagine the casualties involved at that time, let alone the primitive conditions and lack of supplies of food, clean water and medical equipment.

The Irish community also continued to be a great support, all of which would turn out to be extremely important at the time of my car accident a couple of years later.

In December we went with two friends to Hamadan (the ancient city of Ecbatana). We stayed in a most unusual hotel which was also a turkey farm and we woke each morning to the sight and sounds of turkeys running around the gardens. Our first site to visit was to the famous stone lion, a sad misshapen lump eroded by more than 2000 years of history. It is reputed to have been commissioned by Alexander the Great for one of his top generals but now seems to be a playground for young children. Another important location was a Jewish mausoleum revered as the tombs of Esther believed to be the Jewish wife of Xerxes I and Mordechai her uncle. This used to be Iran's most important Jewish pilgrimage site. Professor Llewellyn-Jones quotes Polybius a Greek historian who describes an Achaemenian royal residence at the ancient site of Ecbatana near Hamadan. He suggested that not one part of the woodwork cedar and cypress was left exposed as everywhere was plated with silver or gold. During the invasion of Alexander most of the precious metal was stripped off. In fact little remained of this stunning city of Ecbatana; once again Alexander and the Macedonians had caused serious damage to the works of the Achaemenian dynasty.

As we left this ancient site a veil of sparkling snowflakes drifted across the frosted landscape as if time was attempting to erase the splendours of the empire of Cyrus and his successors.

Bus journey through the mountains of Northern Iran

Northern Iran

Bazargan Border with Turkey: Any one for Chai?

Niall with six-fingered Yousef and friends enjoying freedom in Turkey

Hotel Ornek Erzerum – Eastern Turkey

Mountain pass in Anatolia

Changing buses near Antakya

Haji the Greek at the Citadel in Aleppo

St Paul escaping from Damascus

Grand Mosque

Grand Mosque in Damascus

Roman Theatre in Amman, Jordan

Israeli Customs post at the Allenby Bridge - (Human rights for chocolate)

The Church of the Nativity In Bethlehan

The Western Wall – Jerusalem

The Lebanese border near the Golan Heights

The American Colony Hotel, Jerusalem, 1920

The Bahai Temple – Haifa

Ship on the Suez Canal - 1981

Tomb of Tutankhamun - Valley of the Kings

Tomb of Tutankhamun - Valley of the Kings

A photo of myself cycling down to the Temple of the Female Pharaoh, Queen Hatshepsut

The Temple of Queen Hatshepsut

An old photo of Agatha Christie and her writing desk at the Winter Palace Hotel

Hatshepsut's temple at Karnak

Sphinx of Memphis

Statue of Ramesses II

The Temple of Amenhotep III, Luxor

Luxor Temple:
Pylon with Obelisk

The Great Pyramid of Giza and the Sphinx

The Step Pyramid of King Djoser, Saqqara.

Camel man in Tehran selling camel dung outside Embassy Gate

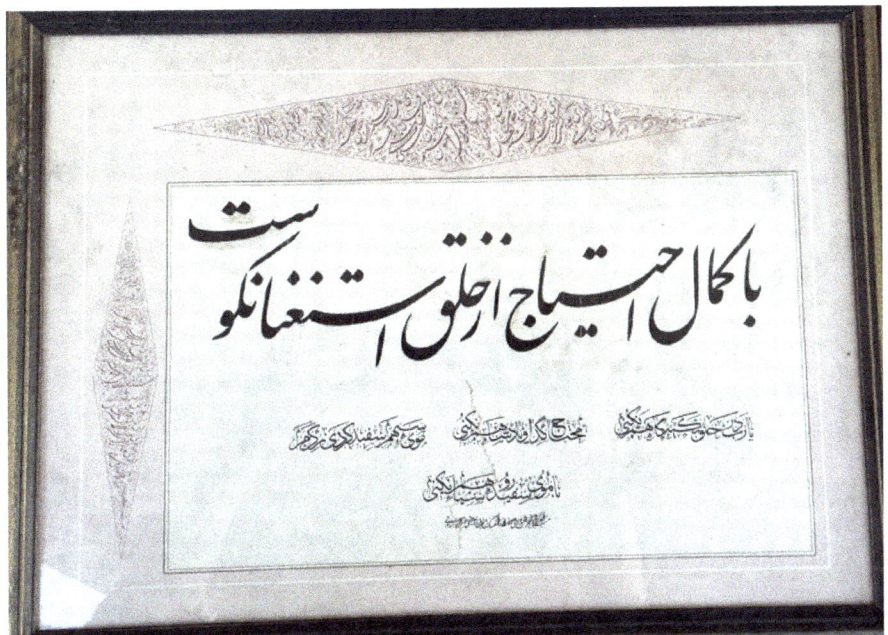
Template for Omar Khayyam Mausoleum

The Mausoleum of Omar Khayyam at Nishapur. Calligraphy by Abdol Rasouli.

The Mausoleum of Omar Khayyam at Nishapur

Tari-Khana Damghan - The 8th century

Pir-i-Alamdar Damghan AD 1021

Gonbad-e-Qabus – tomb tower

The stone lion of Hamadan (šir-e sangi-ye hamedân)

Tombs of Esther and Mordechai (Hamadan)

*Mausoleum of
Baba Taher Hamadan*

*Painting by
Hossein Mahjubi*

PART 3
-1983 -

39. BALL ON A WIRE
January 1983

When new diplomats arrived in Tehran, among their first tasks was a round of 'courtesy' calls on the different embassies. One winter morning, Niall telephoned to ask would I bring down some tea and cakes for the Palestinian Ambassador who had just arrived at the Chancery. Devji and I carried a tray with the necessary items down the outside stairs. Ambassador Zawawi was a dignified elderly man with a pleasant smile. He was accompanied by armed guards who waited beside the car at the front of the embassy. Devji poured the hot chai for the ambassador and I went upstairs to prepare another tray for the guards. I was used to taking tea to the drivers but this was definitely different. The two men were prowling the street with lethal Kalashnikovs, although it seemed to me that the only marauders on the road were several scruffy cats, looking on in bewilderment at this show of force. The tea and biscuits were given to the guards and I tentatively accepted an offer to handle the guns. Being totally accident-prone this maybe was not a wise move and my rejection of a 'Che Guevara moment' would probably have been the best course of action. Certainly the guards realised this quite quickly as they hastily took the gun back and returned with sighs of relief to their tea-drinking. A little tricky maybe but nevertheless, this occasion was definitely more memorable than taking tea to all the other embassy drivers over the years!

We decided to go to the ski slopes at every possible opportunity in the winter of 1983. The ski resorts were only a short drive away and the snow condition and weather usually excellent. On a Saturday the ski slopes were empty apart from a group of Pasdaran who were there to check that we did not get up to anything other than skiing. Just to underline this we had to ski on different slopes, which were divided by a rope into male and female.

The Pasdaran of course were allowed to patrol the women's slopes with, as I soon discovered, large packs of safety pins. On one occasion a button was missing from my raincoat. It was obviously quite a long coat but the last button below the knee had fallen off and the lower part of the raincoat was flapping open. As I skied to a halt at the base of the slope, two Pasdaran ran up to me pointing to the coat, which was open well below the knee. To my amazement one of them knelt down on the snow, got a big safety pin from his pocket and carefully pinned the ends of my coat together. He stood up smiled and waved me goodbye. I turned to return up the mountain not quite sure what was happening. If a western man had behaved like that he probably would have received a slap. Yet here was a feared Revolutionary Guard being kind but intrusive and I was waving and thanking him. It was really good, however, to finally meet a Pasdar who was not a threatening figure.

In diplomacy, as in every cultural exchange, it is always so important to know the rules and traditions of the country; but after a new revolution that was difficult. This action in the west would probably have been regarded as insulting or at the least patronising; but the Pasdaran seemed to think they were keeping me safe, though safe from what, I was not quite sure. Maybe the wife of the New Zealand Ambassador had the right idea when she dressed as a man and skied on the men's slopes.

Tehran's wonderful weather was always a delight mainly because there were four distinct seasons. Spring and autumn were temperate and the flowers and changing colours on the trees were like an artist's palette. In summer the heat was dry rather than humid and in winter the air was crisp and fresh and there was abundant snow for several months, which was great for skiing.

Apart from the dress code, however, strict Islamic rules applied in other areas on the 'his' and 'her' slopes. On one occasion, we and another couple were stepping into a small, round, cable car cabin to go up to the higher slopes when a Pasdar demanded our identity cards to check if we were married. If not, we would have to split up and wait for another cabin. Very annoyed at this stage, we all started to complain vociferously about the ridiculous situation. We continued to complain as we ascended the mountain until suddenly the equipment came to a grinding halt. There were a few rasping noises and then there was just silence. Initially the silence was wonderful as we looked down at the pristine snow way below us and up at the cloud covered mountains above us. Suspended, we swayed gently, a small ball very high up on a slender wire. It was almost a spiritual experience.

That feeling did not last very long, however, as we began to realise that this was potentially an unnerving event which might not be too serious in Austria or Switzerland but in Iran it was a very different matter. Whether the breakdown was caused by divine intervention or the bad temper of the Pasdaran or was just a mechanical failure, the question we were facing was, with bad maintenance and lack of spare parts, could it be fixed before we froze to death. After a tense half hour, the machine whirred back into action and continued up the mountain; we lived to tell the tale. Nevertheless, we did decide not to complain too loudly again.

40. MINISTRY OF POTATOES

Soon it was time to see more of the ancient sites of Persia. Driving with our friends, Andrea and Klaus, we went to Yazd, Kerman and on to Bam. Moving on from Kerman we passed along the road through the Dasht-i-lut desert. Roger Stevens described this desert area as "forbidding and immense with spring gales more cruel than the sea. In winter calm or summer heat the very distillation of deadness." No gales materialised but it certainly was a long cold journey. Finally there in front of us lay the incredible medieval ruined city of Bam. Since our arrival in Tehran, I had been anxious to visit Bam and I couldn't believe I was there at last. The walls of this oasis town were well preserved as was the magnificent Citadel looking down over the old town. I was filled with awe at the beauty of the view and sad that so few people would be able to enjoy this experience. Roger Stevens suggested that "The ancient Citadel and its surroundings are Iran's most photogenic ruin." Passing through the new town we wandered through the narrow streets and climbed up to the Citadel. Many of the remains are from the Safavid era although Bam is thought to have been founded much earlier in the Sassanian period.

At this point we decided to return to Tehran although I would have liked to travel further east along the road to see Baluchistan and the border with Pakistan. Sylvia Matheson writes, however, that it is essential for anyone travelling further to take adequate fuel and water. Sometimes on this route there are travellers who didn't take adequate precautions and are forced to beg for fuel and water to complete their journey. Our own supplies for our return to Tehran included boxes of delicious, plump dates, a speciality of Bam. (There was a big earthquake years later which destroyed more of Bam, although how much I am not sure.)

On our return the skiing season was finished and we began to play tennis in our spare time. Once again there were lots of funny stories. One story emerged from one of the embassies about a husband who had no time whatsoever for his wife's complaints over being rudely forced to cover her hair and wear a chador especially in the heat of summer. He would explain to her time and time again that it was the law; he could not therefore make an official complaint about her treatment - she should just get used to it!

Most of our husbands were sympathetic even if they could not do anything about the situation; but we all knew of this woman's predicament. This would all change, however, when on one particular occasion the husband was walking down the road to play tennis at another embassy in the north of Tehran. Suddenly an old lady covered with a chador came up to him and hit him hard on his bare knees and elbows with her umbrella. Apparently she was upset that his arms and legs were not covered. I think that most people find that the knees and elbows are the least erotic part of the body but maybe she was of a different opinion. Of course it is also possible that she was making a bid for feminism, perhaps she thought that if she had to wear a chador, he should cover up too. In any event, the next day the husband was on the phone to the Foreign Ministry with his complaints early in the morning. At that point we came to realise that sometimes a principle is no longer a principle. Anyway the wives definitely thought that at least some poetic justice had been achieved.

The stories were becoming more amusing by the day so I decided to put them down on paper and write a play. It would centre around a mad chargé d'affaires and his even stranger wife and would obviously have to be based in our embassy, as we could not accuse anyone else of being peculiar. So we based it on a fictional Minister of Potatoes who came to Iran but somehow mislaid his potato samples, which were found too late in a shed at the airport. Everyone was used to the play-readings so we had lots of available actors. I tried to get Devji to play himself but he did not want to. After the play was performed he said he was sorry he had refused because 'I thought it would be very silly but in fact it was very good.' Praise indeed!

We were asked to write some more episodes so I was kept busy for the next few weeks. There was never any shortage of material on which to base stories or plays. The next play was based on the idea of an Iraqi plane flying over Tehran and a sonic boom causing great panic at an embassy dinner party. The more important people immediately headed for the door to the basement only to be told that the basement faces Baghdad and contains the boiler so it was probably the most dangerous place in the house. Everyone was therefore resigned to staying put and taking their chances with the rest. The next sketch 'The Final Breakfast' was about a diplomat who had told everyone about his departure six months before he was due to leave. He consequently had subjected everyone to an endless round of farewell parties. At the end the only dates he had left when everyone was trying desperately to get out of any more parties were one or two mornings for breakfast.

People appreciated that story because in a small intimate posting like Tehran most diplomats feel they have to give or attend a farewell party and it can get really out of hand. Like all the sketches written about our life in Iran and performed in different embassies, the sketches were accepted as good fun - but definitely more Father Ted than Oscar Wilde.

41. PLANNING AN ESCAPE

Meanwhile the birds were settling in nicely. Squeaky and Tweaky were still rather nervous but they regarded the bad-tempered parakeet as their big brother or protector and gazed up at him with adoration. The irritable parakeet, however, thought that he was greatly superior to the canaries and looked down his red beak at these inferior beings. When the weather got warmer they all seemed very content sitting in their cages on the balcony. What I should have noticed were the mean looks the parakeet was giving to his fellow birds flying in great numbers around the numerous trees in the grounds of the British Embassy at Golhak. I should have known he was planning his escape.

Soon a series of books started arriving at all the embassies. At the start of the American Embassy hostage crisis, the embassy staff had shredded all the confidential documents so that the Iranian students who were storming the embassy could not get their hands on them. They had underestimated, however, the ingenuity of the students who rescued the shredded material and painstakingly set about reconstructing the documents. These secret documents were assembled into various books and delivered to the different embassies. This task of reconstruction was mostly carried out by the female students because the male students, it was thought, had more important things to do. All the local diplomats found these books fascinating as they provided a clear insight into the views and policies of the Americans in the period leading up to the Islamic Revolution. Their publication was of course totally contrary to the practices dictated by international diplomatic conventions.

The front and back covers of one of the books contained the following statements.

Front Cover

Imam Khomeini:

The Shah has been carrying out a plan to deceive the nation for some time, He has negotiated with some people but failed, he has tried to deceive the nation, but the nation is not willing to let itself be deceived by the Shah, no matter how much he retreats.

Back Cover

Espionage nest documents No.12

US intervention in Iran (3)

Muslim students follow the line of Imam

The confidential documents in these books had been written by US diplomats in Iran (prior to the hostage crisis) and covered all aspects of the local situation at the time - such as the way the Shah was viewed by his people, the likelihood of his remaining in control and what might happen if he did leave the country. The documents were then transmitted to Washington and to other US Embassies in the region. Despite the illegality of their actions, the students had carried out an amazing task, piecing together minute strips of paper, a task which was later to be documented in a riveting Hollywood movie called Argo.

Another pamphlet we received contained the text of correspondence between Khomeini and Pope John Paul II who had offered his services as a mediator in an attempt to resolve the hostage crisis.

In one letter to the Pope (November 12, 1980) Imam Khomeini writes 'Our people were massacred for fifty years, and the best sons and daughters of our nation were thrown into inhuman prisons where they died under brutal tortures, yet the question of mediation never arose, nor did it ever occur to His Eminence, the Pope, to show any concern for our oppressed people or even to mediate with the plea that oppression cease.' He went on to say 'Yet now they wish to mediate, now that the young people of our nation, after long years of oppression and misery, have decided to hold, in that nest of spies, a few individuals who were spying on our nation and conspiring against it. Or rather, against the whole region.'

According to his letters, Imam Khomeini demanded from Pope John Paul that he request President Carter to send Shah Mohammad Reza back from the US to Iran, otherwise the American hostages would not be released. Needless to say, this request would have put the Pope and President Carter in an impossible situation. In fact the hostage crisis did indeed bring down the presidency of Carter and he was replaced by Ronald Reagan in the next election. The Shah had been receiving cancer treatment in America and was to die a few months later in Egypt. The hostages were finally released in January 1981, a short time before our arrival in Tehran.

42. NOW RUZ

17th March – St. Patrick's Day

We did not have too many visitors from Ireland apart from businessmen because the Islamic Republic was not on the list of top world tourist destinations in the early eighties. Two friends of ours, Dr. Joan Mullaney and Niall's school friend Ciaran, did come out to Tehran for St. Patrick's Day that year to find that Niall had bent down the wrong way to open the diplomatic bag and had injured his back, which was already his 'Achilles heel'. He and I stood beside Esther in the reception line for a time and then in, great pain, he went to lie down. The foyer was just beside the bedroom so some of the guests went to join Niall who was reclining like a Roman Emperor, giving out the odd groan for the benefit of his audience who had decided that sitting on his bed was more fun than joining the main party.

The following morning, Niall jumped out of bed declaring himself cured and despite our protestations headed off in the direction of the tennis court. Needless to say, he returned in even greater pain and had to stay in bed for a week, apart for trips to the physiotherapist.

When Niall recovered, we drove to Isfahan with our friends. We passed by The Great Salt Lake, Dasht-i-Kavir which is described in 1902 as covered in parts "by a glittering ice-like sheet of salt efflorescence on which rest pools of brine, intensely blue. Under the crust lurks water, and round its edges is its foul and dangerous slime". A century later, that Dasht-i-Kavir didn't seem quite so unattractive as the earlier description. Stopping in Kashan we wandered through the lovely gardens there. When we reached Isfahan, we stayed in the old *caravanserai*, the Shah Abbas Hotel. In 1902, Mackinder felt that "under modern conditions Isfahan is probably doomed to an inevitable decay". This was because Isfahan would become isolated due to lack of adequate roads and future railways "appear likely to avoid it, passing far to the northward from Kashan to Hamadan and Baghdad, or to the eastward by Yazd and Kerman to Bander Abbas". Despite this lack of infrastructure this "inevitable decay" did not occur because the incredible palaces and mosques built by Shah Abbas make it one of the most magnificent cities in the world. Like us, Joan and Ciaran found the culture fascinating, but I have to admit that it was not enough to entice anyone else to come out to visit us in Iran.

The most important holiday in the Iranian cultural calendar is that of Now Ruz or Persian New Year. Falling on the twenty first of March each year, it marks the spring equinox, which goes back thousands of years and signifies the planting of new life. For the first time since our arrival we were in Iran for this festival period and were very honoured to be included in the family of our friend Kian who worked in the Danish Embassy. Kian was a wonderful cook and the sight and aroma of Persian food was magical, as garnet red jewels of pomegranate mingled with pieces of lamb and dark green herbs, while golden strands of saffron, sultanas, flakes of almonds, and pistachios laced the rice dishes. At the end of the evening we sat talking and drinking coffee beside the swimming pool in the beautiful moonlit garden. Mostly the conversation centred on political matters, a topic which was depressing but also intensely relevant. To my delight, on the branch of a big tree I observed a motionless silver grey owl studying us intently, his huge eyes aglow, as he appeared to be wondering what we were doing in his garden. That night was another memory stored forever.

43. THE FOREST OF PHILIPOPOLIS

October 1983

Another Trade Fair had just finished and we were due for our annual leave. We flew back to Europe for an endless round of visits to family and friends in England and Ireland. Meanwhile Niall had meetings with trade officials and different businessmen who were trying to break into the Iranian market. We decided to try another adventurous trip back to Iran through Turkey by car. The first step, of course, was to buy the car. Peugeot was still a popular car in Iran so we thought there was a better chance of servicing this brand there than any other. Consequently we went to Paris to buy a Peugeot 505 and continue on from there to Tehran. We stayed in Paris with friends from Foreign Affairs and then drove to stay with our German friends Margot and Otto in their house in Munich. Margot had been the best student in my psychology classes when I lectured at Sophia University in Tokyo and also became a very talented artist of Japanese Sumie or Zen painting. Her husband Otto was a very accomplished flautist and we had not seen them for several years so there was a lot of catching up to do.

As well as long discussions we had to make trips to the shops to buy food for the journey back and the fun part was buying lots of German cakes and chocolates to take back for Christmas. The pharmacist was another port of call as I had been quite ill on the trip after a stay in hospital in Ireland and needed some medicines for the journey.

Refreshed after our stay in Munich, we set off again on what would be the most stressful part of our journey. The famous historian Arnold Toynbee, in his book 'Journey To China' states that 'the motorist en route from London to Constantinople may reckon that he has put about one-third of his road behind him.' However he feels that this will be 'remembered like some dream of a golden age, as he trundles through the middle third and labours through the last.' For us, the most difficult part of the journey would be from Istanbul (Constantinople) to Tehran as we were watching the time very closely: we had to reach the mountain passes of eastern Turkey and northern Iran before the winter snow might block them. Time was running out because we had started our journey a little too late. We were constantly thinking of the previous winter when more than twenty people had died in their cars as a result of being trapped in their vehicles in the snowbound Iranian mountains.

Driving through Yugoslavia to Bulgaria we then stopped for the night in the ancient biblical town of Philipopolis named after the father of Alexander the Great, Philip of Macedon. It was of course Alexander the Great who was to bring an end to the glorious era of Persepolis. We arrived late at night at the hotel, which was surrounded, by a huge dark forest. There were no lights anywhere and the hotel staff were standing expressionless in a line in the dimly lit foyer to greet us. It was actually quite scary and we expected the solemn-faced staff to change into monsters at any moment. In fact we were the only guests and the staff were probably scared of us.

The following morning everything looked normal in the daylight and the hotel was just a big modern concrete building in a forest, not a hiding place for ghouls. We ate our breakfast in the big communist-style dining hall set out with long wooden tables and we still appeared to be the only guests. Eating in the large silent room we felt quite uncomfortable, watched from a distance by the expressionless hotel staff. We could not wait to escape outdoors into the fresh air.

Our exit from Bulgaria and customs clearance into Turkey caused no problems unlike the journey of Professor Toynbee in 1929 who was held at the Turkish customs for several days. Arriving full of excitement at the frontier post he had glimpsed the city of Adrianople with the 'minarets and dome of the Selimiyeh Mosque' which were 'the chef-d'oeuvre of Sinan, the architect of Suleyman the Magnificent.' His excitement waned somewhat when faced with a fine display of Turkish bureaucracy. As well as being unable to pass through customs, the Toynbee family had been forced to arrange for a Turkish chauffeur to come from Constantinople in order to drive their car through what was then a military zone, while they all had to travel by train. Fifty years on, passing through customs was much easier and we arrived quite rapidly at Hadrian's city, Adrianople, now called Edirne. Hundreds of trucks were waiting in line to have their papers checked but we crossed the border quickly without any problems.

44. THE FIASCO OF GALLIPOLI

Despite the necessity for speed to miss the snow we decided to go to Gallipoli to see where the First World War carnage took place. It was raining which seemed appropriate as we recalled the groups of young men rushing to near-certain death as a result of Churchill's flawed decisions and mis-management by the generals. Churchill, who was at that time First Lord of the Admiralty, had to take responsibility for the fiasco and resigned from his post. He, of course, survived and moved on to better things but so many young men died as a result of misguided patriotism in a meaningless war - that is still glorified by so many people despite so much evidence to the contrary. Of course the bravery of the soldiers should be honoured but not the war.

We searched for the name of my mother's uncle who had lied about his age and was mown down, a child, in this man-made disaster in far-off Turkey. I was told by my father, when I was very young, about the shameful mistakes made by politicians and the military, especially in the first word war. My father became a pacifist and conscientious objector in the Second World War even though as a scientist he did not have to go to war. He conducted his own court case and did not go to jail. Instead, as a valuable government research scientist, he was sent to the Department of Agriculture food science centre in the north of Scotland for the rest of the war. He also spoke out about the treatment of the Jewish people but the consequences of his actions, sadly, lasted all his professional life.

From him I learned that it is necessary to speak out for an important principle, in spite of the, usually negative, consequences. I felt this again so strongly as I stood in the rain in Gallipoli, a rather desolate peninsular overlooking the mouth of the Bosphorus and the calm expanse of the grey Aegean Sea. I finally found the name of my great-uncle – Ernest Bates – and thought sadly of the pointless slaughter as I read all the names of the young men who had died in this senseless war not, as they initially thought, for the country they loved but for the egos of the military and government leaders. Unfortunately, nothing has changed so many years on. We still go to war for senseless reasons including, even now, the egos and unbridled desire for power of craven politicians.

Across from Gallipoli we explored Troy and as I stood in the windswept plains I thought of the battles, described by the great Greek and Roman poets, Homer and Virgil, that had taken place here many centuries ago among the heroes of the ancient world. It was here that the Greeks are reputed to have dragged their huge Trojan horse filled with warriors which led to Virgil writing in his epic poem 'The Aeneid' the timeless warning: be fearful of Greeks bearing gifts.

We stopped at the Hilton Hotel in Istanbul for several days. Here we could park the car and once again visit the Blue Mosque and Hagia Sophia along with the Topkapi Museum. Istanbul had been one of my favourite cities since my first visit several years before. In the evening November light the whole city was misty and blurred, reminiscent of an Impressionist's painting. In the mid-19th century, Ida Pfeiffer had described the view spread before her from the tower in Galata: 'The glorious hills with their towns and villages, the number of palaces, gardens, and kiosks, and mosques, Chalcedon, the Prince's Islands, the Golden Horn, the continual bustle on the sea, the immense fleet, beside the numerous ships of other nations, the crowds of people in Pera, Galata, and Topana - all unite to form a panorama of singular beauty.'

It was not all beauty and culture of course in Constantinople in the 1800s, just as there was much poverty and tragedy elsewhere at that time. Her visits to the slave markets were obviously very upsetting and in the harbour there was a wooden barrier separating those who were going to or returning from countries where the plague was rampant. (This of course means a lot more to us now after experiencing the ravages of Covid-19.)

For me in 1983 it was such an exciting feeling seeing the bridge over the Bosphorus, beside a backdrop of such beauty and culture. This was the gateway between Europe and Asia and every time I went to Istanbul I would rekindle the same sense of adventure that was felt that day as we crossed the bridge over the ice cold Bosphorus on the road to Iran.

We were getting very worried about the weather in the northern passes of Iran because by now it was the end of November. We made a mad dash for Ankara, a city which we had not visited on our other trips to Turkey. Unfortunately the capital city, previously called Angora, had none of the beauty and mystery of Istanbul and the main site of interest was the tomb of Ataturk, which was quite stark and militaristic. We did not stay too long in the capital city and on the road again we were relieved to reach Erzurum. On this occasion we stayed in the Grand Hotel which although not too grand was much better than the Ornek Hotel of our previous visit. Our night in the hotel was thankfully without incident although the ghost of six-fingered Yousef lingered on and we would always wonder exactly with what dicey projects he had been involved.

Again we passed by the ruins of the eighteenth century Pasha's Palace high up on the mountainside invoking ideas of the glory of previous centuries. We drove up the narrow path and peered through the gates but it was undergoing renovation and at that time was closed to the public. Ahead the cloud-covered mountains of eastern Anatolia and northern Iran were looking very menacing, as we got closer to the border at Bazargan. Fortunately the snow held off until we got to the city of Tabriz in Iranian Azerbaijan. The only modern hotel in the city was a large concrete block but it was warm and very adequate for an overnight stay. In the nineteen thirties, Robert Byron was not too impressed with Tabriz and wrote of it; 'The features of Tabriz are a view of plush-coloured mountains, approached by lemon-coloured foothills; a drinkable white wine and a disgusting beer.' Sadly we did not have any wine or beer, drinkable or otherwise!

45. THE DIPLOMATIC BAG IS LEAKING

By the time we got back to Tehran it was snowing quite heavily and discussions about the skiing season were already underway. We had shared a mountain chalet in Shemshak with Roger and Jennifer Martin and had some wonderful skiing weekends there with them. Unfortunately Roger had finished his posting in Iran and had been transferred as Ambassador to the FAO in Rome but we still had the use of the chalet. Roger would be greatly missed, as would Jennifer, especially her charitable work with the bazaars. We would also miss their friendship, but sadly this happens all the time and this transient nature of relationships is probably the most difficult part of diplomatic life.

Shortly after our return the diplomatic wives held another meeting to discuss the disposal of money collected from the bazaar held in the Korean Embassy while I was away. Every year the amount of money we made increased although the number of people needing help also increased. Everyone was sad to lose Jennifer but, on the positive side, we had gained more recruits for our charitable endeavours and the bazaars seemed to have become a permanent fixture. We had all decided from the first day that any money collected would be divided between Christians and Muslims. My Indian friend Livleen was the treasurer and the decision was made that most of the money collected that year would go to the Nuayin Institute for the Blind in Isfahan and the rest would be divided between several other groups. The Nuayin Institute produced for sale a lovely selection of colourful bags, tablecloths, cushion covers and place mats that were decorated very tastefully by their blind artists. All these items were sold in the bazaar and we were all very happy that some groups were willing and able to attempt to become self-sufficient.

The small food bazaar I had started in our embassy with Jennifer, Pat and Livleen the year we arrived in Iran had turned into a large annual affair and was a great way of providing money for the group of needy people that came looking for help. This group was growing each year because of the instability caused first by the revolution and then by the war with Iraq. The terrible disease of leprosy had been eradicated but had re-emerged after the revolution and the special group we had supported from the beginning was the Sisters of Charles de Foucault who cared for the leprosy community in Tehran and Tabriz.

We were all looking forward to a quiet period over Christmas when Archie suddenly appeared at the door of Niall's office holding the diplomatic bag at arm's length. "I think there is a problem with the bag - it's leaking" he said wrinkling his nose with distaste. Niall quickly got the key, unlocked the bag and taking out the official papers laid them out on his desk. They smelt very definitely of whiskey and they were a little crinkled. Niall was confused and very worried until he finally found the answer at the bottom of the bag. It was a hand made wooden box containing a smashed bottle of Irish whiskey. The people who had set up the stand for the Trade Fair over the last few years had apparently felt sorry for us because of our lack of 'proper' alcohol and decided to lend a helping hand. They were a great group and it was really kind of them. Their gesture was appreciated but it was quite risky and hopefully would not happen again. That story was reminiscent of the apocryphal tale we heard coming from Saudi Arabia where the Foreign Ministry were supposed to have told the British Ambassador that his piano was leaking. In fact that story probably was true because books and furniture were usually the labels given to any items which were questionable and the story was confirmed when we were posted to Saudi several decades later.

Roger Martin, the Belgian Ambassador had told us how engineers who were building motorway flyovers smuggled alcohol inside the metal pipes. It was very interesting to see to what lengths people will go in order to acquire alcohol in a dry country. Some years later, of course, sophisticated scanners were to be put in place, so alcohol could no longer be hidden. Even more frightening were stories about some Iranian doctors who - when given their allowance of medical white spirit - mixed it with orange juice at their parties. After those tales we steered clear of any suspicious looking orange juice at any parties we attended!

Kian and I at Dizin ski slopes

Men's ski slopes separated from female slopes by rope

Tower of Silence - Yazd

Wind Towers in Yazd

Jabalieh Kerman, Iran

Bam Citadel

Arg-e Bam ancient citadel of Bam and ruins of old town

A "superior Parakeet"

Cover of confidential U.S files from the American Embassy. (compiled by Iranian students from shredded documents)

A copy of Mahjubah Magazine for Muslim Women

A shredding machine to shred routine Embassy work??!!

American Embassy Tehran - "Shredding machine to shred Embassy Documents" – Mahjubah

"The Amercians celebrate Christmas in the Den of Spies" – Mahjubah

The American Embassy front gate in Tehran

Importance of a USA Diploma

Defaced building fronts in Tehran

Niall at the Irish Embassy entrance in Tehran

Caravanserai on the road to Isfahan

Imam (Shah) Mosque (Isfahan)

The Shah Abbas Hotel empty swimming pool (swimming is not revolutionary)

Special items laid out for Now Ruz

Mount Damavand -17,000ft

Staying with Margot and Otto in Munich before driving to Tehran

The Hagia Sophia Istanbul

Gallipoli first world war 1915

Replica Trojan horse on the ancient site of Troy "I fear the Greeks even when bearing gifts" Aeneid by Virgil.

Niall at Troy

PART 4
-1984 -

46. CAT KILLER

February 1984

The rest of the year went by with not too many incidents, much to our surprise. Probably that was also a great relief for the officials in the Department of Foreign Affairs. The attitude of most people at the top of the Department basically was that they did not want to know what was going on, especially in a place like Tehran. As long as there were no major diplomatic incidents that would cause them trouble or embarrass them, everyone was more or less left alone in unimportant faraway places. Therefore as the trade relationship was now soundly established and exports were increasing, we were once again left more or less to our own devices.

The bird population in the residence was thriving too. Tweaky and Squeaky were very happy rolling around the cage on their tiny claws. They seemed especially happy when they were out on the balcony in the sun from time to time. They still looked adoringly at the parakeet, their elder brother in the cage beside them, not seeming to notice that he was unwilling to acknowledge them apart from a condescending nod of his head, from time to time. What they probably did not know was that he was attempting to escape.

After he experimented by pecking different parts of his cage for many months he finally found the weak spot and was able to open the cage door and with a triumphant squawk flew off in the direction of Golhak. The canaries appeared a little upset but got even more attention now that the bad-tempered parakeet was no more. Jacqui and her daughters dropped in to see them regularly and promised to look after them when we went away so they had a much better life than in the back room of the badly lit pet shop.

A bird had been lost but there was a new addition to the street cat group. It was a beautiful fluffy Persian cat which we named Taghouti, a Koranic word used by the new regime to describe all the haughty, wealthy or just cultured and educated Iranians whom they thought were opponents of the regime. Taghouti certainly would not have fitted into the revolution at all. She was special and knew it. She would arrive at the embassy for dinner and then glide silently off into the night, her bushy tail sweeping behind her. A mink and white ball of fluff that no one could tame.

A government minister and his entourage appeared at one point and there were a few nail-biting moments especially when both the water and electricity were cut in the middle of a ministerial dinner. We managed to cope because both Irish and Iranian Ministers continued to talk across each other for such a long period of time that the electricity had come back on before they had finished their speeches!

We were all delighted when a UN military representative, Captain Kieran O'Loughlin, was posted to Tehran. He was a great asset to the expat community and enjoyed going on all the cultural and archaeological trips. As we were all used to the same faces at dinner parties any new arrival was immediately pounced upon and showered with dinner invitations. Apart from being a delightful and knowledgeable dinner guest, Kieran was soon to help save our lives in a serious car accident in the autumn.

The summons came early in the snowy afternoon. "The Armenian family next door want to see you for coffee tomorrow morning," announced Esther. "Why?" I asked, very puzzled. Our only dealings with the family in the villa next door had been complaints from the husband on just about everything.

The *ashrali* man had also told Esther that the neighbour had burnt two stray marmalade cats in his boiler in the garden. The cats, Thomas and Thomasina, had been very gentle cats that we all fed until one day they just disappeared. So I suppose the news was probably true. Our police guards had threatened to kill the neighbour but that had not happened yet. I decided to test out the house of evil to see what was really going on.

The following morning I went to the corner and turned into the garden of the next-door neighbour. I paused with trepidation at the infamous boiler and was met at the door of the house by the wife of the arch-enemy. She looked very normal and seemed in fact quite anxious to please. Maybe she was trying to make up for the bad behaviour of her husband.

The house was quite dark inside; long curtains were held back with velvet ties exposing lace curtains, which kept out any glimmer of sunlight. The furniture was ornate and heavy with glass and porcelain ornaments scattered everywhere. The husband's sister entered the room quietly. She looked very gentle her dark hair curled tightly at the nape of her neck. No sign of the ogre himself; so far, so good.

I sat down gingerly on the edge of chair, feeling very uncomfortable and trying to think of something to say. I suppose one topic of conversation, which would be a good start, could be "does your husband kill cats often?" On seconds thoughts, perhaps not.

A big plate of sticky cakes arrived followed by delicate gold tipped cups of delicious Turkish coffee. I was just starting to relax and then the bombshell dropped. The sister looked at me sharply. "I want to read your coffee cup," she demanded. "You do?" I answered a little weakly. "That's fine." Actually it was not fine, I did not want my future being read by a family of cat killers; but I felt to escape alive I had to agree to this seemingly innocent request.

Putting on a seriously studious look, the sister drained my cup into the saucer. Swishing everything around, she let the grains settle and then peered at them intently or short-sightedly, I was not sure which was the case. There was a period of several minutes where she appeared to be looking into my future. Then she pronounced the verdict, "you will be here for several years." That is possible if the embassy police guards or your brother don't kill us first, I thought grimly. Then she paused theatrically, "you will have a baby soon." Again, that was quite possible for someone of my age. Then that was it apparently, time to go, she had said her piece.

I was shown the door into the garden and back past the dreaded boiler. What a relief! I never did find out, however, why I was invited in for a coffee cup reading nor did I see them again over the next few years. The husband continued to sit in his garden eavesdropping on our conversations when we sat on our patio. We were only aware of this because of the smoke signals he was sending up over the wall from his constant stream of cigarettes.

47. CYRUS THE GREAT

April 1984

Sadly our Indian friends Livleen and Arun had returned to New Delhi the previous February. Livleen like Jennifer was greatly missed for her wonderful social gatherings and work with the charity bazaars. In difficult postings it was particularly important to have close friends with whom to discuss work and the political situation. We had also discussed with them the possibility of adopting an Indian child, which was something I had always wanted to do. Livleen thought it would be quite simple but had promised to check out the situation on her return home to India.

When she got back to India she found out that the rules had changed and that no one could adopt a child without a home study carried out by social workers in their own country. That of course was impossible in a country like Iran but we decided to go for a holiday anyway as we had already booked the tickets and it would be good to see Arun and Livleen again.

Niall had arranged to go to see a group of Irish surveyors who were working on a project building a port in Bandar Abbas on the northern side of the Persian Gulf - so we decided to combine the two trips. The idea was that Mahmoud, our new driver who had replaced Archie after his heart attack a few months earlier, would drive us down to Bandar Abbas. We would fly to Dubai and then go on to New Delhi.

Once more we set off along the road to Qom. It was going to be a tiring trip but the thought of passing through Isfahan always made me feel better about the journey. The Elborz mountain range faded into the distance and the magnificent cone-shaped Mount Damavand still tipped with snow could soon no longer be seen. Dasht-i-Kavir, the reddish salt lake desert, a vast expanse of swathes of dusty, grime streaked salt seemed to go on for ever delivering up, as if in sacrifice to the gods, some sun-bleached bones of dead camels and sheep.

Fortunately the road from Tehran to Qom was more boring than grim, unlike the journey made on horseback by the adventurous Isabella Bird, one hundred years previously. She described passing caravans of the dead on their way to the holy city of Qom and how, on one occasion 'a mule collided with another and fell, and the loosely put-together boxes on its back gave way and corpses fell out in an advanced stage of decomposition.' After reading this account I was quite happy to see only the odd sheep or camel bone on our route.

Passing through the village of Kashan we went to see the gardens of Shah Abbas, which always seemed an oasis of calm in a chaotic world of revolutionary fervour, even though everywhere was plastered with pictures of war victims and violence. We stayed for a night in Isfahan and visited the miniaturist once again to buy presents for our friends in New Delhi. He was always pleased to see us and as there were no tourists any more it seemed that we were his only regular foreign customers. Nevertheless he appeared quite happy, painting away on his own regardless of whether he sold any or not. I suppose that is the sign of a true artist.

On the road to Shiraz we stopped at a little cafe for lunch. I was feeling very hungry and even looking forward to the ubiquitous kebab and rice when we sat down outside at small tables covered with plastic table clothes. The meal was carried out on tin dishes by a smiling young man who placed the dishes on the table and then returned with three bottles of Pepsi Cola. We started to serve ourselves from the serving dishes and began to eat. Suddenly I saw a group of small black objects scurrying across the table and attempting to climb onto the food plates. I could not believe it; the table was suddenly covered with small cockroaches apparently hoping to join us for lunch. Mahmoud made valiant attempts to dislodge the roaches from the table onto the ground but it didn't matter - I had definitely lost my appetite.

After lunch or rather our failed attempt at lunch, we again visited the tomb of Cyrus the Great, the founder of the Persian Empire, who was buried at Pasargadae, 'the Persians Camp,' and the military capital of the country for most of his reign. The large stone sarcophagus was very impressive and I found it quite moving, maybe because reports of this ruler had concentrated on his kindness and compassion as much as on his military ability. Maybe equally important for me was the location of the tomb which is set, a little off the road, in the solitude of the desert plain. We parked the car and walked towards the monument with a quite strange feeling of reverence for this military ruler who died more than two and a half thousand years ago. The sun was beating down as we approached the heavy stone sarcophagus, standing silently, a lonely sentinel in the windswept plain. In the time of the Shah, this area would have been filled with tourist buses as crowds climbed the stone steps vying with each other for photos beside the resting place of one of the greatest emperors of all time. The silence, and the sense of being alone, invited contemplation. I gazed across at the mountains and thought about the achievements of Cyrus II who had chosen the site for the Imperial city of Persepolis towards the end of his reign so very long ago. It has been reported that Alexander the Great 'visited Pasargadae and, horrified at the condition of Cyrus's tomb – touched, according to Plutarch, (the Greek historian) by the inscription of 'Grudge me not this little earth that covereth my body' – ordered it to be conserved, and punished the Magi who had guarded it so incompetently.' (Roger Stevens)

A little further on are the remains of the Pasargadae military city where there is very little left except for various broken columns scattered all around. All that remains of the Reception Palace is a single tall, column at the very top of which is located a huge stork's nest. We continue to the necropolis of Naqsh-e Rustam, the cliff that contains four rock-cut tombs. These are thought to be the tombs of the Achaemenian rulers Darius II, Artaxerxes I, Darius I and Xerxes I. Only one, the largest facade, is identified by an inscription, that of Darius the Great in which the royal throne is supported by individuals representing the nations of the Achaemenian Empire. The king is facing, in worship, the fire altar of Ahura Masda. A few metres from the cliff is a square-shaped building. There is controversy as to the purpose of this building. Sylvia Matheson suggests that Darius probably built the 'Ka'bah-i-Zardusht' or 'Cube of Zoroaster' as it is called. It might have been a fire temple containing the sacred flame or a provisional royal tomb. Again there is no one else around and the total silence makes the visit even more special.

That night we once more stayed in the former Intercontinental Hotel in Shiraz, warily on the look out for anyone who had been around for our vodka-bottle rolling trick three years earlier. All the staff in the hotel seemed to be new, however, and there was no sign of our over-friendly Revolutionary Guards. The following morning we decided to pay our respects, once more, at the tomb of the Sufi poet Hafez.

Sitting beside the dark green cypress and slender poplar trees in the sun-drenched garden induced a sense of peace which reminded me of my time in Tehran studying with the calligrapher Abdul Rasouli. The calligrapher himself was a Sufi and he revered the work of Hafez much more than any other Sufi poet although in later years the work of Rumi and Omar Khayyam probably became better known worldwide. Sitting in the garden we admired again the memorial with its beautiful coloured tiles depicting the flowers and birds of Shiraz. The great number of Persians who sat reading books of poetry or just came to stand by the tomb showed what a special place the lyrical poetry of Hafez had in the hearts of the Persians.

48. IRANAIR FLIGHT 655

Soon we reached the Gulf city of Bandar Abbas where we were met by a mass of colour as bougainvillea bushes of all hues of pink lined the two large carriageways. Before the revolution this port city had been a winter beach resort for wealthy Iranians but now it was rather forlorn as unfinished buildings littered the landscape. Work was still continuing in the port, however, and we went to stay with a group of Irishmen who were working as architects and surveyors on a new port project. We were shown around the new construction site by our friend Brian whom we had met on his frequent visits to Tehran and later that night we went to a party where we were introduced to a female worker at the camp, a European woman who seemed very understated but apparently was well known for her attempts to seduce as many men as possible. It seems that this was regarded as her main job and according to various accounts her record was already quite impressive.

After breakfast we headed for Bandar Abbas airport, breathing a sigh of relief as we left the intense atmosphere of the construction camp behind us. There was always a lonely feeling associated with foreign workers, even professionals, when they are away from their families for long periods. This was often disguised by partying and appearing to have a fun time but it could not hide the loneliness for long.

The airport was an undistinguished concrete building built by the Shah. Persian women in the gulf area had a most interesting form of hejab, the nose and top part of the face excluding the eyes, were covered with a piece of fine black leather or in recent years plastic, which gave an illusion of a black-beaked bird of prey. The suggestion was that it had been used in the past as a form of skin protection from the sun rather than a religious practice. There were a few local handicrafts in the small shop but nothing of too much interest so we sat down and waited for flight IR 655 to Dubai.

As we walked across the tarmac in the scalding heat of a Persian Gulf afternoon to board the plane, I was reminded of the stories about the lack of maintenance on Iran Air because of money being diverted to the war effort. The plane certainly did not look in too great shape, the upholstery was torn and the seats kept falling backwards, which was particularly annoying when the air hostesses repeatedly asked me to pull the seat up for take-off. Nevertheless it was a pleasant trip across the Persian Gulf looking down at the tiny dhows in the deep blue sea below us and, somewhat to my surprise, we actually arrived safely in Dubai.

Tragically three years later on the third of July 1987 the 290 passengers including 66 children on flight IR 655 were not so lucky. The Airbus was shot down by the American warship USS Vincennes. The American version of the incident, which would change many times, was full of excuses and blamed the Iranian pilot of the plane for the catastrophe.

Later in the psychology textbooks this incident appears as a case study in the chapters on stress. This "unfortunate mistake" - it was suggested in the books - could be attributed to stress which could lead to perceptual and cognitive distortion: the plane was ascending but appeared to be descending, the plane was a passenger plane but the captain of the American warship believed it was a F-14 fighter plane, mistakes apparently understandable given the difficult situation in the

Gulf.

The psychology books, however, were probably not aware of the whole political picture and were selecting an easy solution to the problem, namely stress can cause mistakes: therefore this tragedy had to be caused by stress. The problem, however, was much more complicated. It was, given the antipathy of America to Iran after they had been humiliated by the hostage crisis, probably more likely a combination of a stress reaction with a distinct cavalier approach to an untrustworthy enemy.

An investigation by Newsweek suggested there was 'an overeager captain, panicked crewmen and a cover-up.' The journalist Bob Fisk, who spent a lot of time in Iran, carried out an analysis of this tragic incident in his excellent book *The Great War for Civilisation.* (Fourth Estate, imprint of Harper Collins 2005). He also gives interesting insights on editors and newspapers who want to take a certain line regardless of what their journalists write. His piece for The Times on the shooting down of IR 655 describes the inefficiency and aggression of some of the American warship crews and says that the information from Dubai traffic controllers had been drastically cut. Fisk wrote that anything negative about the Americans had been left out. He also felt it was one thing to have a piece cut but quite another to risk one's life for a paper, only to find that the courage necessary to report wars is not in evidence among those whose task it is to print those reports. So Fisk's investigation appeared not in the Times (London) but in the Irish papers.

Years earlier at lunch with Niall in the embassy, on one of his trips to Iran to investigate the progress of the war, Fisk was bemoaning the fact that he was getting little help from the British Embassy. Maybe like the British papers it was too uncomfortable for them to acknowledge the true facts, especially as there were rumours flying around about the defection to the UK of a Russian spy aided by MI6. At the time, few people in Tehran knew the details but the spy had been smuggled across the Turkish border by one of our colleagues in the British Embassy who, it turned out, was in fact a MI6 agent and not a regular diplomat. He also disappeared back to London very shortly after the event. The Russian who defected proved to be of significant value to the Western powers at that time.

49. THE PINK CITY
May 1984

From Dubai we boarded an Air India flight and arrived in New Delhi in the middle of an extremely hot and humid spring. We were staying with Penny and Justin, our friends from the Department of Foreign Affairs who had been posted to the embassy in India. When they heard that our original plan had been to adopt an Indian child, Penny leapt into overdrive and decided to find us a baby. She had qualified as a social worker before she married and was an amazing person, able to adapt extremely well to different cultures and help with social issues as well as carry out her responsibilities in the embassy. In between the usual Delhi sightseeing, Penny and Livleen fitted in trips to various orphanages. We visited one of Mother Theresa's orphanages where our views on the position of females in Indian society were sadly reinforced - there were twenty-three girls and just one boy. Fortunately we were very happy to take a girl but at that particular orphanage all the children were going to be sent to Germany, so we had to look elsewhere.

By this time it was beginning to seem as if everyone in the house needed a break from the stress of baby-hunting, on top of which, the humid weather was becoming oppressive and difficult to bear. The hot weather in Tehran felt more comfortable because the air was much drier. We decided to see some more of India and travel by train to the pink city of Jaipur. The train was called the Pink City Express and our carriage was meant to be air-conditioned - not that it made much of a difference as I was so busy watching rural India pass by that I did not even notice. The journey took most of the day and the village life was fascinating although the most exciting part for me was from time to time spotting a group of elephants drinking from olive-green pools of water.

Jaipur was an incredibly beautiful city. The buildings were built of different shades of pink stone and on a hill overlooking the city was a huge pink fort. We had booked into the Rambagh Palace Hotel, which had been one of the palaces of the Maharajahs of Jaipur over the years. This palace had recently been converted into a five star hotel and the Maharani, the wife of Jai the last ruler who died in 1970, was living in a house in the grounds. Later walking through the magnificent gardens we encountered one of the sons of the last Maharajah. He was on his knees tending the exotic plants. Initially we mistook him for the gardener, only realising our mistake when he stood to greet us in perfect English and we could see he was wearing an elegant beige shalwar chemise (cotton trousers and long top), definitely not the uniform of a gardener. He was very passionate about the garden and happy to tell us all about the bushes and colourful flowers.

The palace had changed very little since the days of the British Raj and was still decorated in the style of that era with big comfortable armchairs; huge fans on the ceiling, heavy engraved wooden side tables and richly coloured, handmade Indian carpets thrown across the floor. Tropical plants in large earthen wear pots dominated the open spaces, while a heavenly scent of freshly cut flowers permeated our bedroom. A four-poster bed, covered with embroidered silk material and cushions, took up much of the room but there was also a sitting area, with a chaise-long and a view of the garden where we could watch the graceful peacocks strolling proudly around the garden. It was a wonderful place to unwind after a stressful few weeks and we were very happy to spend some time just wandering through the gardens or swimming in the cool, blue-tiled swimming pool in the courtyard. We also saw the city sights and of course fed the local monkeys. In her memoir the Maharani describes the city as an 'intricacy of domes and towers, lattices and verandas, with all the buildings coloured a deep oleander pink.' Walking around this stunning city and visiting the huge fort which proudly overlooks it, we dwelt for a short time in a long gone world.

On the train journey back we ate lunch and then slept most of the way. Unfortunately I was greedy and ate the Indian curry, Niall sensibly did not eat it and was fine. I was really ill, however, on our return to Delhi and continued with a bad stomach for the rest of our stay in India. This combined with stress and some iron pills I had been prescribed, meant that I started to bleed from my colon which added a further complication.

While we had been away Livleen and Penny had found the Head of Foreign Adoptions, Mrs Batra, who wanted to meet us. She turned out to be a strongly built forceful lady in her sixties who looked as if she would take no nonsense from anybody, especially bureaucrats. As soon as she learnt the problem of the social worker report she decided to find an alternative legal way to adopt a child. She recalled a case the previous year when a French filmmaker had obtained a letter from the French Embassy, which said he would be a suitable candidate to adopt a child. That part was the easy bit, as we were staying with Justin and Penny; the next stage was more difficult - to find a lawyer who would accept the case and finally to find a judge who would pass everything. Mrs Batra, who seemed nearly as keen to help as Penny had been, immediately had another solution. Her nephew, who was a lawyer and had already adopted a child would, she was sure, be willing to take the case and would also be able to find a judge. In fact the only real problems seemed to be that because the High Court closed in less than two weeks we had very little time to find the baby.

The realisation then hit us; we had, apparently, overcome the bureaucratic problems but still had not found a child! That would have been depressing apart from fact that Mrs Batra was a very determined lady and also a bit of a miracle worker. Sure enough, when we were attending an embassy reception two days later, a phone call came through to Penny. Excitedly Penny turned to us saying that a baby had been found and we could see her the following day. The next day came and went as did the next day with no news. We were beginning to get worried when a message came through from Mrs Batra that the baby was quite sick but from a very good family! This *non sequitur* was all we needed to hear as it suggested bad news. Depression was really beginning to descend on all of us.

The next morning with very heavy hearts we set off for Ganga Ram Sikh Hospital to see the baby. It was a rather ramshackle place with various small buildings opening onto little stone paths. Finally we met someone who seemed to know what we had come for and we were shown into a room where three babies lay in cots. Two plump babies looked quite healthy and the other in the middle was tiny and emaciated. She had a tube in her head, a bandage on her leg and a look of world-weary resignation on her face. I muttered to Penny as I entered that I hoped they had given us one of the fat babies, although I had a feeling ours was the tiny sad one in the middle. That of course was correct, our baby was the sick one in the middle. We then went to meet the doctor in his room. He was brutally honest and told us that they could not guarantee anything about her because she was so sick and possibly eight or ten weeks premature. She was two pounds at birth and three weeks old when we first saw her. She had not really put any weight on and was still very sick. The doctor informed us that she could be blind or brain-damaged, they could not tell because she was too young. She needed extra care to survive and we would have to pay for an air-conditioned room with round-the-clock nursing. That was the easy bit and we signed the papers immediately.

50. GIN AND TONIC

Staggering outside into the hot sun, I drank lemonade from the stall at the gate and tried to comprehend the situation as hysterical laughter was interspersed with tears. We were all both amused and shocked that up till then the only information we had received was that she came from a good family and was sick. Previously we had not been informed that she might die or could have serious disabilities and we were not sure whether we could cope with this uncertainty. (Despite this negative prognosis, Clare went on to obtain First Class honours both in her degree and MSc in Human Rights.)

Back at Penny's house, we all collapsed on a sofa with a very welcome gin and tonic in our hands while telling Justin the story and trying to decide what we were going to do next.

Once again we decided to give Penny a break and go to Kashmir for a week. Penny had been wonderful, not only was she putting up with the stress of our visit but she was also looking after her own four children including Eoghan, aged two years, and an Indian family who had a terminally sick child, Shoba, and nowhere to live. Justin and Penny let them live in a hut in the garden and helped with their food and medical aid. For me that was true diplomacy and a wonderful way to live, especially the idea of sharing a life of privilege in the midst of such poverty. The stress was compounded for all of us by the unbearably humid weather so it was a relief to leave the heat of Delhi for the cool mountain air of Kashmir and try to work out whether we had the strength to cope with a potentially blind or brain-damaged child.

As we descended the aircraft steps we were met with the invigorating air of the Himalayas. Kashmir was so beautiful with its clear blue sky and breath-taking lakes reflecting the snow-tipped mountains. The air at this altitude seemed so fresh and pure after the stifling, dust-laden atmosphere of Delhi. Srinagar, the capital of Kashmir, was still a bustling Indian city filled with people running in all directions but there was not the same frenetic feeling as in other Indian cities. An air of solitude and peace reigned which in some ways did not make sense because - with the Pakistan/Indian conflict always on the horizon - violence was only a step away. There was already a very heavy military presence as a consequence of the objection by the local Muslim population to Indian rule. Armed military seemed a little incongruous amid the stunning scenery of the snow-swept Himalayas. A short time after our visit violence did erupt which meant that all tourists, even Indians, were discouraged from travelling to Kashmir. We began to wonder if our presence, wherever we went, might be a signal for the start of violence!

The first night we stayed in a small, cramped guesthouse on the main street and the next day went into the local bus station and asked for two tickets to Ladakh, which bordered on Tibet in the Himalayas. Niall had hoped to go to the capital city Ley with its imposing, fortified monastery, when we were living in Japan but we hadn't managed to get there - whereas from Kashmir it was only a bus ride away, albeit a long one, through the snow-covered Himalayas. Unfortunately we were met with blank stares, not for the first time I'm afraid, and informed by the bored ticket man that we could buy tickets but there was no point because the high pass was totally blocked with snow and did not open until mid-June.

Our disappointment did not last too long because not going to Ladakh meant that we could spend the rest of the week on a house boat on one of the lakes - which was probably a more sensible option. Heading up to the snow-bound Himalayas on the local bus at eleven thousand feet along one of the most dangerous passes in the world did not seem wise, especially in our stressed-out condition.

When a few years later I read an account of past explorers, I realised how lucky we had been. In 1715 on May 17th two Jesuit explorers set off from Srinagar with three servants and an interpreter. The travellers report of this route stated that 'it led through narrow defiles and along steep dizzy precipices to the Sodshi Pass, three thousand five hundred metres high. The mountain path, hardly practicable even to pack-animals, then led to a wild mountain torrent, which proved in the end to be a tributary of the Dras.' Other explorers centuries later in 1906 and 1934 found similar problems with this snow-bound pass.

The Jesuit, Father Desideris, also described the suspension bridges of Ladakh and his descriptions have been confirmed by modern explorers: 'These bridges are made of loosely twined willow ropes, which serve both as footway and side-rail. The travellers passed over the roaring mountain torrents in single file. The bridges swayed alarmingly under their feet and the height made them dizzy. After crossing the last precipitous gorge and still following the pack-trail they finally entered the magnificent valley of the Indus and followed its course upwards across treacherous slopes towards the local capital of Ley.'

Although obviously the pass was now able to accommodate a local bus, at certain times of the year, the descriptions of a forty day journey through the treacherous pass to Ley in 1715, which was still the same two centuries later, was inspiring but did not provide too much encouragement for day-trippers.

Having booked a lovely houseboat on the main Lake Dal on which Srinagar is located, we then wandered around the town looking for souvenirs amid the usual piles of tourist bric-a-brac. The whole place seemed imbued with the heavenly scent of sandalwood and it was easy to find interesting presents such as pretty wooden carvings and incense sticks.

The following morning after a very substantial breakfast of freshly baked bread, eggs and honey, we set off to find the houseboat. The boat, with the rather grandiose name of Buckingham Palace, was very pretty and the smell of sandalwood, which permeated throughout the bedrooms and sitting and dining area, was overwhelming. It was probably good that we were both quite fond of the scent otherwise it would have been a disaster.

We were sharing the boat with a sociology professor from America whom we met at mealtimes when a friendly Kashmiri cook would present us with delicious local cuisine prepared on board the boat. The professor was an interesting academic and we had many good discussions on the political, sociological and psychological impact on the world of the Iranian Revolution. What none of us probably realised at that time, was how far-reaching, long-lasting and ultimately devastating that impact would be. It is now believed in some quarters that even the seeds of the suicide bombers were sown by the way child soldiers were sent to the war front to test out the area for mines before the main Iranian army went into action. At that time, however, we were unaware that this was happening.

We went over to the Shalimar gardens on a boat laden down with flowers. In Kashmir there were garlands of flowers everywhere and the gardens were so beautiful, signifying paradise and based on the ideas of the Persian Moguls who had ruled there for several centuries. The boatman smiled non-stop as he guided the shikara, happy to have customers in an unstable political climate. I too was very contented as I lay back against the cushions and trailed my fingers in the ice-cold water coming down from the mountains. This was indeed paradise! At the back of our minds, however, was the ever-present anxiety about whether or not we could cope with a potentially very sick child. I was still bleeding quite profusely and was not sure what my own diagnosis might be.

51. BABY IN A PEG BASKET

When we got back to Delhi, Penny was still looking after the sick child in the garden and was awaiting our decision about the child in the hospital. That first night back I spent a sleepless night trying to decide what was the right option. If my diagnosis was not good I wondered could Niall cope with a child who might turn out to be very sick. Niall was also awake so I discussed my thoughts with him but he pointed out that we now had a new dilemma: if we left her we would always wonder what had happened to her and we would never come back to adopt another child. At that point I realised that either way our lives had been changed forever. If Niall also felt that way we had our answer.

The following morning having made the decision to go ahead with the adoption, everything suddenly seemed much easier. We went back to Ganga Ram hospital to tell them of our decision and called in to see the baby. For the first time she seemed so much better and the look of sadness on her face had softened almost as if she realised she was going to be taken care of. Whatever was going to happen we would have to face it together. A few days later, a High Court judge had been found by the marvellous Mrs Batra. Our next task was to go to down to the Delhi Law Courts, which presented us with a scene resembling a Charles Dickens novel. Lawyers and clerks scurried around in long black gowns and stiff white collars, carrying endless sheaves of papers inside the gloomy court. We sat down in heavy wooden high-backed benches as specks of dust danced in the few rays of sunshine forcing their way through the grimy windows.

Fortunately everything went well, the judge and lawyers were very kind and the legal proceedings were completed without undue complication or delay. The only difficulty was that we could not leave India until the baby was at least five pounds in weight: with only a few days left to our flight that did not seem likely. Clare Simran (the latter name meaning 'Gift of God' in Punjabi and bestowed on her by the Sikh hospital) had been just two pounds at birth and had been seriously ill in the previous three weeks. We were due to fly a week later and she still weighed only three pounds. On the last afternoon, which was Niall's birthday we did not know what to do. Niall had to get back to work and by then I was still bleeding badly and feeling too ill to stay behind. Once again Mrs Batra provided us with another solution – we could fly a doctor with us as far as Dubai.

A doctor, who had friends in Dubai, was found and he was delighted at the thought of a free trip to see his friends. This was all arranged within an hour and meanwhile Penny covered a small peg basket with material as a kind of carry-cot. We packed our belongings and Justin brought us to the hospital to collect Clare Simran, two bottles full of baby milk and a tin of baby milk powder. We then all went with Justin to the airport to queue for a plane ticket for the doctor. Once on the flight, the doctor drank champagne and promptly fell asleep and - in a state of some considerable anxiety - I was left, literally, holding the three-pound baby for the rest of the trip.

As soon as we arrived in Dubai the doctor left the airport as quickly as he could and we began what seemed an interminable wait for the plane to Tehran. Even all those years ago the duty free section was amazing especially the jewellery section but I had seen enough gold in Iran to last me a lifetime so I was quite happy to sit still. Watching the passengers rush by we were visited by a constant stream of passing Arab business men resplendent in their freshly starched white robes. They all wanted to see the tiny baby in the peg basket and expressed amazement at her size. I could not imagine any Western men in a busy airport stopping to examine and chat about a baby they did not know but as I found out later, when living in the Middle East, no successful discussion with Arab businessmen starts without a long chat about family life.

The ten-hour wait finally came to an end and the IranAir flight was called. We were obviously very relieved but also worried because although we had sorted out the Indian bureaucracy and managed to get Clare Simran out of that country we still had not got through the even more difficult part of trying to get her into Iran. The flight was fine and the only thing I remember about it was that I had to hold the baby precariously on my knee and one of her two feeding bottles rolled down the plane never to be seen again. I think that Niall and I were just too preoccupied with the problem of entering Iran with an undocumented baby to notice anything else.

The Iranian Immigration rules were extremely tough and the baby, of course, had no Iranian entry visa. With his usual diplomacy and not a little desperation, Niall managed eventually to sort this out with the immigration authorities at the airport; it was nevertheless an extremely stressful experience all told. In India, Niall had written Clare's name into my passport, which he was entitled to do at that time as chargé d'affaires responsible for consular matters in Iran. Fortunately her date of birth was May the first, which was several weeks after we had left Iran so we could pretend that I had delivered her prematurely in India. Clare was clearly premature and still weighed only three pounds, so her size tallied with what we said. I had my fair hair covered with the mandatory headscarf and Clare was bundled up in a blanket with her dark hair hidden so we managed to get her into Iran - although I am not quite sure the authorities believed us.

There had been several tense moments when a phone call was put through to the Foreign Ministry but fortunately everything was fine and the originally stern-faced official handed back the passports with a big smile. Thankfully, despite the revolution, Iran remained a child-friendly country and we had arrived back from holiday with three saris and a tiny baby in a peg basket.

52. SLEEPING ON THE ROOF

Kristie and Kian were waiting for us at the airport and we all then went straight to Tehran Clinic where Kami had arranged that Clare Simran would be observed in his neurological ward for the next five days. I was still losing a fair amount of blood so Kian stayed the night in the hospital and I was to come back the next day and stay for the rest of the week. When I got back the following morning Kian was in a terrible state, having stayed awake the whole night worrying that the baby might die.

In fact everything was fine and Clare Simran was beginning to look better every day. It seems that the nurses were also worried because as soon as Kian left they brought in an incubator and placed her inside it.

Of course I had seen the terrible state of Clare several weeks previously so I tried to explain to the nursing staff that she was getting much better and that she had been for the past weeks in an air-conditioned room not a heated incubator. My explanation was ignored and the incubator was plugged in. I felt slightly uneasy as I sat on the bed and watched her. After about half an hour I noticed with horror that she was going very red and appeared to be quite distressed. Quickly running into the corridor I found a nurse who took one look at her and immediately removed her from the machine.

We were once again very lucky. I thought about the stories the women in the Irish community had told me about there being really good doctors in Iran but how some of the nurses were not trained and could be really incompetent. Fortunately that was the last of the scares for that week and for the next few days I would sit in the hospital room reading and taking care of Clare Simran. She had to be fed every hour and a half but she always woke up with a smile and dropped off to sleep immediately afterwards which made the feeding less tedious. During the nights after feeding the baby I would wander across to the window - watching people sleeping out on mattresses on top of the flat roofs of the surrounding houses. It was the only place they could get a good night's sleep away from the suffocating heat of their houses.

Clare and I soon left the hospital very grateful to Kami and the other medical staff for the treatment we had received. Almost immediately I had to return to the clinic for investigations to work out why I was still bleeding from the colon after all that time. Once again, like nearly all of the medical staff in Tehran Clinic, the doctor was very well qualified and experienced having trained in America. The facilities, however, were quite primitive. This meant that the procedure involved standing on a shower dish, a camera and a long piece of rubber tubing. To be fair, the medical staff, because of the slaughter in the war had much more to worry about than my minor complaint and I was treated very well. It was a great relief, nevertheless to find that my diagnosis was colitis and my treatment was cutting out coffee, fibre and all milk products, except for natural yoghurt, for ten days. This treatment worked and I was very quickly well again.

Meanwhile Fathi, a cheerful Iranian woman, began working in the residence, several days a week in order to help Devji with the cleaning and me with Clare Simran. To my relief Kristie also came over on many occasions to bath the tiny baby in a small plastic bowl. Clare was so fragile that most people were too terrified to even touch her but Kristie had been a professor of nursing at George Washington University and was extremely sensible and competent. Many people over recent years have had similar experiences of adoption in different countries and hopefully for most of them the stress has been worth it. Others, however, have experienced long-term problems in the context of their adoption process – whether of a psychological, bureaucratic or physical nature. We were very grateful that at all stages we had so many caring people to help us through this traumatic experience

53. AN UNDIPLOMATIC LUNCH

September 3rd 1984

Went to an embassy lunch today to meet the new first secretary's wife. The hostess was twittering away as usual and everything was 'super' and 'very exciting'. The new wife seems quite nice but unfortunately appears to be taking too seriously the task of becoming a diplomatic wife, which often means being more interested in image than being an authentic human being. Certainly the charming image dropped halfway through the lunch when she turned to Jacqui and asked why she had been so long in the country. Jacqui replied that she was married to an Iranian and the new wife with a look of total amazement then asked how anyone could possibly want to marry an Iranian. A verbal argument ensued as one of the other Iranian wives suggested that a course in good manners was needed and suddenly the table was in uproar.

Everyone was shouting at everyone else while the hostess was trying to pretend that the situation was still 'super' as she attempted in vain to keep the peace. 'How marvellous it is to get some friendly discussion going' she trilled as she ducked a piece of bread, which was coming in her direction. Usually diplomatic lunches are not so overtly antagonistic and are usually more sophisticated with subtle barbs rather than overt attacks but, to be honest, that lunch was definitely much more fun than most.

That summer went by very quickly. By now we had another staff member joining the embassy, a very pleasant young girl called Roya who had been brought in to help Esther as business was improving. Roya, fortunately, was full of common sense and to our relief was easily able to counteract the bible attacks coming from Esther.

For several months Clare continued to be fed every hour and a half but soon was starting to put on weight and showing great improvement. Baby milk was very scarce but some Irish businessmen would help out and bring in powdered milk and disposable nappies, which were also not available. There were not many young children among the foreigners in Tehran because it was not a family posting and Don and Pat and their baby son Stephen had been transferred home so Clare Simran was on her own until Bill and Mandy arrived to live in Golhak with their baby daughter, Hannah. They were another great addition to the group as they also liked to make adventurous tours of the country.

We decided to hold a small christening ceremony for Clare in the embassy. Fr. Mulligan was happy to officiate and Kami and Kristie would be the godparents in Tehran and Justin and Penny in New Delhi. It was a good mix of Muslim and Christian godparents. Everyone was very fond of Fr. Mulligan, a very sweet old man who had given his life to looking after the Christians in Abadan on the Persian Gulf. He really loved Iran but after the revolution he was regarded as a spy and threatened with expulsion. Niall helped him to be reinstated but when Niall left, he was finally expelled and had to move to Damascus.

54. THE SKULL

November 1984

On Saturday November 17, a group of foreign diplomats set off on a day trip to see archaeological sites close to Qasvin. Devji and I packed a picnic lunch of huge flasks of tea and coffee, fruit, his tasty samosas, sandwiches and cakes. We placed them in a cooler bag with bottles of water and bottles of sickly over-sweet Pepsi products which were made locally in Iran. Sunglasses, loose long-sleeved shirts over tee shirts and cool baggy trousers were a suitable Islamic uniform and would be perfect when the cool early morning air changed into the blistering heat of noon.

Everyone arrived at the embassy at 6:30 am and we began to pack different cars and jeeps on the road outside. We had purchased a Chevrolet jeep from the Australian Embassy because a strong car was useful for travelling over tough treks in the desert and stony paths. A few hours later it would also have another use - that of saving lives. Finally the cars were ready. The new British head of mission and his wife came with us in our jeep as well as Kieran the Irish UN captain, all of us driven by Mahmoud the cheerful young embassy driver. We waved goodbye to Devji, who was holding Clare in his arms; little did I know that I would not see either of them again for some time.

Mahmoud was always a delight on this sort of outing. He could help with translations and enjoyed seeing sites that he would not normally visit. There was no room in our jeep for our other friends Bill and Mandy, which was good because their tiny daughter Hannah was with them, and she would probably not have survived the trip in our car. None of us had any idea of how the day would develop as we drove out of Tehran on that lovely sunlit morning.

The other cars contained the Australian chargé d'affaires, John, and the Norwegian chargé d'affaires, Peter and his wife Inge. We had had many interesting trips with John, Peter and Inge. Other friends from various embassies came as well as Martin Charlesworth, the friendly and knowledgeable archaeologist from the British Institute of Persian Studies.

The dusty streets of Tehran were covered with pictures of martyrs from the Iran/Iraq war and huge murals showing soldiers, guns and mullahs adorned the walls. The piercing eyes of Ayatollah Khomeini were soon left behind as we headed up Ali Shariati, the large tree-lined road passing the stately British embassy summer residence, into the cool, leafy suburbs of North Tehran. We then passed by the towering

Elborz Mountains along the main road to Qasvin.

The conversation was fast and furious as we all discussed the political situation. Much of the conversation centred around whether there was any improvement in the Iran/Iraq war and whether the violence on the streets in Tehran was escalating. These topics were always on our minds, along with the usual food shortages.

In the front seat, I watched the picturesque villages flash by. Tiny sand-coloured houses and mosques were surrounded by elegant poplar trees as groups of sheep rested under their shade. Unfortunately life in those small country villages was not as idyllic as it appeared to be from a distance. Life was very hard, with few if any amenities and not much food. Certainly unlike the cities, there would be no luxuries at all in these isolated villages. We stopped by the road and sat on a crumbling stone wall as we drank hot coffee and ate pieces of honeyed baklava, watching the sheep nimbly balancing on the rocky terrain.

We moved on past the town of Qasvin, which we had visited many times previously. At first sight it seemed an uninteresting modern town but founded by Shahpur I, it had a fascinating history and was filled with ruins and fine buildings from different periods of history. From the Seljuk period the twelfth century Madresseh Haydarieh remained behind a high wall. The historian Pope wrote that this Madresseh or college contained the finest piece of Kufic writing in Persia.

Another reminder of times gone by was the Friday Mosque, the Masjid-i-Jumeh, which was partly Safavid partly Qajar and contained an earlier Seljuk prayer hall. Unfortunately our memory of Qasvin would shortly begin to centre on the local hospital rather than on the historic ruins of the town.

Soon we arrived at one of the many archaeological sites that surrounded Qasvin. Parking the cars along the road we climbed over the small wall clasping our assortment of rugs and picnic baskets. Bill carried Hannah on his shoulders and she was delighted to be out in the fresh air and particularly delighted to see the sheep who were soon scattering in all directions. The rugs were laid out on the stones under a small tree and we sat down to eat our lunch. Everyone seemed hungry and immediately tucked into the delicious selection of food from the different countries. Packing up the leftover food for later, we rolled up the rugs and left everything in the shade of a clump of thorny bushes.

As we descended a set of ancient crumbling stone stairs I held on to the wall to keep my balance. My hand clasped something hard I looked down and saw that I was clutching onto the skull of a ram placed in a small niche in the wall. His sightless eye sockets stared straight at me and his blackened teeth seemed to be fixed in a mocking smile. I shuddered and moved on quickly. Several hours were spent climbing over ancient stones and wandering through rooms open to the sky, thinking of the people long gone who had spent their lives there. It was really good to see these sites with Martin because the ruins really came to life as he explained the history of the surroundings.

55. TEHRAN CLINIC

We returned to rest in our original shady spot and finish the remains of our lunch before we set off back to our embassy where we had arranged to meet for dinner. The idea was that everyone would make their own way there and we would follow at the rear in case there were any breakdowns or other problems. This indeed was ironic as we would be the vehicle with the problem and we would not arrive back at the embassy at all. This being the era before mobile phones, no one would know what had happened to us.

Everyone was nicely drowsy as we drove along the Qasvin to Rasht road, about 100 miles west of Tehran. The British chargé's wife was sleeping in the back seat with her head against the window. Her husband and Kieran sat beside her; while I sat between Niall and Mahmoud and watched the cars stream past on either side of the narrow road. The dying sun disappeared, casting a rust red glow on the bleak Elborz Mountains range as it dropped out of sight. The road seemed much more busy than on the outward trip and later I read that the road could be very dangerous especially at twilight. Tired from the sun and exercise I fell asleep - and woke up a day or two later in hospital in the intensive care unit.

My first image on waking was of an Iranian doctor standing at the foot of the bed holding an x-ray. The doctor's white coat was black while his black hair and beard were white. My vision had turned everything into a photographic negative. Oliver Sachs describes these symptoms in one of his neurological books but fortunately these symptoms of damage done to my brain did not last long or at least not long enough to worry too much about them at that time. These symptoms lasted just long enough to register that something was wrong but there were other injuries, which were more pressing. The main problem was the terrible pain I was experiencing in the right side of my body. The doctor examined the x-rays and started to speak. He spoke softly and kindly as he told me of a terrible car accident outside the town of Qasvin. He looked at the x-rays again and told me I was severely fractured on both sides of my pelvic area but the fracture on my left side was more severe. I was quite puzzled because the really bad pain was on my right side. The doctor looked equally confused and re-examined the pictures. He finally decided it was necessary to take new x-rays.

A nurse and porter came into the room and I was rolled onto a trolley. I started to feel a little panicky as the lift closed behind me and I descended to the x-ray room. It was confirmed that the right side of my pelvis was more badly fractured than was the left side. My right hip and ankle were also cracked and I had head and facial injuries from crashing into the windscreen, which had shattered into tiny fragments on impact. Six weeks later I was still picking splinters of glass out of my face. On my return from the x-ray I was wheeled into a new room and was relieved to see Niall in the other bed.

56. 'IN THE HANDS OF ALLAH'

The Iranians were notorious for their bad driving. Everywhere we travelled there were rusting wrecks of vehicles on the roadsides. Mahmoud, our driver was the first visitor to the hospital. He was very shocked and sat beside the bed with his head in his hands. He told me that there had been at least two deaths, and probably more, of the four

Iranians in the other car. I was very upset to hear of the deaths but relieved to hear it had been the Iranian driver who was to blame rather than our driver.

In Iran if there was a death in a car accident or if an Iranian was involved then the foreigner would always be blamed. Our driver Mahmoud, therefore, had been very afraid that the police would take him away. In our case, however, that night on the television it was announced that the Iranians were to blame for our car accident, so it must have been very obvious indeed. Apparently the local police had blamed the accident on the van driver's carelessness.

Slowly the picture was beginning to unfold and it appeared that the four Iranians had been buying pistachios at the local market for a wedding party. Speeding back along the crowded, busy road in an open-backed, locally made Paykan truck they had recklessly moved out from behind a lorry and crashed straight into our jeep on the other side of the road. The strongly built Chevrolet jeep had saved our lives but sadly had caused the death of the occupants of the other car. The driver of the Paykan and his companion in the front seat had been killed instantly and the men in the back of the open truck had been seriously injured and at least one of them, and probably both, had died later.

It seemed that the UN Captain Kieran McLoughlin was the hero of the hour. Fearing that the British chargé's wife was the most seriously injured he lifted her out of the car and tried to flag down several vehicles to take her to hospital. Car by car they refused to help. This was probably because they were afraid that they might be implicated in the accident. At one point a car window opened and a silk scarf was thrown out of the window to cover her hair.

Finally Kieran threatened the driver of one car saying that if the wife of the British chargé d'affaires died, the car driver would be held responsible. This driver took the husband and wife and Kieran to Qasvin hospital where apparently Kieran became very anxious about the angry mood of the relatives of the dead Iranians who had gathered there. An ambulance then took them to a hospital in Tehran and the following day the injured wife was flown back to Britain. Fortunately she recovered but it took a long time.

In the ambulance Kieran phoned the British Embassy in Tehran to explain the position about the accident and to ask the staff of the embassy to send someone to help us as he had to leave us behind and I was also very seriously injured. It was a Saturday night and no one came to help but fortunately the medical staff and Mahmoud took good care of us.

Outside Qasvin a truck finally arrived at the site of the accident and we were loaded onto the open truck on top of the dead Iranians and taken to the hospital. At Qasvin hospital the medical staff thought I would not survive because I was showing no vital signs. They thought that I was suffering from internal injuries because of severe pelvic fractures and that as a result peritonitis had set in. Despite this belief, the doctors who treated me continued to patch me up and stitch my face. One of them came to visit us in the embassy several months later and explained how he had felt I was in the 'Hands of Allah'. He must have had a lot of practice because although my face would never be the same and I would always have some numbness in my upper lip, he did a really good job.

I remained in Qasvin hospital for several hours because there was no other ambulance available. Eventually one was found and Mahmoud, Niall and myself set off for Tehran. On the way Mahmoud heard the ambulance driver on the radio to one of the hospitals in Tehran, which had a very bad reputation. He had the presence of mind to tell the driver that we were related to Doctor Kami Fatehi who was our close friend and godfather of Clare Simran. He was also one of the top medics in Tehran Clinic, the best medical facility in Tehran.

Kami was phoned and he and his wife Kristie went immediately to sit and wait for us in the clinic. They had to wait several hours because in this comedy of errors the ambulance in which we were travelling broke down on the way and we had to wait for a replacement. On our arrival Kami sorted out all of the medical arrangements and Kristie, although I was still unconscious, immediately washed me down, removing all the congealed blood and preparing me for the radiology department.

The first night after I regained consciousness in my new room in the hospital I was in terrible pain and in an attempt to ease this pain I tried to move my right leg. As a result of this I stretched it a little out of the bed and it got stuck. I could not move it one way or the other. I tried to call for help but to no avail. Finally Niall, in the other bed, was able to press a button and a nurse appeared. She pushed me back onto the bed and gave me some pills to relieve the pain.

The following morning when Jacqui, my friends from the Irish community and Kian and Kristie heard this story they arranged a rota so that someone would be with me day and night. I really appreciated that because all of these women had very busy lives with their jobs and families and they really did not need any extra tasks on their agenda.

57. GRATITUDE

John, the Australian chargé, came into the hospital to tell me his part in the story on the night of the accident. He explained how, when all the cars arrived at the Irish Embassy that night, Devji came down the steps carrying Clare and told them that there had been an accident and he had heard on the radio that at least two people were dead. Very shocked, they all thought that we had died and Clare was an orphan once again. John and Peter, despite having been out since five in the morning set off immediately to see what had happened to us.

 On the way to Qasvin they saw two ambulances stopped on the far side of the road. Crossing over they saw that we were being transferred from the broken-down ambulance to a new one. John told me how upset he was, that although unconscious I was groaning in pain.

What I felt most when I listened to all these stories was gratitude. Gratitude for surviving the accident against all odds and for all the people who had helped me. I think this feeling helped me to heal much quicker than I should have. I also felt that I could learn something from this experience. I could learn how people coped with intense pain and because of this could be more understanding as a psychologist. Maybe humour and gratitude are two of the most important factors in healing, although I must admit humour was not top of my list at that time.

A friend from the Australian Embassy, who was looking after Clare, brought her into the hospital. Clare looked terrified when she first saw me because my face was very badly bruised, swollen and covered in bloody stitches. Apparently everyone thought I would be completely disfigured for life. When I spoke, however, Clare finally recognised me and smiled.

After six days, Niall discharged himself from hospital because Ireland held the presidency of the European Community for six months and he was still the only Irish diplomat in Tehran. In those days the presidency was particularly important because it was the responsibility of the country holding the presidency to call and chair meetings not, as in later years, the responsibility of the Commission representative. It was difficult for Niall because, although not badly injured, he was terribly bruised and shocked.

After ten days I felt stronger and although I was still not able to sit up or turn over in the bed I felt it would be easier for everyone if I went back to the embassy. So I returned to one of the guest rooms and Clare was left beside me in a little cot so I could talk to her, although I could not bend over to reach her.

Since the revolution there were more groups needing money; leprosy, which had been eradicated, had re-appeared. Sister Maryam and the other nuns of the French order of Charles de Foucault did a great job looking after people suffering from leprosy and the diplomatic wives tried to support them and other groups as much as possible.

When I was in hospital my friends from the diplomatic corps came to see me every day and told me all the news. We had been preparing for a new charity bazaar, which that year would be held in the British Embassy, in Ali Shariati.

After leaving hospital a group of wives came to the house to tell me about the preparations for the Christmas Bazaar which, obviously I would be unable to attend as I could not yet even move in the bed due to my fractured pelvis. There would be a food stall and coffee shop and lots of items from our different countries. An Indian friend, whose husband worked for the UN, donated saris and woodwork from India, other wives donated special teas from all around the world, home-made biscuits and clothes but sadly we would be missing Jennifer's good humour and her Belgian chocolates.

Devji, our wonderful cook, who had travelled the world at one point with the Indian Foreign Minister and later with various Ambassadors, made quiches and samosas. The bazaar was a great success and I was happy to get a stream of visitors at my bedside talking about the day and discussing the money earned for all our projects.

After five weeks I was healing very well and the orthopedic surgeon decided it was time I started walking again. He and Niall stood beside my bed and tried to coax me to sit and stand up for the first time since the accident. Even sitting up caused terrible pain and nausea and after several attempts at standing I decided that was it – I was not going to bother ever walking again, it was all too painful.

Fortunately they would not give up and eventually, although I could not manage crutches very well, a walker was produced and I was able to stand and lean on that. Enough was enough; I gave up for the day but promised that I would try again the following day. Soon, thankfully, I was able to move around more easily.

At the beginning of December my father sent a letter from England through the diplomatic bag wondering what had happened, as he had not heard from us for some time. Because the Irish newspapers had reported that we were fine no one had thought to tell him about the accident and the telephone was rarely working in Tehran. He was very relieved to hear we were recovering.

Christmas was a quiet affair. We held our usual small Christmas Eve party although I was still on my walker. The church choir from St Abraham's came to sing Christmas carols which added to the atmosphere and a few friends came to dinner on Christmas Day. I was still in a lot of pain, however, resting and trying to recover; in fact I just wanted Christmas to be over as quickly as possible.

Snow was falling fast throughout the Christmas period but sadly I was not able to walk properly, let alone ski. From time to time we went with Kian or other friends to the little chalet in Shemshak which we had previously shared with Roger and Jennifer. We went at the weekend so I could sit in the sun and watch everyone ski down the slopes. There were cafes in the resorts of Dizin and Shemshak but in no way did they resemble those in Austria or Switzerland. It was kebab and Pepsi on plastic plates and cups not sacher torte and gluhwein in fine china and glassware. We had just survived one potential disaster. Another would soon be on the way.

Bagh-e-Fin Kashan

War Mural, Kashan

*The Stork's Nest
Pasargadae*

The Tomb of Cyrus the Great - Pasargadae

Face Covering of women in the Gulf - Bandar Abbas

Rambagh Palace Hotel, Jaipur

The Wind Palace (Hawa Mahal) in Jaipur, the pink city

Srinagar – Kashmir

Buckingham Palace House Boat on Lake Dal, Kashmir

Niall, Sociology Professor and Buckingham Palace staff

Mountain area in Kashmir

Niall at Shalimar Gardens, Kashmir

At Humayun's Tomb in Delhi with Livleen

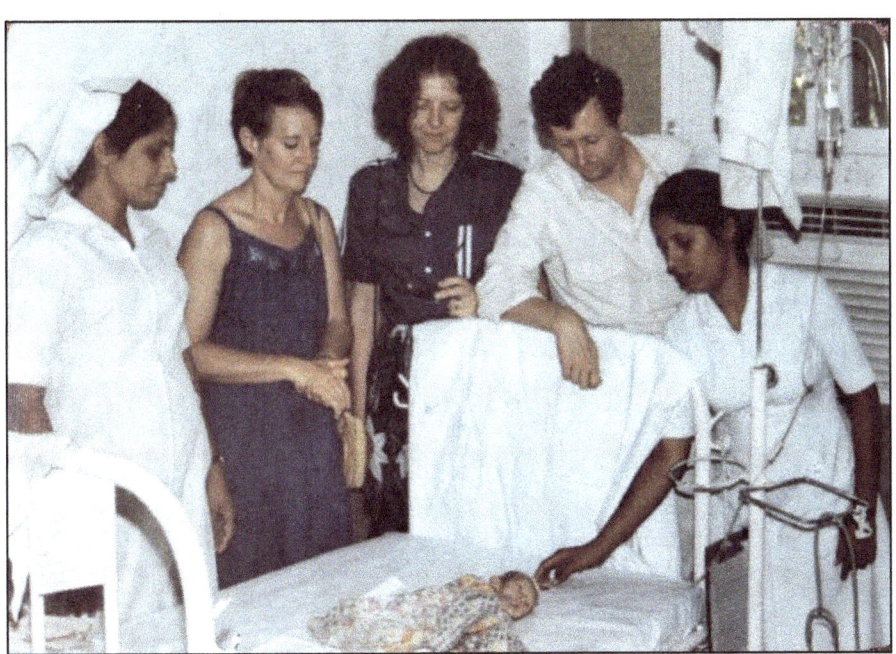

Penny with Clare Simran in the Ganga Ram Hospital, New Delhi

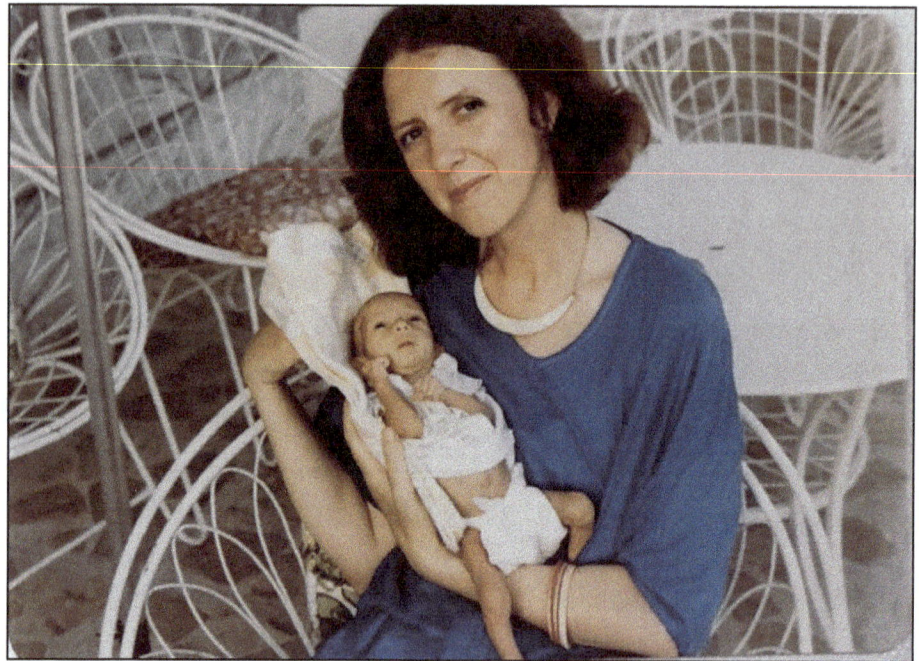

Myself and Clare Simra

Clare's christening – Father Mulligan, Dr. Kami, Kristie, Ramin Fatehi and myself

Niall, Kristie, Clare and Farimah Abdol Rasouli

Christmas 1984- St. Abraham's Choir with us at the Embassy

Evening Press Front Page: Monday 19th of November 1984

Diplomat survives death crash

THE Irish diplomat involved in a car accident in which two people were killed in Iran on Saturday escaped with cuts and bruises, the Department of Foreign Affairs in Dublin confirmed yesterday.

Dr Niall Holohan, the Irish charge d'affaires in Tehran, and his wife, Felicity, were among six people travelling in a car which was in collision with a small van. Two of the van's three occupants were killed instantly, and the third was seriously injured.

The official Iranian news agency reported yesterday that local police had blamed the accident on the van driver's "carelessness." The Department of Foreign Affairs said it understood that the car in which Dr Holohan was travelling was in no way to blame.

An Army officer, Captain Ciaran O'Loughlin, who is attached to the United Nations in Iran, was also travelling in the car. He escaped uninjured.

"It was a miraculous escape," he said yesterday. "We were travelling on our own side of the road when a truck went to pass us out. Another vehicle was coming. I cannot remember much about it except that our car was a total write-off."

He said the size of the car in which the group was travelling was responsible for saving them.

The Department of Foreign Affairs said yesterday that Dr Holohan and his wife were expected to be released from hospital in Tehran very shortly. Both suffered cuts and bruises, but no serious injuries.

The accident happened on the Qazvin to Rasht road, about 100 miles west of Tehran. According to the Iranian news agency, the other passengers in the car were a British diplomat, Mr Christopher Rundle, and his wife and a US diplomat. Mrs Rundle sustained serious head injuries, according to the agency, and was flown home with her husband yesterday for medical treatment.

The Irish Times: Tuesday 20th November 1984

PART 5
1985

58. THE IRAQIS ARE COMING
March 1985

It was March 1985 and my recovery from the accident was going well. I had discarded my walker and was feeling much better. Everything seemed to be fine. Clare Simran was also doing very well and seemed a happy child and every few months I would write a report to Mrs Batra in India telling her how she was developing. The embassy appeared to be functioning smoothly and business was improving. In two years Irish exports had gone from four million to sixty million pounds, which seemed to justify the reopening of the embassy. There were still food shortages but some Irish beef was available as, of course, was caviar. Niall's sister, Renagh, and other friends would send us treats from time to time and Martyn Turner, the cartoonist with the Irish Times, published a cartoon of Niall in dilapidated top hat and tails kneeling in the desert begging an imported Irish cow for coffee and cheese.

Once again everything changed one day when the piercing wail of an air raid siren ripped through the still air of the Persian night: the Iraqis were coming. An eerie silence fell as - windows taped in case they broke and lights off so no target could be identified - we sat in the large room. What we were waiting for we were not quite sure but we did know that the siren signified bombers were on their way from Baghdad aiming to hit the centre of Tehran. For some months now, Iranian towns and cities had been bombed by the Iraqis and we knew it was only a matter of time before long-range missiles would be targeted on Tehran.

For a psychologist who for many years had been working both with hospital patients and Olympic athletes, helping them to deal with stress, this was indeed poetic justice. It was definitely a case of practise what you preach! I had already lived through four years of violence and food shortages since my arrival in Iran but the possibility of bombing raids on the cities, by Saddam Hussein, was something that the foreign community and Iranians alike had feared since the start of the Iran-Iraq war.

(Sadly, years later the world would await in nervous anticipation the "shock and awe" tactics to be employed against the Iraqi people by the world's only remaining superpower. The world would watch another conflict develop suggesting that the human race would seem to have learned little from past experiences. This was confirmed again in 2025 when Israel and the US launched a surprise attack against Iran rather than engage in diplomatic negotiations.)

We were waiting every evening in 1985 for bombs to drop on Tehran, waiting for explosions that would tear through concrete and human flesh with equal impartiality. Our diplomatic passports could no longer be relied on to save us from weapons that made no distinction between foreigners and locals. For the next three or four weeks the whole of Tehran was transformed into a defenceless target - we could not escape from Iraqi weapons or the concomitant psychological terror. Life virtually came to a standstill as we could think and talk of little else. The waiting period and uncertainty were probably the worst aspects of this stress-filled time as we tried to anticipate what might happen and our fevered minds dwelt on what might so easily befall us.

Every day and every evening anti-aircraft guns shot fiery arcs into the night sky, attempting to search out and destroy the enemy. Indoors, we sat quietly in the dark as the harsh noise drilled into our brain. This scenario would continue for several more weeks at random periods throughout the day and night.

We sat clutching our ten-month old daughter Clare who giggled throughout this noisy game. Our perceptions of this 'game' differed. What for us was a terrifying life or death situation was for her just great fun. Her perception was obviously guided by lack of knowledge but it certainly could be considered a healthier approach. There were no bomb shelters and nothing could be done to alter the situation - getting upset would cause more distress and possibly faulty action. In order to protect her, we had to try to keep calm; otherwise she would sense our anxiety. There was nowhere to flee. It was just a case of sitting and waiting and experiencing the most frightening feeling of all - a total lack of control.

I was very aware, from my psychological experience, that at times like these when we feel out of control, we may panic and lose clarity of thought and often make faulty judgments. As the bombing wore on, many Iranians did panic and left the city every afternoon to camp on the roadside or in the surrounding Elborz Mountains. More than a few were sadly killed in road accidents as they left the city – these were victims of fear itself rather than Saddam Hussein's military aggression.

After a few days of constant bombing the foreign airlines refused to fly into Tehran and SwissAir arranged for a last flight to airlift out the foreign women and children. The Department of Foreign Affairs suggested that I leave the country with Clare but I felt it would be more stressful to leave my husband and friends at that time than to stay. When I had been injured in the serious road accident a few months previously my Iranian friends and members of the Irish community in Iran had nursed me night and day because of the poor hospital facilities. It would have been very difficult to leave them at this time.

The reports of scenes at the airport were pretty horrific and distressing as families clamoured to get on the plane; although the stress became more intense by the day, I did not regret my own decision to stay. Years later my friend Elizabeth told me how she had come out to Tehran for a holiday when her father was working in Iran with an international aviation company. Her timing was not great and she had been caught up in the revolution. Trying to leave just before the arrival of Ayatollah Khomeini from exile in France she had queued up at the airport in an attempt to catch one of the last planes out of Iran. She described how it was total chaos as people fought to get tickets, throwing dollars in all directions. They were desperate to get out before the retributions started. Elizabeth, who was always extremely helpful to everyone, carried a case for a pregnant woman who was in front of her. It turned out that this woman's husband was on the ticket desk and on this occasion Elizabeth was rewarded for her act of kindness. Both women managed to get on the last PanAm flight out of Tehran.

In 1985 stories soon abounded personalizing the facts that were reported in the news. Sixty children killed at a birthday party as a building hit by a bomb collapsed in downtown Tehran, an apartment block around the corner from the Irish Embassy just near the book shop in Zafar crumpled to the ground trapping and killing many people after being hit by a missile. Business continued in the city, although concentrating on anything other than the bombing was difficult for most people. Trying to view the bombing as a distraction, I used the Zen meditation programme that I had adapted years before for sports and mental health problems and arranged to meet with my friends to meditate and talk over the daily events. In these ways we attempted to impose some meaning on the insanity of our daily existence.

Requests for psychotherapy were coming in frequently as many people were traumatised by the uncertainty of this violent situation and children still had to prepare for their exams. As a result of their anxiety they naturally found it even more difficult to concentrate. With children I used the meditation therapy to calm them down and help them focus on their schoolwork rather than on the trauma surrounding them. Sadly most of the drawings they produced consisted of dead and broken bodies lying amid piles of weapons. Iranian children had seen too much tragedy over their childhood years. (Decades later, horrific sights and experiences have been lived through by thousands of children in Iraq, Syria, Afghanistan, Sudan, Ukraine, Lebanon and Gaza, leaving generations traumatised.)

That year, most embassies cancelled their National Day receptions but we decided that the Saint Patrick's Day party should go ahead as usual although it was held in the dark because of the blackout in Tehran. Just a few candles helped to light the way up the external staircase. Attendance was down but those that did attend remembered the night very vividly. In fact it was very hard to forget because of the sense of camaraderie heightened by anticipation and fear.

Shortly afterwards we decided to leave Tehran to seek refuge with friends at a chalet in the mountains for four or five days during the Iranian Now Ruz holiday period. This happened to coincide with a particularly heavy bombardment of the city which resulted in several deaths. When we returned to Tehran, Niall found that the embassy telex machine had almost run out of paper as a result of frantic messages from the Department in Dublin demanding to know if we were still alive. A somewhat red-faced Niall had to apologise that he had abandoned the embassy for the safety of the mountains without informing Dublin in advance!

Day by day, night after night, the endless round of brightly lit skies and mind-numbing explosions continued. Slowly this began to take its toll with tearful episodes and headaches as the stress continued to build. At times it felt as if I was treading in a jar of treacle, head clouded, unable to free myself from a situation that continuously pulled me down and seemed like it would never end. The responsibility of looking after Clare and meditation helped me to get through this terrible period.

59. MYSTERIOUS POET
April 1985

The bombing did end. It stopped as suddenly as it had started, and a week later we left by train for London and Dublin via Moscow. This was partly because the Iraqis regarded IranAir as a legitimate wartime target and threats had been made to shoot the planes down and partly because we still found trains an interesting and enjoyable way to travel. Settled in our compartment we could relax at last. The villages of Northern Iran passed by, stuck in a time warp hidden from the gaze of the twentieth century by groups of slender poplar trees. At the border with the Soviet Union, the Revolutionary Guards came onto the train to check our passports; we held our breath as they found a fault in Clare's paperwork and looked at us suspiciously as if we were kidnapping an Iranian child. There was no such thing as adoption in Iran and we feared they would refuse to let us leave or at least try to take Clare from us. Finally we breathed a sigh of relief as they handed back our passports and we shunted across the border.

Once again the Soviet guards came aboard checking for escapees under the seats and in the space above our heads. Obviously they did not see the irony of the situation which we had observed on our arrival in Iran several years previously. Four years on there still did not seem to be any great advantage in migrating to communist Russia even from war-shattered Iran. The lush scenery of Azerbaijan passed by, blue and red exotic birds perched on telegraph wires and Russian soldiers in lookout posts surveyed the countryside as the reality of another grim world dawned. Surreal scenes were played out on the station platforms along the route through central Russia. Girls in ankle socks and 1950s style dresses and old women wrapped in colourful shawls with baskets of produce on their arms walked by. Men in army uniforms swaggered along the platform like actors on a stage. The silent action was viewed through the grime-covered windows of the train with fascination. In the dining room we were again served bowls of borscht soup and roughly baked bread while waiters dressed in white jackets brought us hot tea in tiny Russian gilt-topped glasses, a glimpse once again of a bygone age.

After four days on the train we finally arrived in Moscow where our friend Adrian kindly put us up again in the embassy. Italian diplomat Daniele Vare's description of Moscow in 1931 suggests that not much has changed: 'And there, in full view, lay one lemon and a roll of toilet paper. Two items which he was told 'we would pay for in their weight in gold, and cannot get.'

We did some sightseeing and even attended the Bolshoi ballet, which was wonderful. Still not satisfied with our surfeit of Russian culture we took an overnight train with Adrian to Leningrad (Saint Petersburg) to see the Hermitage Museum with its priceless art treasures and Fabergé silver work and enamelled eggs. For most of the time, however, we were very tired and we just rested.

On one occasion, Clare and I were driving along the road with the wife of an Irish colleague and her young daughter. We were going to meet Jan Butler, the Irish translator wife of Yevgeny Yevtushenko, the great Russian poet whose volume of poems sat on my bookshelf beside the works of Solzhenitsyn and Pasternak when I was a student. In the sixties, Russia was an unknown entity and attracted many students with its literary giants and ideological fervour.

The long straight road through the deep forest was bordered on both sides by huge pine trees towering over us. The fresh pine air seemed to cool the car and scent our skin as a deep feeling of peace and renewal reigned. As the car turned into a clearing we saw several wooden dachas (country homes) huddled together against the velvety dark green backdrop of the forest. Going inside we drank sugared Russian tea as Clare Simran and her small friend played happily together on the floor. Unexpectedly the door was flung open and a figure strode in, long, dark coat flapping, eyes searching the room until they came to rest on the tiny children. Slowly Yevtushenko looked down and fascinated they stared up at him, dark and fair hair mingled together. "A snow princess" he mused quietly as the blonde child looked up and "depthless dark pools" he smiled as he gazed into the eyes of the dark-haired child. A few brief words of introduction were uttered and then the mysterious poet was gone, leaving unfinished lines of poetry hanging in the air.

We travelled back to England on the train and stayed in London for a week. Aiveen gave a party for Clare's first birthday but unfortunately Clare was suffering from a bad fever. It was a fever that led to another drama in our lives. Two days after the party we got a message from the Irish Embassy in Moscow to say that one of the children in the embassy had meningitis and they were worried that Clare might have contracted the disease. Because of her fever we could not rule out that possibility and that meant that everyone at the birthday party was also at risk. I rang Great Ormond Street Hospital and discussed the situation. The sensible advice was that if Clare's temperature was not reduced by medication then we should bring her into the hospital.

In fact Clare's fever did go down a little after her medication but it was decided that because she had been exposed to so many people at her birthday party, it would be safer for everyone if she was checked out at the hospital. Everything was fine so we were then able to carry on to Lancashire to see my great aunt before we left for Dublin. I had always been very close to her especially since my mother died twenty years previously when I was a student at Manchester University. She had been a great support and I liked to see her as much as possible. Now she was all alone because her only grandson had drowned a few years earlier and her only child, his mother, had died of grief shortly after. It was her first time to see Clare but by now Clare had developed an ear infection and, in great pain, was crying continuously. This initial introduction did not go down too well until we discovered why she was crying and sorted the problem What we also did not know was that my great aunt was suffering from cancer which despite many hospital tests (and prayers from Father Mulligan) would not be diagnosed until shortly before she died 3 years later in 1988.

60. A WHITE HOUSE

The bombing in Tehran started again and we stayed in Ireland for several months waiting for it to stop. It seemed as if we were getting used to enforced stays in Ireland waiting for instructions. At least I was able to start working again with the Irish crossbow champion Richard Delaney and the Olympic team for the next Olympic Games in Korea in 1988. Time seemed to flash by because I loved what I was doing and in Iran there were no sports teams at that time. The Tehran Times proclaimed on the back of the newspaper that 'Archery and Swimming' were games of the Holy Prophet but there was really very little chance of organised sporting activity there at that time.

The first archer I had worked with for the Moscow Olympics invited us to his farm in the country. When we discussed the recent bombing he was very upset and suggested that I go to see a clairvoyant he knew in Dublin to check if it would be safe to return. I do believe that some people are able to predict the future but I also believe that many more people are just charlatans. Phil was a very stable sensible individual, however, and when he explained that she was a very simple woman who did not do readings for money but rather because she had a special gift, we decided to go ahead. Phil made the phone call in front of us and made no reference to what we did or where we had been.

A week later we arrived at a house in the suburbs of Dublin. The clairvoyant was a quiet, unassuming woman but I still felt a little nervous as we sat at her kitchen table. Would she be a charlatan or, if not, would she see something terrible in our lives. Either way it did not look too good. Pensively she took Niall's hand and stared at it as if she was puzzled. Finally she spoke with great uncertainty, suggesting that she saw an ayatollah. She obviously did not know what an ayatollah was but this was no different, at that time, from most people in the West. I held my breath, realising immediately as Phil had implied, that she may have some sort of psychic ability. Niall was not so sure until the end of the session, when he admitted that she did see things that she could not logically have known.

She suggested that Niall would be involved in a war at some point because she saw lines of bearded men marching beside tall buildings.

Five years later in August 1990, Niall did in fact find himself in the middle of the Iraqi invasion of Kuwait.

The clairvoyant looked at my hand and saw me walking around carrying both a pen and notebook. This was exactly what I usually did when we went on our trips! She suggested that I would have many careers but she did not know what they would be. She saw something to do with sport, hospitals, massage and beauty. The first two suggestions made sense as a clinical psychologist working with the Olympics but massage and beauty made no sense at all. Years later massage and beauty may have been explained by the fact that I started to do some Japanese healing and in Saudi Arabia I helped to produce perfume which I sold to support a charity I had set up with my publisher the poet, Seamus Cashman, for children with disabilities in Palestine and areas of conflict across the world.

That day I was still feeling uncomfortable but also felt that she did have some form of psychic ability. Another of her claims was to see a white house in America surrounded by huge trees. We informed her that we had no intention of going to the US because we liked 'funny' countries. Seven years later, however, although Niall did not put New York near the top of his list, he was posted to the United Nations in New York for five years. After several months in Roosevelt Island, an amazing strip of land in the middle of the East River, which could only be reached from Manhattan by cable car, we moved out to Westchester County. The only house we found, at that time, which seemed suitable to accommodate all our belongings, was in fact a white house surrounded by huge trees. We had forgotten about the clairvoyant's words and only remembered them when we had moved in.

Niall was loving his job and doing well so we were a bit surprised when she told him that his career would have problems. Her reason was that he was too honest and would not play the necessary game of self-promotion. Although at the time we did not take her too seriously, her warning turned out to have some substance. He was often given relatively unimportant posts but we did not mind because we enjoyed everywhere we went and Niall managed to turn everything around for the better, far more than might be expected in the circumstances.

The clairvoyant suggested that I would have difficulty walking as I got older and more than thirty years after my car accident there has sadly been a definite change for the worse in my mobility, although several operations have now improved the situation. She appears to have got one suggestion wrong, however, when she told us Niall's mother would die before long. The following year Niall's aunt, who had lived with his parents all her life, did die unexpectedly. The clairvoyant also missed the fact of Clare's adoption even though Clare was sitting quietly in a corner eating an apple. She was in fact very surprised to hear she was adopted and said she had never before missed an adoption or a fostering. At the end of the session we told her where we were living and asked was it safe to return. She replied that she saw no danger for us in Iran.

It had been an interesting experience and we felt reassured. Like Phil I felt she was genuine, although it was not something I would want to repeat too often.

During the next few months Clare was happy playing in the Irish rain and getting to know our friends and neighbours. Finally instructions that we were to return to Iran were issued. We were told, however, not to enter the country until the latest bombing raid had stopped. Consequently we decided to drive back which would give us more control if we had to hang around waiting for Saddam Hussein to stop his missile attacks. Once again we set off meeting up with friends across Europe, while watching the news to see when the bombing might stop. Although this was a little unsettling, the good news was that we could visit the fascinating historical places in Turkey, which at that time were quite difficult to reach.

61. RUMI

Roger and Jennifer Martin invited us to Rome so we drove down to stay with them. Roger was very happy with his interesting work as Ambassador to the FAO (UN Food and Agricultural Organisation) and he and Niall spent many hours discussing various issues. Jennifer and I were equally interested in discussing the charity and social interactions in Iran although the recent Iraqi bombing played a big role in all our conversations especially as the bombing was still continuing. Clare was having a great time playing with Elias, Jennifer's young son, who had been born on Christmas Eve, a few months before Clare. The only drama we had on this occasion was when Clare disappeared and was nowhere to be found in the embassy. Finally she was located, fast asleep on the floor of the bedroom, hidden under one of my 'special piles' of clothing. Roger always referred to my 'piles' whenever we met after that. One evening we all went out for dinner with Ambassador Mezzalama and his wife whom we knew from the Italian Embassy in Iran. They were both very interested in the news from Tehran.

Promising to see everyone again the following year when we would be finishing our posting, we set off to drive across the spine of Italy. Passing through the lovely medieval city of Assisi we stopped to view the mummified body of Saint Clare before rushing down to the port of Ancona. Once there we were just in time to board the car ferry for Izmir. The positive side of this somewhat nerve-wracking journey was that we would spend three marvellous weeks wandering around central and Eastern Turkey before we were given the all clear that the new spate of bombing had finished and we were able to return to Iran.

In 1845 J.L.Stephens arrived at the city of Smyrna (Izmir) on his horse and described it as follows:

'I entered the long-looked for city of Smyrna, a city that has braved the reiterated efforts of conflagrations, plagues, and ruins; the queen of the cities of Anatolia; extolled by the ancients as Smyrna the lovely, the crown of Ionia, the pride of Asia.'

The stunning bay with its backdrop of wooded hills and verdant surrounding countryside was our first view of Izmir. It was from this harbour that the famous Greek ship-owner, Ari Onassis was forced to flee, as a child, with his family following the expulsion, by the Turks, of all Greeks from Anatolia in 1923 after the defeat of the Greek armies.

L.J.Stephens congratulates the Greeks 'in selecting the sites of their ancient cities, on the declivity of a mountain running down to the shore of the bay, with houses rising in terraces on its sides; its domes and minarets, interspersed with cypresses, rising above the tiers of houses, and the summit of the hill crowned with a large solitary castle.'

As I stood on the deck of the boat from Italy watching the sun-dappled mountain terraces decked with an abundance of colourful flowering bushes, it seemed the ancient Greeks had indeed chosen a beautiful setting for the city of Smyrna. This city of 'figs and raisins' is also reputed to be the birthplace of Homer, the first Greek classical writer, famed author of the Iliad and the Odyssey.

From Izmir we drove to the crowded beach resort of Kusadasi. It was the tourist season and the only memorable event was when we heard the charity concert Live Aid on the little radio, which we always carried with us so that we could keep in touch with news of the bombing in Tehran. It was an inspirational concert arranged by Bob Geldof. Listening to the Who, Queen, Paul McCartney and all the other artists really lifted our spirits as we prepared for the most stressful part of the journey. The beach at Kusadasi was lovely and a welcome respite from our time on the road but it was so packed with sun-striped bodies, in different stages of pink and bright red sunburn, that it was difficult to reach the sea.

On one of the days, instead of fighting for a place on the sand with the old Turkish man who oversaw the beach like a sergeant major, we set off to see the classical remains of Ephesus. Unlike the writer J.L.Stephens who travelled for three hours by horse from Smyrna, we drove. On this occasion I had remembered to pack some toys for Clare to keep her occupied for the trip - although Niall probably still felt that she should be taking an interest in the local ancient statues rather than teddy bears!

Tourists thronged the ancient Roman site of Ephesus which was the city of the Goddess Artemis later renamed Diana by the Romans. For travellers in the past, much of this huge city had not yet been excavated and there was little to be seen at the temple of Diana. In the early 1800s, J.L.Stephens could not even reliably find the site of the Temple of Diana asking in frustration 'where is the temple of the great Diana, the temple two hundred and twenty years in building; the temple of one hundred and twenty-seven columns, each column the gift of a king?'

Stephens felt that this was a place of desolation. Pieces of columns and blocks and fragments of stone were scattered everywhere. Over the years later excavations uncovered some impressive finds and a great deal of work had been carried out on the site by the time we arrived. It seems that some of the columns had been removed from the Temple of Diana and placed in Hagia Sophia in Istanbul. Ida Pfeiffer mentioned in 1842 that 'In the Sophia mosque we find a few pillars which have been brought hither from Ephesus and Baalbeck (Lebanon)'.

Ephesus is a particularly important location for Christians as it is said to contain the house where Mary, the mother of Jesus, lived in her old age. It is also known for the New Testament writings of Saints Paul and John. It is therefore a very special site from both a spiritual and an archaeological point of view.

Passing through the amazing sights of central Turkey we reached the town of Konya, which is associated with the Sufi poet Rumi. This for me was another highlight of a wonderful trip. The museum at this time was just a little wooden structure containing some life-size models of whirling dervishes and glass cases filled with books of Rumi's poems and information about his life. In the west, the widespread interest in Sufi poetry would not really materialise for a few more years. My own fascination with Sufism had arisen from studying Buddhist mysticism in Japan. I understand that the old primitive 'shed' has now been replaced by a sophisticated museum but I will always remember the old authentic building with great affection.

The account written in the letters of Gertrude Bell when she visited Konya makes a fitting tribute:

'My visit to his tomb was a real pilgrimage for I know some of his poems and there are things in them that are not to be surpassed. He lies under a dome, tiled with blue, and sombre Persian enamel and lacquer. On either side of him are rows and rows of the Chelebis. The Dervish high priest and his direct descendants - all the Chelebis who have been ministers and over each is the high felt hat of the order with a white turban wrapped around it. "Ah listen to the reed as it tells its tale: Listen, ah, to the plaint of the reed."'

Cappadocia was our next port of call. A region of Turkey like no other! It is a haven of caves, monasteries and churches hewn into the rock. It is a fairy tale place strewn with huge rock chimneys that look like giant man-made mushrooms but in fact are sculptured naturally by millions of years of erosion. Reaching the pretty village of Goreme, surrounded by hills which appeared to consist of streams of fragile rock cobwebs, we decided to use it as a base for a few days to explore this amazing area.

On our first day in Goreme we explored the open-air Museum to see the Byzantine chapels and churches carved into the rock. Probably the most famous was the stunning Karanik Kilise or Dark Church, which contains painted frescoes of various scenes including Christ on the cross. There were so many churches that it almost became overwhelming. For the next two days we travelled around Cappadocia, a fantasy land of fairy chimneys and nature's weird and wonderful rock sculptures. This amazing area was very calm and quiet as there were few tourists. It was here that we heard on the radio that the bombing had stopped in Tehran and after six weeks of travelling we were able to return to Iran. It was a really exciting to feel that we could at last get back to 'normal' whatever 'normal' was. It would also be good to discuss all the news that had happened in Tehran while we had been away.

62. HELICOPTERS IN THE DESERT

August 1985

Shortly after our arrival back in Tehran the usual organisation of the Trade Fair started. Food and consumer goods were still not very plentiful but some meat, including Irish beef, was now available in the shops so the dinners and big receptions would be easier to cater for this year. Once again smoked salmon was brought in by some of the businessmen and by the Irish Trade Board officials. It now seemed that Clare's favourite foods were smoked salmon and caviar!

Our tenth wedding anniversary was at the end of August so anyone already in the country to set up the Trade Fair came to dinner. We had a lovely evening eating out on the terrace and after dinner we cut the cake. It was a huge elaborate-looking frothy cake covered in the usual synthetic sugared frosting. Most cakes in Iran looked delicious but were rather sickly and tasteless and this cake was no exception. We only ate half of the cake and I took the remaining part into the foyer and placed it on Mahmoud's desk until we cleared everything away later that evening.

We all settled down with a cup of coffee enjoying the warm night air until at one point I stood up to get something from the foyer. To my horror entering through the glass doors I saw a heaving black mass on the table and soon realised that the top of the remaining part of the cake was covered with cockroach icing. Not a centimetre of white frosting could be seen. Reinforcements were swiftly called to deal with this unexpected invasion and the cake and its occupants were rapidly dispatched into the bin.

For some time we had been thinking about crossing the desert to Mashad but had been warned against it, as it might be too dangerous. I think the idea of danger was more about crossing the desert than anything else, although there were a lot of other things to worry about in Iran.

In fact this was the desert that the Americans had used for their disastrous and tragic attempt to rescue the American hostages some years previously in 1980. The plan had failed partly because the Americans found to their great surprise that it was not an isolated desert but had a road running through it and a bus appeared on the road just after the transport plane landed. This meant that the Iranian bus passengers had to be taken prisoner. It is difficult to work out who was more surprised that day, the Iranians or the American military.

According to some news reports, the rescue attempt was a disaster from start to finish. The Americans had no idea where in the embassy the hostages were being kept. It was only by accident at the very last moment that a CIA operative happened to be sitting on a plane beside the chef who had cooked for the hostages. For some reason he had been released and as a result of questioning him the Americans found that the hostages were being kept in the Chancery. How they thought they could land helicopters in the middle of Tehran, unseen, and evacuate the hostages was beyond me but apparently that was the plan.

Eight helicopters were involved but one had problems and another one crashed into a fuel transporter plane, which burst into a ball of flames, resulting in eight Americans being killed and four being badly injured. Not the US Air Force's finest hour!

Our idea was to cross this same desert with our Norwegian friends Peter and Inge and drive on to Mashad, an important city close to the Afghan border. The Friday Mosque in Mashad contained the tomb of Imam Reza, Shia Islam's eighth Imam, and was a major pilgrimage site. Foreigners were not allowed into this mosque but could enter the outer courtyard. At this stage, however, Niall was looking very much like an Iranian pilgrim because since the accident he sported a beard; even one-year-old Clare had her own little chador.

The desert was as had been reported - a large desert - which did contain a small sandy windswept road for at least some of the journey. There was not an enormous flow of traffic - we did see cars on the road but no buses. At the expected location we came across the site of the American helicopter accident which was now signposted for the benefit of visitors! It was sad to see hundreds of pieces of rusting helicopter pieces scattered all across the ground and to remember that people had died there. According to contemporary reports, the attempted rescue mission was probably doomed from the start. Indeed, in the context of the walled well-guarded American Embassy it did not seem a very sensible idea to attempt a rescue in the centre of Tehran starting from this distant isolated outpost.

In sombre mood we carried on to the holy city of Mashad. The following morning, Inge and I carefully wrapped ourselves in our chadors, making sure our hair was completely covered and we all set off to see the tomb of Imam Reza. Fifty years ago, Robert Byron went to a great deal of trouble to gain entrance to this forbidden site. He tried to disguise himself as a Persian (not very successfully) and managed to see some of the courtyard but the hot sun began to destroy both his composure and his charcoal make-up so he decided not to continue his plan. It seems that life at the time of Reza Shah, whom Byron called Majoribanks (in case his diary fell into the wrong hands) was no different from the current time. Nevertheless the always poetic but often cynical Byron was totally enthralled by what little he did see in the courtyard; 'Glimpses of arabesques so liquid, so delicately interlaced, that they looked no more like mosaic than a carpet looks like stitches of larger patterns lost in the murk above our heads; of vaults and friezes alive with calligraphy - these were its actual words. But the sense was larger. An epoch, the Timurids, Gohar Shad herself, and her architect Kavam-ad-Din, ruled the night.'

Excitement was uppermost in all our minds at the thought of seeing this special shrine but we were also somewhat nervous in this epoch of revolutionary fervour. Mahmoud carried Clare in her tiny chador, Niall and Peter attempted to stroll nonchalantly and Inge and I pulled our chadors around ourselves, trying not to trip while keeping our eyes firmly fixed on the ground. This important mosque is a complex of buildings, courtyards and blue and golden cupolas. One of the buildings contains the tomb, encased in a gold covering, of Imam Ali Reza the eighth Imam, who was reputedly assassinated in AD 817. While the rest of the city was not too interesting, it was a special experience to walk from the courtyard of the mosque into the beautiful building containing the shrine amidst the genuine devotion of the Shia pilgrims.

On our return to Tehran we arranged several cultural evenings. Niall played his guitar and sang Irish folk songs, while other diplomats sang songs from their own countries. The highlight of these events was when my sehtar teacher Jamal gave a concert in the embassy for friends and diplomats. We made a small stage and draped a colourful Persian carpet over it. Jamal's performance was outstanding as he played Iranian classical pieces on the tar and the sehtar. Music was discouraged under the new regime so it was a wonderful chance for everyone to experience true Persian culture instead of the usual talk of death and fear. It was a memorable evening and during dinner an interesting discussion about art and music continued into the early morning.

63. BOBBY SANDS STREET
Thursday October 10th 1985

We are still sharing our bedroom with several mosquitoes who are trying to escape from the increasing cold outside. Every morning we awake to painful lumps on our arms and faces, not to mention blood-splattered walls, evidence of nightly attempts at mosquito assassination. Niall has received a request from Ireland to check out some names in an Armenian graveyard on the road to Ardebil. Unable to contact the Armenian Archbishop he thinks it is probably going to be an unsuccessful trip but at least he can try to track down the graveyard. An extra reason might be that Mahmoud has not seen his father for a long time and would like to return to his village in Ardebil. It sounds like another adventurous journey to a part of the country with which we are not familiar so I am very happy to tag along. Although Devji has lived in the country for years he has seen very little of Iran so we invite him to join us.

With one eye on the ominous-looking cloud formation descending over the Elborz Mountains I start to pack up the car. Devji has baked some pizzas for a picnic and we all start carrying down armfuls of Persian guidebooks, bags of clothing and various toys and 'boggies' for Clare. Niall suddenly notices that the tyre pressure is not sufficient and one large screw is missing from the back wheel hub. When this is shown to Mahmoud he protests in true Persian style with a shrug of his shoulders and an upward flick of his chin - 'ab naderi' (it doesn't matter) - and this despite the fact that we had been involved in a fatal accident less than a year before! But it did of course matter and our first port of call would be the Peugeot repair shop.

This delay is unfortunate but it is early in the morning so we are still in good spirits as we set off for the road to Tabriz. We move swiftly down the expressway into Abassabad, renamed since the revolution as Shahid Beheshti, past the large wall painting of Khomeini, a huge standing figure outlined against a deep blue background - a mass of tiny people at his feet and the Al-Quds (Jerusalem) mosque in the background. Young boys pop out from nowhere with cartons of Winston cigarettes, thrusting packets into car windows. This week apparently the price is a little cheaper - 550 rials. The open-fronted Peugeot shop is opposite the Museum of Modern Art, which removed the calligraphy artwork of Abdul Rasouli possibly because of the Sufi influence that permeates his work. Today, however, we are concentrating on the car problem but as we expected the Peugeot agent couldn't help us so we set off again to look for spare parts elsewhere.

Downtown the traffic is very heavy especially as it is Thursday, the last workday of the week. One near miss after another occurs as cars screech to a halt inches away from other cars, in a dazzling display of brinkmanship. As we inch alongside the cars, a distinguished grey haired Iranian driver ostentatiously twirls his moustache, very aware of himself and his status symbol - a huge, bright red Chevrolet. One of many in pre-revolutionary days, it would not have been given a second glance. Now, however, it is an incongruous sight in the midst of battered Paykans and the sleek black Mercedes of the new elite.

We reach Kairosh Kabir and turn off into an amazing scene - a whole street is taken over by open-fronted shops containing spare parts for different cars. Men are rushing in all directions, shouting, arguing, gesticulating wildly and peering under car bonnets. This busy centre is probably where the Embassy's Mercedes headlights were brought after their clandestine removal, prised from their sockets, six months ago. Since then the lights have been temporarily shaded by the 'peaked cap' fitting of its Paykan replacements.

It is getting late by the time the tyres are finished. So we turn swiftly into Manucheri - the most popular tourist trap containing a mixture of expensive antique shops and cheap bric a brac. As the car passes we can see the shops, their windows festooned with long strings of hand-worked gold, brass and copper bowls and brightly coloured miniatures. In some shops ethnic dresses hang limply from doorways, while sheepskin jackets and hats are piled in dusty windows, scattered with the spindly bodies of long dead mosquitoes. A few years ago, the traffic would be held up by groups of Americans in shorts and tee shirts haggling with hard-voiced intensity over a piece of (so-called) pre-Islamic pottery or copper bowl. Now only locals dart across the road, head down, a teapot or sheet of barbari bread in hand, women wrapped in mud-spattered chadors clutched between their teeth to keep the material in place. Without tourists, for me, Tehran is a quieter more attractive city but for the locals it is an economic disaster.

At the end of the street we pass the imposing iron gates of the British Embassy. On the stone pillars repose a lion and a unicorn. Smiling Pakistani gate guards run out of the gate lodge to open the gates for some official. Maybe this building is impressive but I preferred Golhak, the Embassy's summer residence which seems to have a much more relaxed atmosphere. This is probably because any visits I paid to the downtown embassy building were to official dinners which often can be stilted and even boring. Driving along the side of the embassy we passed Bobby Sands Street, which was formerly named after Sir Winston Churchill. It was re-named by the new regime in honour of the dead IRA hunger-striker (a typical touch of Iranian irony!).

64 BLACK FLAGS

Around the corner the stark entrance to the Russian Embassy comes into view; the impassive bulky gate guards are out of sight as light rain mists the windscreen, the rain barely kept at bay by the mechanical scraping of the windscreen wipers. (The original wipers had also been stolen and had to be replaced by another legacy of scrapped Paykans.)

Heading in the direction of the airport, we turn off for the Karaj road as shambling concrete buildings sprawl before us, their grim grayness softened by the mist. They are overshadowed by the giant Shahyad monument, a relic of imperial days. It stands out, an unusual modern construction, unlike anything from ancient Persian culture. Beneath it, rows of half-finished high-rise buildings stand forlornly, cranes rusting outside them, as if several years ago a giant finger plucked workmen from the scene leaving behind a crumbling ghost town. Everywhere black flags, representing the mourning period of Ashura, hang limply in the rain. Outside the Azadi sports centre stands a huge gaudy replica of a gilded mosque dome. There is again no sign of the gracious splendor of Islamic and pre-Islamic architecture.

At the toll gate, khaki-clad Pasdaran normally open all the car boots. This morning the checking seems to be quite serious but for some reason we are just waved through. As we speed along the Karaj Road to Qazvin, the barren mountains stretch out, their stark bareness contrasting with the colourful noisy movement on the busy road. Clare loves the honking of the horns and the waves from occupants of other cars.

At last we reach Qazvin, a town full of difficult memories because of our accident. An ancient town, whose elaborate tiled gateway now leads to nowhere but stands alone on an isolated piece of green. A small dried-up river runs through the town, its sandy bed filled with debris. Packs of red onions lie in piles outside a crumbling warehouse, ready for transportation to the capitol city. On the side of the road we find a resting place for crashed and abandoned cars (a testament to Iranian driving) heaped carelessly on top of one another like a gigantic modern sculpture. An old bearded man, on an equally ancient donkey plods slowly by, content no doubt, in the knowledge that his means of transport is probably the safest way to travel.

Along the road are scattered tiny tea houses, outside tables covered with plastic table cloths and the ubiquitous plastic bowls of sugar lumps attracting huge numbers of flies. Oil-rich Iran has long been the world's biggest plastic kingdom, although everything is changing. Stacks of tins of motor oil and old tyres line up outside open-fronted motor repair shops.

The weather is now starting to get hot and humid. Clare is getting bored so she starts to play her favourite game of 'boggie', which entails trying to catch any floating object accompanied by squeals of delight. Boggie, her first word was a combination of birdie and dog. She rips up small pieces of tissue paper and lets them flutter around the car. This was a game devised out of desperation to keep us all from going crazy when I forgot to pack enough toys on our six week car trip through Europe to Iran. A few months ago, when just one year old, she was a much more passive observer but now she joins in shredding the tissues with great enthusiasm.

Stopping for a picnic we sit down gingerly on a patch of dry scrubby grass, carefully avoiding the painful-looking thistles. When we passed by during the summer on our way back from Europe, every inch was filled with Iranian families enjoying picnics in whatever scrap of shade they could find. We eat the leftovers from the embassy supper including pizza and Devji's tandoori chicken while drinking coffee from a huge flask, which is a fixture in every Iranian's picnic basket. Suddenly the sky is lit up with jagged flashes of lightning and great splashes of rain dilute my cup of coffee. This definitely gives us the impetus we need to start packing up the remains of our meal and get back on the road.

An old tractor slowly winds its way through the churning mud while the dull sound of heavy rain changes to a sharp rattle as large hailstones bounce ominously against the car windows. Gentle mountain peaks are hazily silhouetted against the cloudy sky as the freshly harvested fields are interspersed with sandy patches and slender trees, reflecting the constantly changing landscape of Persia, which is a major factor in its fascination.

In the streets of Takestan there is an unusual bright atmosphere that takes us by surprise. We soon realise that the reason for this is because the women are wearing pretty pink, flower-patterned chadors, it's very simple but it seems to cast a carefree light over the whole area. This is such a welcome relief from the dismal pieces of black material sweeping the floor in the other dull, drab towns. A typical scene soon greets us, however, as we see pictures of Khomeini, Montazeri and Khamenei on the stone pillars, which once bore statues of the Shah. Although I was never a fan of the Shah, whose regime was quite brutal, revolutionary fervour really dampened the lightness I was feeling when I saw the coloured chadors.

This is grape country and all the fruit stalls lining the road are displaying piles of bunches of mouth-watering deep red grapes. In pre-revolutionary days, wine from the Qazvin region was famous and even now people drive out to buy grapes in order to make wine secretly at home. The fields have disappeared, leaving sandy stretches, punctuated by groups of tall wispy poplar trees and walled orchards, so reminiscent of Persia and typified by the ethereal paintings of Majubi. Moving on we pass by the unusually shaped memansara of Takestan beside the petrol station and the tea house where two months before we stopped for a bottle of coca cola on our way back from Europe.

The terrain has become completely sandy, hills in the background a purple and grey mass of weird shapes. A small mining construction stands starkly against the hills. The rain has cleared by now, bringing out a swarm of birds perched high on power lines, sleek black crows and blue, black magpies strutting along the roadside scavenging in the piles of wet leaves and mud. Passing the village where Mahmoud's wife was born, we are now surrounded by impressive mountains. Mahmoud points out one in particular, Camel Mountain, so called because of its hump-like shape. It seems like an idyllic scene. In the foreground, overshadowed by the imposing mountain range, little oases of dark green bushes, vines and slender poplar trees surround small orchards as young boys offer bunches of grapes for sale on the roadside. While in the fields heaped with piles of watermelons, men move around languidly collecting them in huge sacks. For a short time it is easy to forget that the tragedy of the war with Iraq hangs over the all the villages as thousands of their young men never return from the war front.

Passing through another little village of Abhar I am jolted back to reality seeing black flags flutter everywhere, a railed flower garden in the central square now empty of a statue of the former Shah.

65. SULTANIYEH

Mahmoud drives quickly past a lorry carrying heavy loads of bricks balanced precariously and protected only by a net-like cover made from rope, which is badly broken in parts. It is definitely a worrying moment but once again we survive. Turning off the road for Sultaniyeh I see the blue dome of the tomb of Mongol Sultan Oljeitu, buried there in 1316, rising majestically from behind a row of poplars.

 The village houses are constructed of mud and brick and two little boys appear from nowhere, attaching themselves to us as we investigate the tomb. Unfortunately it is still covered in scaffolding, as it was when we visited it two years ago, although some minor restoration has been carried out on the balconies. The stonework is magnificent and there are the remnants of eight minarets, only one of which is fairly intact. On the ground, turquoise and black tiles are stacked ready to replace the broken ones. In Byron's time the eight minarets appear to all have been intact and he describes the 'pinkish' brick work and the minarets which 'were originally turquoise and trefoils of the same colour, outlined in lapis, glitter around the base of the dome.' It is wonderful to see that renovation work is continuing on this special building. At the car we give the boys some chocolate biscuits and a handful of mints, which they shared with a group of chadoris who rushed across the road laughing and talking in Turkish.

Back on the main road we pass a recent bad car crash, what seems to be pieces of a car and an articulated lorry are scattered around. Everywhere we go we see wrecked cars, another sad testament to Iranian driving and a terrible memory of our own car crash. Passing a graveyard, I can see that most of the graves are marked out by little sharp stones but at the front are a series of graves bearing large photos of young men, while the Islamic Republic flag is standing proudly on each grave. Men and women are gathered around the graves holding flowers. What a waste of young lives! (There were no winners in this war when it ended. Just many thousands of dead young men on both sides.)

We enter Zanjan, a once important town, destroyed during the Mongol invasion. On the sides of buildings are more pictures of Khomeini, sometimes side by side with Montazeri. On the wall of one building, a mural of a Pasdar attending his wounded companion. Women squat on the pavement begging and the usual empty statue bases are everywhere. At the petrol station eight articulated trucks stand in the corner with four ambulances on each truck. Is there no end to this devastating war?

Travelling along a railway line, red hills and mud villages reminiscent of Afghanistan stand out in the fading light. Soon the scenery changes again as the mountains take on a mossy-green hue and a small river winds its way along a huge stony riverbed. A lovely fifteenth century bridge with a broken middle arch, spanning the river, comes into view as the road cuts through the mountain range.

The road to Tabriz is very busy, everyone seems to be going away for the weekend but we have driven this road many times and do not need to stop to see the sights so we make quite good time and we spend the night in our usual faceless hotel in Tabriz.

Friday 11th October

In the early morning we set off for the next part of our journey to the Armenian cemetery. The wind has picked up once again as we finally reach the Archbishop's house, which we enter through open gates into a large Persian garden; various paths and flower gardens are located around the large lawn. It must be really lovely in summer when the flowers are in bloom. The gracious old house appears to be in the process of undergoing a major spring clean, people racing around with brushes, bowls of water, upper windows thrown wide open and a light net curtain billowing out of a ground floor room showing a wooden cross on the wall above a single bed.

A young girl answers the doorbell and explains that the archbishop is not there and she herself has no idea where the graveyards are. At this stage we decide to abandon our quest temporarily and maybe write a letter to the archbishop asking him for more information.

We return to try to see the mosque near the hotel but it is closed. Across the road we are being observed by a group of shopkeepers standing beside sacks of grain and lentils outside their open-fronted shops. Crossing over we ask when the mosque will be open but are told it is full of supplies for the war front. We retrace our steps along the Tehran road to find the turn off for Ardebil. The countryside is a little like Connemara with its gentle hills leading down to long yellowing grasses. This then changes abruptly into a scene from the landscape of eastern Turkey.

Every trip in Iran is a kaleidoscope of changing colours and scenery. Today the clouds are racing hazily across the grey sky. Suddenly to our horror we come upon a very recent accident. A Paykan car lies across the road beside a big truck. The front of the Paykan is open and completely buckled, a body covered in blood lies beside the car. An ambulance stands by with its doors closed as a policeman waves us forward. We drive on, horror reflected on our faces hoping that the car's occupants may have survived but we are not very hopeful as the ambulance seems in no hurry to depart. Any serious accident is very upsetting but since our own car accident I'm much more distressed when I hear the sound of an ambulance; it has become a conditioned response, heralding anxiety.

66. FLY SWATTING IN ARDEBIL

After an hours drive we arrive in Ardebil. The town itself is rather nondescript but is famous for its beautiful fourteenth century mausoleum of Sheikh Safi. Mindful of this, we stop outside the Sheikh Safi Hotel, hoping that this will be a decent hotel. No such luck, if the amazing Shah Abbas in Isfahan has been ruined by revolutionary spirit, how can we expect an ordinary provincial hotel to be special?

The new concrete building is already defaced with revolutionary slogans including the familiar 'Down with the USA' motif painted in large letters across the front of the building. We are given the 'best' room with an adjoining 'bathroom'. The rickety beds and grubby blankets make the tiny room look crowded. In the bathroom we can barely move between a shower that is not working, the cracked grime-covered washbasin without a plug and a plastic bucket. Once again so much for the glamour of diplomacy!

Escaping from the miserable room we go downstairs to drink a cup of tea with bread and honey then Mahmoud and Devji set off to see Mahmoud's family in a neighbouring village. The street outside the hotel is packed with little stalls, lit up by electric bulbs, where the vendors are selling cooked corn on the cob and blood-red beetroots. There is quite a festive air in the main street, which must be because it is a Friday.

Attempting to join in the festive spirit we decide to enter a crowded restaurant full of families out for an evening meal. We attach Clare's small chair to one of the refectory tables and she swings her legs happily. The wooden tables are laid out with various glasses and bottles of Coca-Cola. Big bluebottle flies strut confidently up and down the table top, only bothering to move when Niall and Clare swat them, rather ineffectually. Bearded waiters run quickly along the passages between the tables bearing large plates, loaded with piles of rice and long stainless steel dishes full of sizzling lamb and chicken kebabs decorated with slices of lemon and rings of raw onion. Apart from the fly population, the restaurant itself is fairly clean and bright. We order dough (yoghurt mixed with soda water – a drink which the Iranians say counteracts any lack of hygiene – hopefully!) chicken kebab and mast (yoghurt). The chicken kebabs are succulent pieces of chicken, which are really tasty.

When we finally get back to the hotel, we discover one of our bags with nightclothes and extra warm sweaters is missing. Niall goes to search the car boot but can find no sign of the car so we go down for another chai (tea) in an attempt to warm ourselves. We drink the steamy brew from a glass, sipping the tea in true Persian style through a sugar lump between our teeth. Several teas and sugar lumps later there still being no sign of Mahmoud, we retire to bed. (In those days there were no mobile phones.)

During the night the room was extremely cold and all we have to cover each of the small beds was a single blanket. It was a very uncomfortable night. We slept in our day clothes because of the missing bag and the cold. Upstairs a baby has been crying all night and in the street the noisy traffic started very early just as we were finally trying to get some sleep.

Saturday 12th October

Eventually Devji and Mahmoud appeared shamefacedly at the hotel. They offered some vague excuse about there being no buses the previous night so they took the car and – in an attempt to change the subject – they announced that because of flooding, the bridge to Astara on the border with the Soviet Union had collapsed, which we would see for ourselves later on. The river was in full spate and we had to wade across while cars were pulled along by tractors.

Anyway, we retrieve our bag from the car, change and go down for breakfast. It was a pleasant breakfast with warm barbari bread, sweet honeycomb and sour cream. I would have loved a cup of coffee but imported coffee was still largely unavailable especially in outlying areas so we have to make do with the usual milkless tea and sugar cubes. We then packed up and set off for the tomb of Sheikh Ishaq Safi al-Din.

The façade of the tomb looked slightly Elizabethan with an intricately carved wooden door on which was a notice saying: 'closed for renovations.' We swallowed our disappointment and walked around the back by a small kucheh (lane) where a chadori was lighting tiny candles in a small niche in the wall. Mahmoud explained the lady was performing an act of thanksgiving following local traditions.

We then passed by two beautifully tiled domes and one bare brick dome around the back where we peered over a high wall. Ducks were running around the grounds and a dove disappeared into a hole in the roof. An old man wearing a soldier's uniform stood beside an old brick house with a wooden door and shutters. He told us that the tomb was closed but he offered to show us the location of the Friday mosque.

A lady draped in a heavy black chador stopped to speak to us. I wondered initially if there was a problem with my headscarf (which was usually half falling off me in a state of some disarray) but in fact she was telling us angrily that the man was stupid and that we must not take any notice of him. She then went on to inform us that she had three sons abroad, one a doctor in America and one in Canada. She wonders if we were Americans ourselves and then went on to talk again about her sons, one of whom she says was married to a 'Farangi' (foreigner). She cried softly as she spoke showing her four remaining teeth, two gold and two yellow. Everywhere we were confronted with the tragedies of this country and the enormity of human suffering.

Mahmoud went off to ask the caretaker for permission to take photos. The old man kindly agrees and we enter through the lovely wooden gate into a long narrow garden. A tiled arch at the end leads us through into a small area, all the walls tiled in brightly coloured mosaic. Walking into a big courtyard we saw an ivan at one end covered by a wooden grill. Through the main door into the tomb building two silver doors led into the special room where Sheikh Safi ad-Din used to live. The beautiful carpet that once graced this room can now be found at the Victoria and Albert Museum in London. The ceiling, currently under restoration, bears a mirror image of that carpet. At the far end of the room was an exquisite ceiling painting in jewel colours and gold leaf. Beyond this a chamber contained a big wooden intricately carved casket, that of Sheikh Safi who died in 1334. Beside this was a smaller casket holding the remains of his grandsons, and beside that a metal donation box.

In a side chamber was a glass case containing a beautifully carved wooden casket inlaid with ivory. This was the body of Shah Ismail, a descendant of Sheikh Safi who on becoming Shah of Persia in 1502 gave the name Safavid to a new royal dynasty, the most notable of whom was Shah Abbas. Around the mosque were scattered pictures of the Ayatollah Khomeini – just to make it clear where political power in the country now resided. Finally after posing for photos in the courtyard we expressed our gratitude to the old caretaker for showing us his historic buildings and set off from Ardebil.

On the road the distant hills glowed in the bright morning light. In a short time we reached Mahmoud's father's village and stopped in the rain outside the hammam (public bathing facilities) of which we had heard so much. It was bright and ultramodern but built in the old classical style and we recalled some of the problems of which Mahmoud had spoken in the past – so many difficulties involving bureaucratic matters and large bribes. We entered the brightly tiled entrance area, extensively covered with enormous potted plants. Mahmoud took Niall into the men's area with its individual showers, while I entered the women's area with its communal baths and showers.

The women were standing in the warm water combing their long black hair, which they then wrapped up to dry in their fluffy white towels. Chattering away animatedly they raised their arms to lift Clare into the water where she splashed around happily until it was time to set off back to Tabriz and on to Tehran.

67. EVIN PRISON

November 1985

The weather was still quite warm and it was decided to spend the day walking in the Elborz Mountains with the German Ambassador and some other friends. On our return to Tehran, after an exhilarating afternoon in the autumn sunshine we had to pass the menacing Evin prison. Probably no other words are as terrifying for Iranians and foreigners alike as Evin prison. At the base of the huge prison walls was a dried out riverbed like a moat around an old castle. Walking in a somewhat fearful mood along the outer wall of the riverbed, we all heard a commotion coming from the prison. Above us we could hear guards screaming as they ran around the prison grounds. Armed guards could also be seen peering over a lower wall as they attempted to scan the riverbed.

We looked down into the riverbed and to our horror at the base of the wall; his body flattened against the wall and his outstretched arms clinging on behind him was a young man. Terrified he appeared to be silently begging us not to betray him to the prison guards. For several seconds we stood there transfixed, a silent line of foreigners focused on the sight of a prisoner who had apparently escaped from Evin, a place where political prisoners were tortured and shot and a place whose name struck fear into everyone. Friends had told us how, after they shot the son of a neighbour, the Revolutionary Guards dumped his body outside the home and included a bill for the price of the bullet. We could not understand how this man could have escaped over the extremely high wall into the riverbed but we were determined not to aid his recapture. The German Ambassador hissed that we should move on quickly and not show his location by staring at him. The whole group were all very upset that nothing could be done to help him and that image will always haunt me.

The mood on our return to the embassy for dinner was very subdued. Trying to lighten the mood was an effort and it did not work very well; once more I felt a comparison with photos of the gaiety or attempted gaiety of Germans under Nazi rule.

It is always so much more difficult to deal with a real problem and real person than to see numbers on a page of a newspaper. We had often wondered how we would react if a political prisoner came over the wall into the embassy and claimed asylum. To give them up would probably mean certain death for them and to keep them would mean long-term problems for the Irish Government. Fortunately that was one moral dilemma we never had to deal with.

The next few weeks went by without too much drama political or otherwise. The snow was early this year so we started skiing again although I was much more cautious because of my injuries in the car accident the previous year. As many of our friends had left the country our Christmas party on Christmas Eve was more subdued than usual but we were still looking forward to seeing more of the country before we, ourselves, left in the summer.

68. BLOOD FOUNTAIN

Friday December 27th 1985

Soft snow is falling gently as an assortment of snowflake-covered Christmas cakes and frosted turkey sandwiches are shoved into any spare corner of the car. Then Bill and Mandy arrive and more chaos ensues as the two children rush around shrieking with excitement. Delayed as usual by endless cups of coffee, we are finally ready to set off by late morning. Along with a stream of buses and cars we head in the direction of Tehran University, which is full of people attending Friday prayers. khaki-clad Pasdaran stand in the middle of the road trying to organise the traffic but, as always, cause even greater congestion.

The Russian Embassy looms ahead - grey concrete apartment blocks, so reminiscent of the soul-less Moscow buildings. Today the Afghans are marching to mark the anniversary of the Russian invasion in 1979, so the roads are blocked off around the embassy, which probably contributes to the traffic chaos. Young men, snow-covered car accessories slung over their shoulders try to sell their wares, an old lady covered in a grey, flowered chador wafts a container of incense into the car windows. Turning off to the Qom motorway we speed past piles of rubbish, rusty cars and old tyres.

In the distance the two towers at the entrance of Beheshti Zahra stand out against the heavy clouds. Although this was a general cemetery it has now become a special burial place for the thousands of war-dead. Inside the main gates is the blood fountain - spouting a tasteless stream of blood-red dyed water - quite a disturbing sight. The sky lightens and the grey, snowy sky of Tehran turns blue, as we move slowly along past the walled villages and ancient, crumbling caravanserais. The pale blue silver toned salt lake is glimpsed through the sandy hills.

At the Qom toll gate, a young Pasdar stops us to check our destination. As we circle the roundabout, its huge Islamic sign suspended from rusty poles, a mullah strides over sandy paths to reach the main road. While in the distance we see the golden dome of the Hazrat-I-Masumeh, the tomb of Fatima, the sister of Imam Reza whose shrine in Mashad is the foremost Shia site for pilgrims in Iran. Qom is the religious capital of the country and the second most holy city. Mullahs are everywhere in this holy city, wearing long brown, warm, woollen capes over their robes. One launches himself into the road in a vain attempt to get a lift or maybe to become a *shahid* (martyr). Tourists are allowed to enter this city with its great golden dome and minarets but there are no hotels for this strange breed of foreigners.

Moving on quickly from the stares and fervour of the Shia pilgrims, we leave Qom and stop for coffee beside a pretty newly built mosque. Everywhere it seems, new mosques are springing up, finished or in a state of near completion. These are probably the only new buildings at the moment. Across the country, half-completed office and apartment blocks stand as lonely iron skeletons of previous times. A smell of rotting cabbages rises from the fields. All around, a kaleidoscope of changing colours glide together, heather hues, pinky purples and mossy greens mingling with scrubby desert patches beside grey distant hills. We pass a little walled village, men on donkeys going home for dinner, while in the orchard, wooden boxes are piled up ready for fruit. A new turquoise-tiled mosque stands out against the dusty road as unusual mud domed houses and tall poplars can be seen behind the walls of the gardens.

Kashan

Entering the famous carpet-weaving town of Kashan, we encountered a large screen displaying a garish cartoon. Underneath the cartoon are incongruously placed pictures of violence and war victims. Near the garden stands a large modern hotel. It's not too bad, a little run down as usual but the bathroom has thick towels and a big perfumed soap with a picture of a coconut on the wrapping. It's a bit sad that thick towels and wrapped soap cause great excitement and that this is all there is to recommend a hotel; but this is the aftermath of a revolution. On the walk to the garden in the dark, stalls selling rosewater and nuts stand beside fruit shops and a meat shop, dead sheep hanging at the open door. The entrance of the Bagh-e-Fin garden is brightly lit and its only occupants are several young boys sitting around and looking bored, like teenagers everywhere. This special garden, overflowing with colourful flowers and bushes was created centuries ago by Shah Abbas.

The huge pictures of Montazeri and Khomeini are no longer at the entrance of the garden. A group of people rush past us over to the far wall, open a door and run down steps. It is very dark and the tall cypress trees standing beside the stream with its small bubbling fountains, lend an air of majestic mystery to the silent garden where the murder of Amir Kabir took place. He was a forward-thinking, highly respected, Qajar Prime Minister who was assassinated in 1852 for introducing modern reforms. It is getting cold and I think it is time to return to the hotel.

Apart from the peaceful garden, Kashan is overall a very interesting town, especially with its history of involvement with Shah Abbas who is believed to be buried in the crypt of the nearby mausoleum dedicated to one of his ancestors. It is also claimed that the Magi or the Three Wise Men set out for Bethlehem from this very place.

69. FACES AT THE WINDOW
Saturday December 28th

Fortunately we manage to get some sleep. The next day we stop for lunch beside the broken walls of an ancient caravanserai in front of an orchard of fragrant pomegranate trees before turning off the road to the fertile valley of Abianeh. Leaving the road we have our first view of the old castle. It stands on top of the ridge overlooking the river, which winds slowly through the valley. The little fields neatly marked out like sepia patchwork, the trees are bare, depriving the valley of its springtime beauty. While snow-topped mountains rise majestically in the background.

In the valley the scenes flash by - wispy poplars screening houses, a small imamzadeh and tiny pointed stones in graveyards now changing into mud-covered houses several storeys high. On the hillside wooden doors mark a series of storage caves while three Islamic Republic flags hang limply over the sad scene of war graves in a small cemetery.

Twenty-five kilometres from the main road at the end of the valley stands the village of Abianeh in the shadow of the snow-covered mountains. A villager on a donkey stops to talk to three young men all dressed fully in black with baggy trousers whose design would not be out of place in a Paris salon.

The striking buildings covered in dark red mud with beautiful wooden balconies and open brickwork designs are arched all over the streets like those of a medieval European city. Faces appear at the window amazed at the unusual sight of foreigners. Other windows gape open, displaying piles of wood and sacks of rice and grain stored for the winter.

Old ladies, their heads covered with white shawls decorated with red, green and orange flowers gather at their doors smiling brightly as we pass and offering us a welcome into their houses. The brightly coloured shawl rather than the black chador is the traditional wear of the village but when they leave to neighbouring villages they have to wear the black chador. A woman squats beside the small stream washing her pots.

The tiny mosque has a pretty carved wooden door decorated with white and turquoise paint-work and two brass doorknockers. Above the door, is a picture of Beheshti. Inside pinned onto wooden pillars are the sad pictures of war victims; some pictured proudly holding their guns at the war front. Everywhere we are offered tea by the friendly villagers. Over the arched doorways of the houses, colourful paintings are worn away from time and weather. One of the young men in baggy trousers invites us into his parents' house for tea. He discusses regretfully how many foreigners visited their beautiful valley before the revolution. He himself studied civil engineering in the U.S. and now he works in Tehran. We set off down the valley leaving behind a place so different from anything we have ever seen in Iran, full of friendly villagers with memories of former days.

The main road winds round over the picturesque bridge and on to the pretty village of Natanz which Arthur Upham Pope describes as "one of the loveliest mountain towns in Persia". We stop outside the 14th century Friday mosque with the tall minaret decorated with blue and white mosaic. Descending the steps, we open the door into the main prayer area. A few old ladies follow us; remove their shoes and step onto the carpet. A man talks into a microphone, which relays the prayers to the top of the minaret and out across the village. We are not allowed into the tomb area so we stand outside in the open courtyard. Two men climb into view still dripping water from their ablutions in preparation for prayers.

70. MAIDAN-e-SHAH

Sunday December 29th

The light is fading on the last stretch of the journey to Isfahan. Finally we drive down the famous Charbagh Avenue (four gardens) and across the river.

The Kourosh Hotel has changed its name to Kowsar. The modern pleasant interior is not so elegant or special as the Shah Abbas, but is much cleaner and comfortable, with more of a relaxed atmosphere in the huge foyer. Hannah and Clare run around, delighted to be out of the car. They play with the plastic Father Christmas in front of the hotel shop to the horror of the shop owner who moves quickly to put everything out of reach. The TV shows the usual war front pictures and plays the usual stirring revolutionary music but the bedrooms are amazingly bright and clean with no revolutionary messages or pictures of prophets old or new. A man appears with a cot for Clare and a jug of ice into which we place our cans of warm beer. The bathroom looks quite civilised with soap, clean towels and a bath and shower that seem to be in working order. We clean up Clare and Hannah and take them down to dinner. There is no point in our dressing for dinner. The only necessity is to check that we are adequately covered to pass the scrutiny of any zealous "brother" or "sister". The big dining room is deserted but all the tables are beautifully set and at first sight - with the exception of the lack of wine glasses - it could be any good hotel anywhere in the world. The menu too has more to offer than the usual kebab selection. We order onion soup, beef stroganoff - in fact maybe a kebab is safer - and filet mignon. The onion soup is a brown caramelised mess, the beef in a tasteless floury sauce and the filet rather damaging for the teeth. The children swing perilously in their chairs, the table rocks, sending Pepsi in all directions as we hastily and apologetically leave the battlefield that was not so long ago an elegant table. In fact the Iranians are amazingly tolerant with small children and always show great interest. Certainly, in revolutionary Iran, having a child with you appears to be more positive than negative. In the bedroom after dinner, I add another page to my diary while Bill, Mandy and Niall play board games. We drink a bottle of mulled wine left over from a Christmas party and have a special treat by opening a box of chocolates.

The following morning, the view from the bedroom balcony looks so calm and peaceful, and golden arches of the old bridges stand out against the pale ice blue river glinting in the wintry sunlight. In the distance, the pillars of the Ali Gapu and the domes of the mosques in the Maiden-e-Shah. We choose an English breakfast in the snack bar, which consists of a glass of sickly-sweet tinned orange juice, two eggs, bread and carrot jam, a pot of hot water and a tea bag. Mandy decides to order a 'pile of pancakes' - which turns out to be one rather fat pancake on a plate. Still, the service is quite excellent as the waiters scurry around at top speed, expertly and good-naturedly pulling the children away from hot or breakable objects. We pile up the car with the usual nappies, milk bottles and juice bottles.

Parking the car in the square, we enter first the Shah Mosque. The beautiful entrance is decorated on both sides of the door with the design of a prayer mat; the central motif on one side is now adorned with the picture of Khomeini. This time, no chadors are necessary, but I am looking appropriately monkish in a long wool cape, the tweed woven in Father McGlinchey's farm project on Cheju-do Island, off Korea. Mandy looks fashionably Islamic in her woollen hood hat. We pass through the door and check that it really is oxidised silver. In the courtyard, the green stagnant water in the pool is covered with a thin crusting of ice. Clare spots a little girl and moves off at top speed in the direction of the new face.

A guide whom we have seen on many previous visits appears, his woolly peaked cap pulled down over his eyes, and leads us through the arches to the madresseh built by Naseredine Shah. We then return to the main part of the mosque, the square spoiled by the scaffolding which supports a covering of cloth for summer prayers. Bill stands on a marked spot under the impressive colourful dome and claps his hands. He is rewarded by sharp repeating echoes. The guide lovingly strokes the beautiful blue, white and yellow tiles decorating the walls and explains that the tiles are 400 years old. Through into the tiny garden at the far side of the courtyard, the shrubs are now bare, the atmosphere so peaceful.

We collect the children, Hannah hiding behind the arches, Clare sitting on a mat with a chadori and another *nini* (child). The guide points out one of the stones on the wall whose texture had completely changed due to the constant striking of matches against it. He shows us a plaque of beautifully executed calligraphy, and he talks sadly of how many tourists he used to show around before the revolution - Americans, Germans, English - and how expensive everything now is. A fact we know only too well. All of this said in a very matter-of-fact way, not in the usual whining way. We all give him some money and cigarettes and step out again through the huge silver doors, moving down the square to the Sheikh Lotfallah Mosque. It's a compact little mosque, comprising one single chamber, bare but for the fine work on the walls and a colourful dome banded with beautiful calligraphy, written by one of the finest calligraphers of the day, at the base of the dome. As we go out into the square, we happen to meet the Indian Ambassador and his family, passing through Isfahan on their way to Shiraz the following day.

71. SHAH ABBAS

The next port of call is the Shah Abbas Hotel now renamed the Abbasi, where we stayed with Don and Pat in our first year in Iran. The remodelled hotel had once been one of the best hotels in the world, with its fine mirror work, paintings, mosaic and tile work. In the main sandwich bar, we are all allowed to sit together to eat our chicken sandwiches and Islamic beer, as there no longer appears to be a separate anteroom for ladies. The main dining room, where seven years before on our way back from Japan, we had eaten caviar and drunk vodka, now only served kebabs and Coca-Cola. One of the waiters said he would show us the beautiful paintings covered up since the revolution and recently exposed.

We walk up the winding staircase to the upper floor overlooking the main dining area, and he points out richly painted doors and paintings, one of which was still hidden under curtains. He takes us out onto the balcony where we can see the dome of the Madrasseh. We go down through the attractive metal openwork gates into what was once the bar, and smiling, he points to the recesses in the wall where used to be vodka, gin and whiskey bottles; now they only contain orange juice and Coca-Cola. Outside the bar, the fine Isfahan brasswork shades the light and casts soft, glowing patterns all around the ceiling and walls.

In the corridor, we pass by the black and white drawings of old Isfahan and out into the garden where the gardeners are cutting away the last dying blooms of the year. They cut some chrysanthemum flowers, and with a shy smile, hand them to the children. In the *chaikhaneh* - or tea house - at the back of the garden, Khomeini's picture stands out against the coloured background. The hubble-bubble stands on the floor and in the alcove sits a richly coloured wall painting.

Standing among the fading stillness, we reflect on our visit in August 1978: the festive lights strung across the well-kept gardens, the smartly dressed waiters bearing laden trays of exotic foods, arrogantly threading their way through the tables, the coffee house a hive of relaxed activity. A life so different from the people in the streets and yet, we wonder, has the move to the other extreme really improved the lot of the ordinary people. At the desk, the man who had been so difficult on our previous visit is looking much older and greyer. Maybe the trouble he encounters from both sides, those who resist Islamic rules and those who impose them, is getting too much for him.

Leaving the hotel, we walk past the door of the Madrasseh, around the corner to the bazaar, past the gold and silver shop, and through to the garden of Shah Abbas's harem. This is a typical charming old Persian dwelling, with the rooms leading off the central area and upstairs, the balcony, which leads to other rooms. Unfortunately, the paintings on the ceiling are badly faded and in need of restoration, which cannot be guaranteed until the local finances improve.

We go on to see the Mashid-e-Jomeh (Friday Mosque) in the busy part of the town, passing tiles of rubble caused the previous March by a Iraqi scud missile striking the area. The beauty of the unpainted brickwork in the fading light of the courtyard, a mixture of intricate workmanship and natural simplicity, never fails to fill me with emotion. We try to go downstairs to the underground passages but are unable to do so as there is no electricity; so we walk back through the fascinating covered bazaar, the air filled with noise, colour and scents of exotic perfumes and spices.

Dark now, we drive back and park outside the Abassi Hotel to do some shopping in the government handicraft centre, buying some mats. A small multi-coloured striped cotton and wool mat costs the same price as a kilo of chicken kebabs, and a brightly patterned red and beige wool prayer mat costs only a little more. Little wonder that meat, even if it can be found, no longer figures prominently in the average daily diet.

On the wall leading up to the shopping complex is a ten-foot painting showing the back of a black-cloaked and turbaned figure, standing over the body of the slain Shah, whose head lies beside an axe. A chilling reminder of the continuing hate. Walking past the jewellery and textile shops of the covered bazaar, we experience another power cut and the small gas lamps cast an eerie glow over the sheepskin jackets and cotton dresses hanging in the windows.

The old miniaturist we first met in 1978 is our next port of call. When we get to the top of the stairs, we find the door closed as usual, but on this occasion the old painter comes up after us and opens up his little room. The room is so different now, the desk is still in the corner, but the walls are quite bare behind the desk, there are very few pictures, only a few miniatures on pressed ivory or camel bone, none of the Dervishes he did so well. Bill signs the visitors' book. There have only been six signatures in the last four years, ours on the top of the page in 1981.

We return across the river to the hotel. A staircase, six floors high and going nowhere is silhouetted against the darkening sky. On our way into dinner we meet another couple from the British Embassy. We decide to order some caviar. The size of portion was disappointing as it would fit on two teaspoons and was the price of the 100 gram tin from the government fisheries department. Still as this is the best caviar in the world we were not complaining too much. The fish kebabs were also very good and a change from the meat ones. A little boy at the next table was chasing the girls in and out of the chairs. Three pairs of unsteady legs keep hurtling around the room at top speed, three voices shrieking in delight. When the family had finished their meal the boy was picked up and carried off crying, unwilling to leave the other children behind.

Going up to our rooms we spend another pleasant evening playing scrabble and finishing off the beer and chocolates. Then we deposit the bottles and tins safely in the baby basket. The following morning we spent another morning attempting to keep the children under control hoping they didn't cause too much disruption to the Indian Ambassador and his family whom we saw at the far side of the room. We check out of the hotel and set off to try to attend a service in the Armenian area.

Outside the church we park our car and watch the women across the square queuing outside the fruit shop. In this quarter they look like elderly people anywhere, winter coats, thickish stockings and only the occasional chador. The church where previously we had attended a service was closed so we went on to the cathedral. Across from the cathedral was the barber's shop where in 1978 we had drunk our Coca-Cola, enjoying a welcome break from the August heat. The gate into the grounds is locked but when Bill rings the bell an Armenian man opens the gate and tells us we can look around the cathedral. We all get out of the car but, unfortunately just as we reach the open gate, an imposing figure in long black robes appears, striding across the courtyard through the open door and into the waiting car. It was the Armenian bishop whose bushy black beard, glasses and high standing hood we had seen in many photos. He kindly invites to us to attend his service later and waves goodbye as he sets of in his car. We decide to first look at the cathedral, only to find that the man with the keys has also left with the Bishop. We wander around outside the church and read the inscriptions on the gravestones of those who have died over the last century:

Catherine Mary T Ironside M. B.
Medical Missionary of Persia from 1905
Daughter of the late Edmond and Mary Ironside
Nov 11 1921

Unlike during the time of Shah Abbas, the Armenians live in constant fear of persecution, although so far no physical oppression has actually occurred. It is now time to drive back to Tehran to celebrate the New Year.

Martyn Turner's cartoon of Niall published in the Irish Times

Niall shaking hands with President Khamenei and foreign Minister Velayati

Return to Embassy of the crashed Chevrolet

Boarding the train for Moscow

Nearing the Russian Border

A Lookout post at the Iranian-USSR Border

View from Train on journey to Moscow

Niall and myself on the Moskva River boat, Moscow

Adrian and myself in front St Basil's Cathedral in Red Square, Moscow

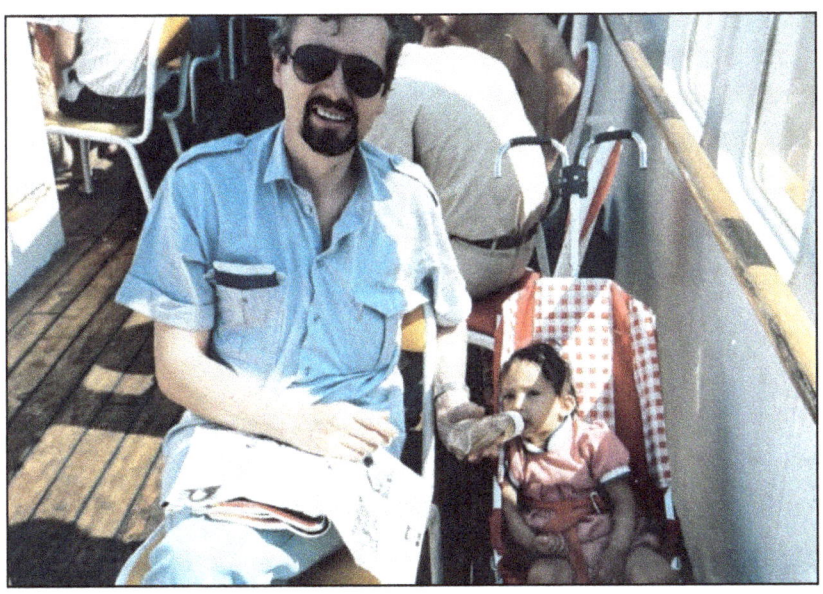

Niall and baby Clare on boat from Italy to Izmir

Basilica Of Saint John, Ephesus (Turkey)

Temple of Diana, Ephesus

Tomb of Mevlana Rumi, Mevlana Museum, Konya, Turkey

Ancient underground chapel Cappadocia, Turkey

Fairy Chimneys in Cappadocia

Cappadocia

Cutting the wedding anniversary cake before the cockroach invasion, Irish Embassy, Tehran

Persian Music Concert at the Embassy

Niall's guitar concert

Niall and exporter at the Tehran Trade Fair

American Helicopter crash site in Tabas desert

Inge with Clare at Crash Site

Inge and I at the Shrine in Mashhad

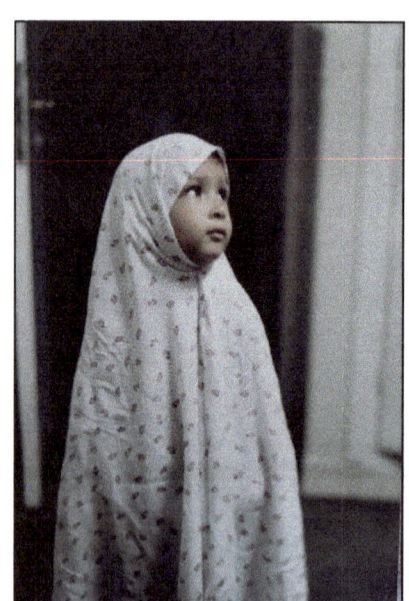

Young Clare in Hijab

Imam Reza holy shrine Mashhad, Iran

The Shahyad, now known as the Azadi Tower in Tehran, Iran.

*Sultaniyeh Dome
- Tomb of Sultan Oljeitu*

The Broken bridge at Astara on the border with the USSR

Hitching the car to the Tractor

Crossing the River without the bridge

Mamoud with his family in Ardebil near the Russian Border

Graves of the War Dead in the Behešt-e Zahrá Cemetery, Tehran

Niall and Bill with Clare and Hannah

Unusual house structures in Abyaneh Village

Bagh-e-Fin, Kashan

Bagh-e-Fin, Kashan

Mandy at Isfahan - Jomeh Mosque

Pre-revolution room in Shah Abbas Hotel

The Armenian Church we visited in Isfahan

Diplomatic Corps in Tehran (1985)

PART 6
-1986-

72. WINDING DOWN
Iran-Contra Affair 1986

There were many rumours going around of Israeli planes landing in Tehran and stories of various arms deals. Most of the diplomats felt that this was the usual Iranian paranoia so no one paid much attention. Maybe, however, there really is no smoke without fire. In November 1986 the Iran-Contra scandal exploded onto the world media.

It seemed that Oliver North and other Americans had flown into Tehran with fake Irish passports to negotiate the sale of American weapons to Iran via Israel. There were American sanctions against doing business with Iran so this deal had to remain top secret. Oliver North was in the process of arranging the arms deal and had come to Iran to complete it. The money was to be used to support the Contra rebels in Nicaragua who were fighting against the legitimate Ortega government.

The reason for the all the secrecy was that the Reagan administration could not get the Democratic-controlled Congress to permit arms to be sent to the Contras. Although we did not know it at the time, our lives and the lives of other Irish people in Iran had been put at risk by the use of fake Irish passports in this highly dubious and illegal operation.

Bandar Abbas March 5th 1986

Niall and Peter, the Norwegian chargé, have scheduled meetings in Bandar Abbas so we set off in two cars for the Gulf. It is an excuse to travel through all the amazing Persian sites, both Islamic and pre-Islamic. Isfahan, Shiraz, Persepolis and Pasargadae, cities and sites of ancient history and stunning beauty, places of which I never tire.

On our arrival at Bandar Abbas, Niall and Peter go to meet the Governor and then on to the Italian Camp for lunch where we meet Brian and other friends. We then pile into three Land Rovers to see a so-called Roman bridge. Stopping at a camel halt we step down onto a sandy area trying to avoid hardened pieces of camel dung. Impossible but at least the dung is not soft and the local children seem quite happy playing around in it while imperious camels look on. There we view a broken arched bridge spanning a large expanse of muddy marsh surrounding a little pool of water. Niall sinks into the mud and has to be pulled out before we lose him forever. It seems from the camel prints that the animals also have had a lot of difficulty at that side of the pool and could only drink standing on firmer ground.

That night there is a party at the house of a Dutch employee to welcome the return of his wife from holidays. Great to meet all the people we met two years ago. Lots of lovely Italian food and their famous grapefruit wine is flowing. The following morning Niall was wishing the wine had not been flowing so lavishly! We all go down to the port and clamber aboard the Bandar in the hope of sailing to Kesh Island Although the sky was clear and the sun of the Persian Gulf warmed our skin, the wind was quite strong and it was thought to be too dangerous to head for the island. Clare is delighting in this new experience and thinks the fluffy, white wake of the boat is snow. Some of the casualties of the Iran/Iraq war come into view: the Michelangelo cruise ship, now rusting in the distance and a cargo ship, exposing gaping holes, the result of an attack by two missiles. Ghosts of a conflict not yet over, buffeted by the waves.

Returning to port we climb the precariously positioned steps back onto firm ground. An old man, white crocheted cap perched on his head, walks along the outside edge of our boat carrying a plastic bucket. Filling the bucket with seawater he pours it over his feet and hands and then goes inside to complete his prayers.

When we return, the foreign contractors at the camp kindly put on a party for us, lots of great Italian food but we are definitely more careful about the grapefruit wine this time. After another late night, Peter and Inge head off to investigate other archaeological sites but we have to return to prepare for our St. Patrick's Day party.

73. TOWERS OF SILENCE

We set off in the direction of Yazd, the desert city, the home of many Zoroastrians and the location of the most important Fire Temple in the country dedicated to Ahuramazda. The whole area of Yazd province is covered by desert. Green patches of vegetation break the monotony and mark out the busy city and other small towns. Today the distant hills are covered in snow. Yazd is a city which experiences great heat in the summer and bitter cold in the winter. The traditional, simple architecture is quite unique in Iran in the way it helps to deal with these extremes. Tall wind towers sit on rooftops and huge domes cover water tanks several metres below the street. Clay is used extensively throughout, turning the city into a uniform grey colour.

Passing the 'Towers of Silence', where the bodies of the dead are laid out to be disposed of by eagles and vultures, we go straight to the Zoroastrian Temple. During the reign of the Shah nobody was allowed to enter the temple where the sacred fire, the symbol of Ahuramazda, has burned for 3000 years. We are a little apprehensive but the embassy apparently was given permission so here we are, in front of the high white walls and the only distinguishing mark we can discern is the winged disc on the walls of the inner modern building. Tentatively we ring the bell at the large door and an old man wearing a Nehru-style hat lets us into the garden. We walk past the frozen pond and tall pine trees into the small room. In the centre, protected by glass is the sacred flame, the symbol of the spirit of the God of Light. I could hardly believe I was in this special room, it was all so simple and yet such a privilege. The whole idea of Zoroaster seems such an ancient and alien concept to the West but it is still alive and relevant to so many people in both Iran and India.

Outside we come back to modern day reality as we pass by the Zoroastrian maternity hospital and school, both with the distinctive winged symbol of Ahuramazda. Our next visit is to the town centre and bazaar to buy boxes of gaz, a type of delicious, chewy nougat, a speciality of Yazd. Then we start our trek back to Tehran for what is probably the most difficult day of the year - St. Patrick's Day.

Monday March 17th

Started making trifles early in the morning but keep getting waylaid by people dropping in for cups of coffee. The cream is not too thick in Tehran and it was very difficult to whip because of its watery constituency.

Go to the UNDP (United Nations Development Programme) building for the new Irish colonel's party at lunchtime. Adrienne from the New Zealand Embassy is busy making Irish coffee for anyone who wants it, which, of course is everybody. The food is prepared by one of the hotels and is excellent. When we return to the embassy, the Spanish Ambassador drops in for a drink to discuss the plight of the nuns and priests. There is no longer any such thing as religious tolerance in Iran.

During our party in the evening the electricity went off for two and a half crucial hours between seven thirty and nine, so it was very difficult to finish cooking the meat or reheat the other dishes. Despite this we survived the evening although we did have the usual one or two people who when offered a piece of shamrock to pin on their jacket crammed it immediately into their mouth! It cannot have tasted too good after a week in plastic wrapping in the diplomatic bag!

At the end of the evening, Fr. Mulligan and the Irish colonel stayed behind for an Irish coffee. Fr. Mulligan was very depressed but there was not much we could say to cheer him up except that Niall will try again tomorrow to stop him from being deported.

Tuesday March 18th 1986

In the morning Niall went straight to the Foreign Ministry to discuss the case of Fr. Mulligan with the Protocol Department. He obtained an extension for him for one month, not enough but a start. At 4 p.m. we go to the Palestinian Embassy. A group of Iranian colonels and the Russian Ambassador are upstairs having a long discussion. The Russian Ambassador comes down to announce to anyone who will listen, which in fact is everyone because it is the Russian Ambassador speaking, that Isfahan was bombed today at 12 noon and much of the refinery was destroyed. Iraq was bombed during the afternoon, probably in retaliation. This is very upsetting; any talk of bombing is unsettling.

I was quite tired but at six in the evening we set off again to meet the new Palestinian diplomat and discuss the possibility of retaliation here. The new Danish Ambassador is very keen to leave the country on Sunday for Easter. We try to persuade him to travel around this wonderful country but I suppose if there is a possibility of retaliation or any further bombing our suggestions will fall on deaf ears. It seems that we are the only ones mad enough to still want to travel around Iran at the present time.

Wednesday March 19th 1986

Went to an Iranian friend for dinner. A marvellous Persian meal was followed with two hand-blown green wine glasses filled with crème de menthe. The guest list was comprised of a great group of diplomats including the Greek Ambassador and the New Zealand chargé d'affaires and his wife Adrienne. On our return I rang my great aunt who had been to the hospital for a check-up. It was worrying because she was still in quite a lot of pain.

74. A FORM OF CLOSURE

Thursday March 20th 1986

There was a surprise waiting for me when I returned to the residence in the evening after going shopping with Mandy. The Indian doctor who had treated me after the car crash was sitting in the main room with his wife and eight month old baby. He explained that he had been worried about me because I not only had the possibility of serious internal injuries but also the possibility of brain damage. In fact, after the accident, I suffered from bad migraine and did have some problem thinking matters through and I found it difficult to make sense of a lot of my cognitive processes. I kept plucking ideas out of the air and I could not put my thoughts together in any coherent way. Fortunately, a year later this had cleared up - although I am not too sure about long-term prospects. (Many of my friends always thought I was brain damaged anyway, so maybe it doesn't really matter.)

The doctor was very reluctant to give details but when pressed he told us how my right pupil was very dilated and my left pupil very small. He said it had been a terrible night; eight people had been in the emergency room of that small provincial hospital in Qasvin. He had been particularly worried about three people that night, the wife of the British chargé, myself and one of the Iranians. Two Iranians in the Paykan had been dead on arrival at the hospital. One died on the way to Tehran and he was not aware what had happened to the fourth man. Niall had been in a state of shock following the accident, was bruised from head to foot and was hallucinating about having to return to Tehran for a meeting. Despite this chaos and the fear that I was not going to survive, the doctor had continued to stitch my eyes and another doctor had stitched the rest of my face, which was so badly battered that no one recognised me for several weeks.

The doctor had not heard about the letter that Niall had sent thanking both him and the hospital for their excellent care and treatment. Often we do not realise the strain and stress the medical profession go through as they try to save lives. Apparently we had received immediate treatment because of our diplomatic status, more out of fear than anything else, I suspect, in the unpredictable new republic. I would like to think that we were treated well because we were seriously ill rather than because of the diplomatic label. As ordinary foreigners, however, we might not have been treated immediately whatever our injuries because of the paranoia towards foreigners at that time. Anyway it was good to have this discussion and try to close that difficult chapter.

Friday March 21st 1986
Today is Now Ruz, the Persian New Year. During the night we heard several shots, the first for some time. There was a great deal of sleet and the snow was very heavy but quite wet and not really sticking to the ground. Although the Elborz Mountains look quite ominous, I had a very restful day and went for a walk in Ali Shariati. The shops were open as if it was a normal day. Back in the embassy Niall was writing a political report. There were suggestions that the Iranians were powerful players in the hostage crisis in Beirut and Niall had been asked to go into the Foreign Ministry and make representations for the release of Irishman Brian Keenan who had been taken hostage by a group believed to be aligned with Iran.

Saturday March 22nd
Decided not to go skiing, which apparently was a big mistake because everyone said the conditions were terrific. I suppose we should have known that from the snow yesterday. Our friend Brian was up from Bandar Abbas and dropped in for coffee. He was pleased with the progress on the new port and said that there were not too many problems now; he was happy nevertheless to escape to Tehran for a short break from time to time.

75. WORSENING SITUATION

Sunday March 23rd

Niall went down to the Foreign Ministry this morning to ask for Iranian assistance in freeing the Irish hostage, Brian Keenan, who was being held in Beirut by a group (later identified as Hezbollah). The response was polite but completely unfruitful. While the Iranians admitted having influence they insisted they had no control whatsoever over any of the Lebanese groups. Niall was very frustrated and tried several times more but, as usually happened in Iran, there was nothing that could be done. (Brian Keenan was not to be released for another four years.)

Palm Sunday at the Italian Consulate. Fr. Piresi told us the situation was very difficult at the moment. He was trying to break the news to Fr. Martini that he may be forced to leave but apparently Fr. Martini would not listen. He was very like Fr. Mulligan, the old Irish priest who had given his life to his parishioners and to Iran and wanted to die there. He would not fit into Italy any more than Fr. Mulligan would fit into Ireland. (Maybe that would explain Fr. Mulligan's unexpected death in Ireland a few years later in 1989.)

Jamal came around to give me a lesson on my sehtar. It is a very delicate instrument, which produces a lovely silvery sound. He also gave a good rendtion of his improvisation of Danny Boy on the sehtar and guitar. He was a little depressed because the authorities had opened some music centres but not his. That was obviously stopping him from building up his own business.

He had other depressing news about new executions in the prisons and how the top military men had been replaced. Also it seems that an important bridge was bombed by the Iraqis last week. They must have tried to keep that bit of news quiet because no one seemed to know about it. The government is trying to make people believe that they are winning the war so any reports of attacks are kept to a minimum. His next pieces of news were that the price of petrol had risen to 20 rials a litre, maybe as a result of the bombing of the refinery in Isfahan. Finally Jamal informed us that a that a plane had been downed in Ahwaz. The plane had been carrying a group of top judges on their way to arrest the commanders of the army at the war front and everyone was killed. It was thought that the crash might have been deliberate because of a tip-off from an inside source. That was the same trip that Niall and the other diplomats made to the war front nearly five years ago, fortunately on that occasion the only mishap was plane failure on the ground.

There was more depressing news when Fr. Mulligan called in to tell us that women were now being sent down to the war front. They were presumably running out of men and boys because the slaughter was so immense. Everyone is starting to feel very uneasy again.

Thursday March 30th 1986
It is an Iranian holiday for Esther and Mahmoud.

Sister Maryam came to discuss the position of the charity, as I will be leaving soon. I am happy to tell her that the wife of the new Swedish Ambassador has offered to take it over so there should not be any problem. She suggests that we go to visit the village for people suffering from leprosy that the sisters run in Tabriz. That would be a great experience; we are driving back to Ireland so we can call in on our way to the Turkish border.

Politically the situation is not good at the moment. Everyone appears pretty negative and hostile and Sister Maryam is worried that there might be a lot of violence on the way and her charity will be deprived of some of its funding. Fortunately my Indian friend from the UN had left some clothes to be sold on behalf of the leprosy group so at least we can hand over some money to her right away.

There is more very heavy sleet all afternoon.

The wife of the New Zealand Ambassador rings to let me know that her friend Zita is selling some dresses made out of antique Turkoman clothing and we should go around to her house at about 6p.m.

The traffic was very bad and the snow was getting heavier as we neared Zita's house in the North of Tehran. At last we pass through the gate into a courtyard, which is surrounded by grass and flowering bushes and overlooked by a huge swimming pool. The house itself is very large and very dark, like a scene out of *Great Expectations*. Clare is very happy to see a big dog and several children so I can safely leave her and go upstairs to a cosy room with a blazing log fire.

Upstairs all the wives from the different embassies are scattered around the room sipping tea and coffee and waiting in excited anticipation for yet another shopping experience. There is a clanging of discarded tea cups as all the women stand up when Zita arrives with bags and bags of colourful tribal clothes and bedspreads which she tips out unceremoniously onto the table. Always a bit slow off the mark I continue to drink my coffee until there is actually a space at the table. I buy a navy and pink long skirt with a matching long top. A very fine gold thread runs through the navy material and although it has a touch of tribal to make it interesting it would actually fit in at any function.

I collect Clare on the way out although she is not too happy to leave her new friends and again we head into the heavy snow. On the way home Mahmoud is doing a valiant job trying to avoid the black-draped chadoris who are dashing, head down, in a suicidal bid to cross the road.

April 1986

We get the sad news that Niall's aunt has died so we return to Ireland for several weeks. While we are there we look for a new house with enough room so that I can work from home. Niall's sister finds us a Victorian house overlooking the sea, with a basement, which could be used as consulting rooms if I wished. It's not in great condition but has a nice friendly atmosphere and the fact that it needs a lot of work means it will not be too expensive. We put in a bid.

MAY 1986
Saturday May 24th

Back from a hectic month in Ireland it is lovely to relax in the garden, in the sun, without having to talk to anyone and then our friendly meat man Gerry rings to say he is back in town. He comes to dinner with the Irish UN colonel and Brian who has come up from Bandar Abbas again. All afternoon I have been trying to find baby milk powder. It is rationed to one tin per person but there is none in the shops at the moment.

Monday May 26th

In the afternoon Kian calls in after her work in the Danish Embassy. I always love seeing her and listening to all her news but today she is in a very dark mood. She tells me how terrified she was over the attack on the Rey refinery and the second bombing alert a few weeks ago while we were away. We decide to plan a shopping trip tomorrow, which might cheer her up or at very least distract her from the ongoing situation.

Tuesday May 27th

Kian and I go down to buy some brass lamps and mirrors in Manucheri. On the way we discuss her plans to move abroad because she is finding the bombing raids too difficult. So many educated Iranians who can find employment in America or Europe are leaving. I can quite understand it but sadly Iran is being drained of its most talented people. The man in the brass shop has no customers and is so desperate to sell anything that he says Kian can name her price.

When I get back I can see there is a funeral in the apartments opposite; it seems that a young boy has been killed at the *Jeppe* (warfront). There is just terrible sadness all around.

76. PLASTIC PLATES

Wednesday May 28th

Gerry is still fighting over his performance bonds (money that had to be deposited in advance to guarantee the delivery of goods from abroad) and the import agency is still refusing to hand back the money.

Go to the calligrapher's house. He has written a beautiful piece of calligraphy which he gave me. I ask him may I come to his house for calligraphy lessons twice a week until I leave the country. His son Soli tells me about an Islamic story explaining how important it is to be true to oneself. Certainly everyone is true to oneself in Soli's family. There is always such a lovely atmosphere in the house, so calm and yet so inspirational. It really is a haven of peace in a mad world.

Leaving to go to the shops I see a worried-looking lady haggling over the price of plastic plates. When I think how things were when we came here for a holiday, on our way back from Japan just before the revolution, I cannot believe that this proud country has come to this - women not even able to afford plastic plates.

During the night the air is filled with chanting and singing in preparation for the next three days to commemorate the death of Hassan, who was the successor of the Holy Prophet according to the Shia tradition.

Thursday May 29th

Ring Jacqui who says her daughters are upset because they can no longer play tennis following a ban by the Revolutionary Guards. Fathi says there were 37 *shahids* (martyrs) yesterday and many injured all from her own small area of Ali Shariati. I saw two 'lights', signifying the death of martyrs, outside the local taxi rank. Again the conversation turns to the availability and price of food, especially meat. I just do not know how poor Iranians can afford meat anymore. More news about one mullah who said women with improper *hejab* (head covering) should not be sent to correction camps but should be dealt with on the streets. That justification of violence against women sounds very ominous indeed. (Forty years later this policy of dominating women through violence has not changed.)

Friday May 30th

Niall went to British Embassy to play football. It is really very hot today so I sit outside with Kian and her young daughter Sanam who came to play in the pool with Clare. Kian says that the mullahs now say if a man and woman are found swimming in the same pool then blood must be shed. She is, therefore, not going to swim this summer. She thinks the exit permit will soon cost 300,000 riyals instead of 50,000 at present; she plans to leave the country as soon as she can.

Kian, Sanam, Clare and I go to visit Hamid Teherantchi. We try to persuade his wife Arus to go to hospital. Teherantchi thinks she has cancer and also thinks it is very serious. Unfortunately she has no passport so she cannot go for treatment in another country. I say I will try to get a British or Irish visa for her if she gets a passport but she should move quickly. She is very miserable because she is in pain and we are all unhappy despite the lovely Russian food. I buy one of Teherantchi's collection of Russian tea caddies in a beautiful burnt orange colour.

77. BURNING CANDLES

Sunday June 1st 1986

Today is Devji's birthday. I forgot, unfortunately, until Esther started hopping from foot to foot and produced a cake ablaze with candles from behind her back. There was a frantic scrabble as Mahmoud attempted to put out the candles, which had already singed Esther's hair. Grabbing a glass of water from his desk he threw it over the cake and Esther's hair. Unperturbed she re-lit some of the damp candles and started singing 'happy to you'. After the celebration she realised that she could have been quite badly burnt and took to reading her bible again in thanksgiving for her lucky escape. Roya meanwhile took over her secretarial work for the day as Esther was now 'indisposed'.

Some blood tests were arranged for me in Tehran clinic where the consultant tells me that Kami and Kristie are now settled in America where Kami plans to start working soon as a neurosurgeon. I hope so because he has had so much amazing experience at the war front that any medical institution would be very lucky to employ him.

Tuesday June 3rd 1986

Niall's birthday today, I heard Devji wishing him happy birthday so, although distracted, I remembered early on in the day. Fortunately Esther did not go near any candles today and she let Roya take charge so everyone was safe. Kian and her husband Hassan are holding a party for Niall tonight and once again chaos is reigning. Gerry comes to do some work on the word processor and lets us know that apparently Kian has forgotten to invite some of our Iranian friends in time and they are now refusing to attend the party. It's very difficult to keep up with the mores of Iranian culture. Kian rings around to apologise and everything is fine. Chaos is Kian's middle name, which is probably why we get on so well.

Gerry is no longer our Irish milkman. He has changed career to become our Irish meat man and is now selling beef. He tells us that at last his company has finally received its money from the government and he will probably be able to leave next week. We may now get some peace, although we will miss his good humour. It really is very stressful for businessmen to broker deals in Iran at the present time. It is difficult to sell goods to the Iranians in the first place and even more difficult to obtain payment for these goods

Despite all of this trouble, beef is getting into the country but meat in the shops is still in very short supply. Fathi told us that she had queued for three hours that morning but when she finally reached the end of the queue, all the meat had gone. In the evening at Kian's party, Bill from the British Embassy confirmed that there had been no meat that morning in the shops. Possibly it has gone to the army or wherever else the government felt it was most useful.

Niall went down to the Health Ministry where they asked him if Ireland could produce various services and training. On his return to the embassy, Roya brought out a cake and Esther did her usual 'happy to you' song. That night Kian's party was very special. She managed to get both fish and meat, although no one knows how she does it because everyone else finds it very difficult to find food. All our friends were there including Soli and Farimah, Gerry, Mandy and Bill and others from the diplomatic corps.

We had a lovely evening but once again as I sat in the beautiful garden, I felt a little guilty that the country was in uproar and like Nero, we were all fiddling while Rome burned.

Wednesday June 4th 1986

Go down with Mahmoud to the Foreign Ministry shop to get some food because once again there is little or no food in the shops. Sadness catches up with me when I see people peering in the window from the outside, interested to see such amounts of food at a time of food shortage. Two chadoris managed to enter the shop and the armed guard on the door was reprimanded for letting them in. That is really upsetting because there is obviously no shortage here although, for some reason, the manager refuses the sale of washing powder for embassies, which is a little strange as the caviar is still flowing.

In the afternoon I go around to Soleiman's house for a calligraphy lesson with his father. After the lesson we talk about his father's friend, the deputy of Hoveida, the last prime minister under the Shah. Abdol Rasouli broke off his friendship because he did not like Hoveida. I had seen what was supposed to be a pair of Hoveida's riding boots for sale after his execution when Kian took me to an exhibition of objects confiscated from Iranians who had either been executed or had fled the country. The Revolutionary Guards excitedly pointed out what they said were the riding boots of Hoveida. There they were in pride of place, standing tall in beautifully crafted burnished brown leather. I felt a little queasy listening to the story. It did sound again so much like the French revolution.

Hoveida had been a cultured man who had finally attempted to introduce some necessary reforms into the authoritarian regime of the Shah; but really it was much too little and too late for the revolutionaries and he had been executed. In retrospect, it was probably good that the calligrapher, who was a truly principled man, broke off his relationship with the friend of Hoveida or else he too might not be alive today.

Niall goes round to the Irish colonel to invite him for Saturday and to discuss the colonel's wine, which unfortunately had not turned out too well.

Thursday June 5th 1986

Fr. Mulligan arrives for breakfast to tell us that the imprisoned Polish priest is now out of jail after 42 days and has been pronounced innocent. Another travesty of justice has been prevented!

In the afternoon I brace myself as Fathi arrives bearing more bad news. She told us that yesterday she saw two young boys in Maidan Mosseini being picked up for military service. The boys were crying because they would not allow them to inform their parents. An older man who was passing by took their address and told them he would let their parents know what had happened. They would train them, said Fathi, send them to the war front and pick up more young boys. What a tragic nightmare for the parents and there is nothing anyone can do. Everyone feels utterly helpless.

Niall speculates that there might be a new offensive in September, which may be why they are picking up more 'cannon fodder'.

I sit and read in the sun; no one is around and I have my most restful day for a long time. I am beginning to feel my old self again. In the evening Jacqui, Ali and Gerry the 'meat man' arrive for a meal and to watch a video which we have just managed to get. A video is still a rare treat in Iran, although the sad thing is that because a few of the foreigners have now brought some videos into the country, the play-readings are no longer so popular. Ali, who is always knowledgeable about the on-going situation because of his position in Tehran University, reinforces Fathi's discussion but adds that lots of young girls and men wearing short-sleeved shirts were also taken away – probably to prison.

After watching our precious copy of 'Gorky Park' we then celebrate our return from India two years previously with Fathi and two candles on a small cake. We had already celebrated Clare's second birthday on May 1st but the fourth of June was her special day when we brought her back to Tehran from India. Well once again I was a day too late with the celebrations.

78. DIPLOMATIC CIRCUS
Friday June 6th 1986

Clare wakes during the night with a very bad nosebleed; maybe it is the altitude or the dry air but she has nosebleeds quite frequently. Gerry arrives at 8a.m. and he and Niall set off for the British Embassy to play football. It is very hot so Clare and I potter around in the pool and I write my diary. Niall's sister rings to say do we want to make a new offer on the house as someone else has put in a slightly higher bid. The house is in a great location but is not in very good condition so we cannot go much higher than our new offer. The men come back from football looking a little the worse for wear. Niall had a bad night last night and he thinks it was generalised anxiety about the situation. I am definitely feeling the same way.

The Head of Personnel rings to say she knows Niall would be disappointed because he was more interested in development aid work but the Anglo-Irish division had asked for him and he should know how important this was at this time. Then she discussed the date of our departure. She thought a sensible time would be after the Trade Fair.

On the television everyone appears to be marching for al-Quds (Jerusalem) Day. It seems as if the whole of Tehran is marching but probably it is the same piece of film played over and over again. Rafsanjani seems to be the main speaker throughout the march.

Saturday June 7th 1986

Do not know who will come around this afternoon so I'm taking advantage of the peace by making two dishes of strawberry mousse. In the afternoon the colonel phones to say he's coming over and Gerry arrives from his hotel. Kami's brother, Bahram, turns up and everyone starts to discuss the state of the economy and more importantly the food shortages! Bahram thinks the country is producing enough oil. Gerry says they are not and at today's low oil prices it does not make much difference anyway. A strong wind and a fierce storm blow up and a game of musical chairs follows as we dash inside and outside again and then upstairs and downstairs trying to avoid the heavy rain.

Sunday June 8th 1986

Trying to get out of the new Belgian Ambassador's swim-lunch, but again I'm not quick enough. The Ambassador himself rang this morning to say that the Dutch Political Director is arriving and he is hosting a lunch for him. Maybe everyone else has turned him down. He is a nice man but a character from the last century who surrounds himself with drama and extremely glamorous Iranian ladies, while insisting that everything has to be on a very grand scale. He is very different from Roger Martin.

Mandy and Hannah arrive but Clare is not in good form today. She seems to be tired and maybe is sickening from something. Fathi arrives to tell us the story of 30 boys from her son's school who were sent to the war front a month ago; 15 came back dead last night. They had been told beforehand that they would automatically get their high school diplomas if they went. She was very upset – as we all were.

Gerry telephoned to say that a raid had just occurred on the telecom centre and all international radio and telephone lines are cut.

Monday June 9th 1986

Today is the end of Ramadan, which means we can now drink water in public – that's a relief as, in the oppressive heat, it was unbearable walking around without water. This morning it's very cloudy and it looks like rain. That would be really good to cool the place down.

News came in that last week 300 men had been apprehended for wearing short-sleeved shirts. Gerry has gone to Isfahan – so once again we might get some peace and quiet.

We arrive at the Belgian Embassy for lunch (to meet the Dutch Political Director) and - to our surprise - there are so many people there that it looks more like a circus than a diplomatic occasion. There are lots of small children and the usual array of 'Persian ladies'. One elderly

Iranian woman has bright blond waist-length hair and is wearing a luminescent yellow dress slashed to the waist and tied in what is probably the latest Parisian fashion with a big bow under the bottom. This makes the whole outfit look most precarious. Chatting to the German ambassador about making trips we start to plan the Varamin journey. His latest news was that IranAir aircraft were no longer being repaired due to lack of cash.

No one seems to be aware of the breakdown in communications, although some colleagues have had difficulty making telephone calls. Each European head of mission has a table to look after – there were 14 tables. One large table nearly collapsed under the weight of three whole sheep complete with heads. I gave that table a miss and piled my plate with vegetables. It was an incredibly difficult afternoon and of course no one talked to the Dutch Director!

Overnight fresh snow reached halfway down the mountains.

Tuesday June 10th 1986

Yesterday was my great aunt's birthday but I cannot phone because the international lines are still down. It appears that Gerry was right: the communications relay station at Hamadan has been hit by Iraqi planes.

I go to Kian's hairdresser and as usual get a little too much cut off. It is a pity hairdressers, everywhere, insist on cutting my hair too short. Anyway I suppose I look, if not better, then at least a little more tidy. I go on to Soli's father for a calligraphy lesson but I am not concentrating too well today. The Portuguese national day followed. We see Jan, the Belgian first secretary, who had been expelled seven days earlier. This was in retaliation for the expulsion by Belgium of an Iranian diplomat who had attacked the Belgian police in a public demonstration. Jan says that after he met with Foreign Ministry officials, his stay has been extended until Friday.

We manage to get the Finnish Ambassador and our Norwegian friend Inge to join us for the trip to Varamin and Rey.

Finally dinner at home with a roasted ham kindly given to us by a local Finnish businessman. Gerry arrives to join us and informs us of a red alert following the Hamadan attack.

Wednesday June 11th 1986

Last night it was announced that the international telecom lines had been repaired and Niall's sister, Renagh, rang to say that our offer had been accepted for our new house in Dublin.

In the afternoon Mandy brought Hannah around again to play with Clare. Everything seems to be getting more ridiculous by the day. Mandy said that two weeks ago her hairdressing salon had been raided by the Pasdaran. As a consequence of that, it was now mandatory for headscarves to be worn in the salon at all times. It was not clear whether the clientele would have their hair under or over their scarves while it was being washed and cut. It all sounds quite insane!

79. CASPIAN COAST

Thursday June 12th 1986

The summer was becoming very oppressive so we decided to escape the draining heat by driving up to the Caspian Sea area to see some Russian friends D and R. (In the early days of the revolution the Russians were not in favour in Iran so it was difficult to socialise with Russians. For general safety reasons therefore I did not put their names into my diary.) As mentioned earlier, Robert Byron used the name Majoribanks to refer to Reza Shah for the same reason; but nearly forty years on I have forgotten the names of the Russian couple.

We had made several trips to the lush vegetation on the Caspian coast to stay with Kami and Kristie in their summer villa but this time we were going to stay in Ramsar at the old Grand Hotel - which was not as 'grand' as its name implied. Ramsar was said to be the most beautiful part of the Caspian where wooded hills reached down to the beaches and everywhere there was a profusion of colour, with palm trees and orange trees scattered among the rose bushes.

Before we left, Niall had to go down to pay a courtesy call on the new female Chief of Protocol. Pashfuirush is now wearing full nun's habit well up on the chin and well down on the forehead and a chador safely stitched up the front so it could not accidentally blow open. Not much hope there then for all the Iranian women who do not want to cover up! Niall had hoped to discuss the renewed repressive measures against women but quickly realised his conversation was going nowhere. It looked like yet another wasted journey to the Foreign Ministry.

It was a busy day for both of us. Before I even thought of leaving for the Caspian I had to go to a Chinese tea party in the Chinese Embassy at 10:30 in the morning. The Chinese were delightful and really tried hard to please and win approval from the rest of the world after being subjected to the tribulations of the Cultural Revolution. Because of that, their behaviour was often so different from the usual blasé diplomatic approach or the officious, arrogant, Iranian way. This was a cookery lesson plus tasting - the food was delicious and I did not need any lunch after that.

While I was there I met the wife of the new Norwegian Ambassador who informed me that it was such a pity that so many of my friends were leaving. I looked back at her blankly because I was afraid most of our diplomatic friends had already left and I really did not know that many of the new diplomats any more. That is another difficult part of diplomatic life: the fact that towards the end of a posting, so many friends have already left that it is not easy to show much interest in new arrivals.

We had hoped to to leave early for the Caspian but this was not possible as Niall had to go to lunch at the Dutch Embassy to meet again the Political Director whom we had already met at the lunch party the previous day. Therefore we had to wait until late afternoon before we could set off.

On this occasion we were using our own car so I drove along the Karaj road safe in the knowledge that any damage caused would not be to the embassy car. We then passed through Karaj along the jade, green riverside. The Casino, an impressive building on the hillside has now been taken over by the military police. On our previous trip, we were stopped and questioned by the police. Today, however, a group of them appeared to be in deep discussion and were not even looking at the road.

This did not last long, of course, before we reached the mountain and the dam, two Nissan Patrol vans drove past us screaming to a halt as they blocked our way. A group of Pasdaran jumped out with guns at the ready. Fortunately, they really were not interested in us but obviously were looking for someone else. There had been a Mujahideen attack in the area the previous week, so this was probably the reason for their edgy behaviour. Once again we set off, in front of us a dark mountain overshadowed the deep, green reservoir formed by the dam, which had originally been named Shabanu Farah after the wife of the deposed shah, Empress Farah.

It was starting to get dark as we drove along the spectacular mountain road to Chalus, finally arriving in Ramsar at 8 p.m. Ramsar's two luxury hotels were set on neighbouring terraces one, the old Grand Hotel, was an elegant hotel full of old-fashioned charm while the modern New Hotel was a white concrete and glass block vividly standing out against the green bushes. Stopping at the front of the New Hotel we met our Russian friends in the foyer and then drove along the road to the back of the old hotel.

It was really beautiful as we walked through the garden filled with palm trees, beautiful red rose bushes and fountains. All around the hills were covered with orange trees and in the background a distant view could be seen of the Elborz mountain range, the outline painted mauve in the darkening light.

Inside we went upstairs holding on to the leather banister and admiring the old maps of the Caspian Sea coast that hung on the wall. At the far end of the entrance hall there were eight-foot crystal chandeliers and beautifully coloured Persian carpets. In the bedroom there was pale grey-flocked wallpaper on the walls and what may have been an original painting by Monet. The tiled bathroom had gold plated taps and the kitchen area contained a huge fridge with an icemaker and cold water taps.

In former times it had been a very famous and exclusive hotel but now it was badly run-down and our first task was to clean up Clare, who had been sick towards the end of our journey, rather than admire the décor. When we had finished washing Clare down we walked across to the New Hotel to meet our Russian friends for coffee in what is really a concrete and glass monstrosity. In the 1960's former British ambassador to Tehran, Roger Stevens, describes Ramsar as the "show place of the Pahlavi Riviera, where there is a larger flamboyant hotel covered with statues on a knoll standing back from the sea, with steep woodland paths behind subtropical gardens, and an avenue a mile long flanked with orange groves leading down to the casino and the beach."

80. THE GRAND HOTEL
Friday June 13th 1986

Early morning we again went across to the New Hotel for breakfast because it seemed that the old Grand Hotel had no restaurant facilities whatsoever and we had only been allowed to sleep there because we were foreigners – a very unusual and exotic species at that time. The waiters speak excellent English and try to make the meal as western as possible by bringing some milk for the tea. By now we have got used to the Iranian way of milk-less tea so we do not use milk anyway, but it was a lovely gesture.

Meanwhile Clare had climbed out of the baby chair and rushed around the dining room chatting to everyone as usual, sometimes in English sometimes in Farsi. When we finally managed to catch her we all went back to the room to collect bottles and nappies for our day out.

Back in the room in the old hotel Clare began playing with the Iranian chambermaid who spoke good English and had not practised the language for a long time because there had been no English-speaking visitors since the revolution. She took us along to show us the former dining room. It had once been very special and was still full of lovely furniture but now it just looked very sad and extremely dusty. If Clare disturbed anything, we all started to cough as clouds of dust from the previous six years rose into the air and settled back making us all look like pre-revolutionary ghosts. Examining all the old photos of the Shah and important foreign guests, we admired the delicate etching on the glass doors while imagining the glory of former days.

Twenty years previously, Peter Somerville-Large had dined in the room when he had been the only guest in the hotel:

'I returned to the hotel and ate alone in the huge dining-room, surrounded by seven waiters. It was a memorable meal; course followed course for several hours, and through the windows I could see the gardens and statues floodlit for my benefit.'

The maid then took us out and surreptitiously led us a little way down the palm tree-lined drive to show us where the casino used to be before the revolution. Inside the windows were covered with plastic sheets and the interior was very dark. We could barely see anything as we tripped over five or six tables and several broken chairs. Even years ago, Somerville-Large was served in the casino by 'a lonely barman' who 'offered me a choice of coffee or soft drinks.'

A door creaked open onto the balcony overlooking the sea and in the garden there was the broken base of Reza Shah's statue below us. Beyond this broken statue sat the concrete and rusting iron remains of a half-completed apartment complex, which would have ruined the view anyway, if completed but is now an even more terrible eyesore. On the balcony there are pieces of broken concrete and lots of cigarette butts and general litter. We move back through the darkened room quickly, worried we might be found in the casino, a now forbidden place.

As we drive out of the gate on our way to Rudsar, a smell of sulphur pervades the air. The town of Ramsar used to be famous for its hot sulphur springs and was visited over the years by many people looking for health cures. Suddenly an old man springs out and takes his hat off his head to demand *'poule'* (money). Used to Iranian tricks we hand over a hundred riyals and he jumped aside delighted with his ruse. Families are picnicking under elm trees beside the sulphur stream. We reach the road and drive over the bridge to admire the inlets of the Caspian Sea, which are a deep shade of midnight blue, rather than the usual dreary grey colour.

Reaching a traffic jam we are held up for a short time because ahead is a setting up point for the *jeppe* (war front). A bus moves off packed with young men for the *jeppe* leaving behind a crowd of chadoris, children and older men, which soon starts to disperse. Ahead an open Paykan is driving away full of chadoris and children with a tattered

Islamic Republic flag flying limply from the front of the truck. Another Paykan passes on the wrong side of the road at full speed with an air of recklessness as it turns off the road to another village. I go silent as I remember our own deadly accident with a Paykan open truck.

We stay behind the bus. I am glad about that because I do not want to see whether the euphoria of the farewells has yet been replaced by the terrible feeling of inevitability of violence and death. In Rudsar the road to the square is lined with huge photos of *'shahids'* (martyrs). There are three lines of metal-framed photos and a fourth line with empty frames still awaiting its death toll.

Outside the police station our Russian friends await us. They live around the corner in a house which has been built in Russian Baku style with a tiled roof and beside it a similar house which had formerly belonged to the agent for the Russian Czar. This was where Reza Shah used to stay before he built his own palace. The old villa is full of character and we eat a snack upstairs before setting off in the mid-day heat.

Our first stop is a large rud, an old bridge, double arched and picturesque. The river, itself, was full of rubbish of all descriptions and Clare decided to try to join in and throw more rubbish down, becoming very upset when we stopped her. The wooden houses overlooking the river were very old and canoes were moored there ready for commercial use. It was all very reminiscent of Kashmir. As I take photos, a family moves into sight waving and smiling as they cross the steep bridge. *'Kheilimam nun!'* (Thank you) the man smiles as I take his photo. We move on to look at some small food shops, which are stocked with vegetables, much fresher and cheaper than Tehran. We get some garlic and eggs noting that the Tehran food shortage has obviously not affected the Caspian yet.

Driving on to Lahijan we all enter a local restaurant, where outside children are flying kites. In the background stands the mountain named Shaitan Kuh or Satan Mountain (a picture of Khomeini was placed on its summit and no one dares name it that any more). In the entrance of the restaurant stands a huge stuffed swan, which Clare keeps trying to feed. Our friends' children are very good at looking after her. The little girl Doren is a very mature four and half year old and the boys at the next table also play with Clare. Kebabs again. These are quite tasty but when there is little else they get a little monotonous.

All around the chanting wails on relentlessly as the Pasdaran try to recruit people for the war front. Despite the bad behaviour of some of the revolutionaries, the Iranians are a really friendly nation and the lady from the next table stops to talk to us on the steps; she also is happy to practice her English while the children play on the see-saw and slides. Her young son who was showing an unusual interest in Clare is in fact a girl. Her mother, it appears, keeps her dressed as a boy with cropped hair and trousers rather than dress her in the usual garb of a chador. What a good idea. It's like the New Zealand Ambassador's wife in Tehran who would sometimes venture onto the male ski slopes in Dizin where she pretended she was a man to avoid the hassle of being checked by the Pasdaran. I did not realise, however, that some Iranians were brave enough also to do this.

81. TEA FACTORY

We arrive in the main square of Lahijan and go to see the mosque. An old lady lets us in. We have to take our shoes off and move onto the carpeted floor. Nothing remarkable inside it, a few dark green curtains hanging down. We ask her how old it is and she says she does not know but we can read it outside. The plaque on the wall has no more information. It says the mosque was built by the son of the minor Sultan but leaves us all none the wiser. A young man rushes out of a nearby shop and laughingly explains that everyone tries to find the age of the mosque and no one can.

We drive on passing the end of a little alley or *"kucheh"* to look at a beautiful window covering which seems like a piece of intricate wrought iron-work, but here it is made of wood. The mansion has been taken over by the Pasdaran and two Pasdars moved forward to the end of the *"kucheh"* to see who is observing them. We drive on quickly. Outside the town we pass the tomb of Kashef-ol-Saltaneh the Iranian consul in India who, we were told, brought the tea plant seed from India in his walking stick. Now it appears to be the Pasdaran headquarters so again we drive quickly past, surreptitiously taking some photographs. Some extra huts are built onto the tall concrete building with the red Islamic Republican sign etched onto the side and back and on the front are the usual printed slogans and a big picture of the head of Khomeini. Islamic Republic flags and a large torn flag with the picture of Khomeini are also flying over the building. Around the building are the usual unkempt grounds strewn with the omnipresent huge motorbikes. A circular look-out post betrays the insecurity of the Guards.

Opposite a tea factory we park our cars. The province of Gilan is the biggest producer of Iran's tea. As yet, however, no leaves have been collected so we move on to the tomb of Sheikh Zahed Gilani, who Sylvia Matheson suggests was the spiritual guide to Sheikh Safi al-Din, founder of the Safavid dynasty. It is an unusual pagoda-type wooden building reminiscent in the shape of a Japanese temple. The roof of turquoise blue and yellow tiles has obviously not been reconstructed even though half of the roof is in very bad condition. Inside the tomb the coffin is enclosed behind an iron cage. In the background are dark green rice paddies and orange pomegranate flowers, while beside the tomb stands a house of a dervish, surrounded by palm trees, with the usual signs of begging bowls outside on the gate.

Women are working in the rice paddies, bent double, long cotton smocks and baggy trousers tied at the ankle while their heads are protected from the sun by small cotton headscarves. The scenery was so like Japan, and even the humid atmosphere was similar. Bending down, they picked out all the weeds. It was a backbreaking job to produce the Caspian rice, of which Iran is so proud.

By now we have moved on to another tea plantation which has a new Japanese machine. Because the machine also picks off too much of the stalk, picking by hand is still regarded as superior. This tea factory seems a bit like any old factory from Victorian England. We watch as the huge sacks of tea are being weighed and then hoisted on the men's shoulders and carried upstairs where they are spread out to dry. Other men are gathered around the table, marking down the weight of each sack.

Everyone kindly stops for several photos. They say that the Gainsborough is the best English machine for dealing with tea and we all stand back to admire the massaging, heavy shaking, rolling and sifting techniques. Finally we go into a room with tea leaves piled in sacks and mounds of tea on the floor. We are shown how to distinguish the different qualities by the feel of different leaves. Clare, meanwhile, is running around playing in the tea mountains scattering the leaves on the slippery floor as we try in vain to stop the destruction. The manager, however, just laughs and tells us the scattered leaves will all be duly brushed again into the pile. We go to sample the delicious finished product in the manager's office and, of course, we then take more photos before we bid farewell and move on to the silkworm farm.

At the farm we see rows and rows of mulberry bushes to feed the hungry silkworms. We climb the wooden steps into a thatched house on stilts. This reminds us of the homes of the head hunters of Sabah in Borneo, but this one houses thousands of silk worms chomping hungrily on the mulberry leaves. Descending the ladder, we find one of the men with a nasty-looking machete decapitating a cocoon, to show a small grub inside. He then brings a handful of fully grown silk worms, which have the appearance of chalky white big fat caterpillars. The children shriek with delight holding and poking them. Clare, very excited but somewhat frightened shouts out 'boggie' and backs away when we come too close. Finally the life cycle of the silk worm is then explained to us and we are told that the silk is sold to a local factory.

Our visits finished, we all set off for the beach where we park the cars and walk along the sand. Clare with great delight runs into the water, shoes wet, dress wet. It's now dark and the silver stars stand out in the clear sky. A car draws up its headlights lighting up the seashore. D's brother jumps out and we all drive off to eat at the kebab restaurant. One is closed because a relative has just drowned, this latest tragedy just adding to the many victims of the treacherous Caspian. Mrs R points out where the waves make swimming very dangerous; explaining how the sand just gives way to a steep drop and of course swimming in chadors is particularly lethal. Sitting outside along the main road we eat kebabs and then drive back exhausted. Fortunately we do not meet any wild Caspian ponies wandering on the road. D warned us that these free spirited animals are a frequent source of terrible accidents along this stretch of road.

82. FOOTBALL-BOSOMED GODDESS

Saturday July 14th

At breakfast a family with two girls, one of whom seems to have a medical problem, called Clare over to sit at their table and eat with them. She is delighted of course and has a great time. After breakfast we set off for a walk around the front garden. Steps are leading up to a pair of silvered lions, but the aluminium paint is cracked and peeling and they just look sad. The garden is filled with huge broken vases, cupid statues, and the half figure of a Grecian female the top part of the statue broken off and removed probably because it was seen as too erotic for the current government. Certainly the description by Peter Somerville-Large[4] of a 'half-naked, football-bosomed goddess' a few years earlier would suggest that was the case.

Griffins and cupids line the steps. At the top of the rust-stained balcony we find two figures from Persian mythology but there is no sign of the broken top half of the female statue, which is now replaced by a concrete Islamic Republic sign!

As Peter Somerville-Large wrote of the Grand Hotel during his visit there just before the revolution:

'All over the fern-filled garden other statues in the style linger beside fountains or hide behind camellias or palm trees.'

Unlike during our visit, the gardens were then in very good condition and seemed to have been quite beautiful, if maybe a little theatrical.

---

[4] Before we left for our posting to Iran in 1981, Lord Dunsany invited us to dinner at his castle in County Meath to meet Peter Somerville-Large. Sadly Peter died aged 97 on October 7th this year just before the launch of this book.

Now the garden is overgrown but at least there are plenty of vine leaves which later Mrs R will pick to make dolmeh or stuffed vine leaves. There are orange trees everywhere and tiny orange fruit the size of fingernails line the floor like a large silk carpet. A huge chandelier appears behind darkened glass. With the overgrown glass and broken statues it now looks like a cemetery. The hotel is still impressive but the paint is peeling off the walls. Parts of the walls are crumbling and overshadowed by a large stretch of discoloured awning which is rotting away. The graceful proportions of the elegant structure are marred and overwhelmed by a huge Islamic Republic sign, not to mention the jarring composition of the ugly concrete block beside it. Soon it is time to return to the New Hotel so we will be there when D and R arrives.

Two old ladies dressed in navy raincoats and trousers with their hair covered, start to play with Clare. Suddenly an old man calls down to them from the dining room and they gesture to me to pull down my headscarf. Moving out to the front we pay the bill. Walking along the road we came across a little glass fronted building, which was possibly for a car park attendant originally, although we are not quite sure. The hut is now cordoned off with a line of broken statue pieces and two bored looking photographers sit on the bottom steps waiting for non-existent tourists.

The family from the hotel arrive and perch the children one by one on the silvered lions. The photographers jump up falling over themselves to produce instant photos, not able to believe their luck. The mother, holding Clare, is delightedly pouring over the results of the two photographers. The family is a picture of contentment despite their problems. We walk around by the stream and buy an ice cream from the vendor beside the sulphur stream. We see the little man from yesterday expectantly smiling but we know we will see him again as we leave so we ignore him. A Pasdaran car races down the lane towards the sulphur paths; we hope it is not going to pick someone up for the war front or for some minor legal infringement.

Niall returns to the hotel to find our Russian friends and when I arrive with Clare I see him pointing at his bare elbows to a man who is wearing a black shirt and sporting the revolutionary black beard. 'What about me?' Niall is saying in Farsi pointing at his bare arms. 'That is not important, it is the Khanum (woman) that counts' replies the Pasdar. I see, it's my headscarf again! The Russians point out that I'm a foreigner but he says it doesn't matter. I will definitely have to get some form of glue to stop my headscarf from falling off, as it seems to cause so much distress to the revolution.

We go back to walking in the garden lamenting the past beauty of the hotel and looking through the windows at the former dining room, now a lounge full of elegant furniture and old prints. Entering the hotel, we walk down the corridor to the breakfast room admiring the fine detail on the glass doors.

Back in the bedroom the chambermaid is already cleaning the room with Clare running after her. We bid farewell to the man at reception and pack up the car. The little man needs to be paid off again and we then drive down to the casino where the blocked up windows are overgrown with trailing plants and thick bushes. There is a stylised Zoroastrian sign on top of the building with wisteria growing over the railings. At the back of the garden the empty swimming pool lies abandoned and broken. We go round to the side of the hotel where we see a series of smashed garden seats and a forlorn-looking rusting roulette wheel and a fruit machine. The two hotels dominate the hillside, as does Reza Shah's Summer Palace beside them. The graceful lines of the old Grand Hotel are ruined by the Islamic Republic signs and the ugly, concrete building beside it.

83. CONSPIRACY THEORIES

Along the Caspian coast the sun glints on the turquoise blue sea. We stop at an open-fronted motor shop to get petrol and do some shopping. The shop was overflowing with a selection of local crafts and cheap plastic items from China. Handmade baskets were jumbled up with plastic ducks, dolls with staring blue eyes and buckets and spades. To our amazement they had tins of baby milk powder so we bought several tins and a big sack of local rice. Driving on we pass tea plantations and rice paddies and skirt the lovely town of Chalus. Stopping at a chelo-kebab cafe for a quick lunch we watch as a jeep drives up and a German man gets out, accompanied by an older German lady and an Iranian man with a bushy beard.

Here foreigners are such a novelty that it is always interesting to wonder about their lives. Maybe she was a hostage, after all she did look quite sad, and was not really communicating with the men or maybe she had been a German spy during the last war when the Germans had been trying to get Reza Shah on their side. Our Russian friends were none the wiser and certainly had not seen them before around the Caspian area. Finally we all agreed that her story probably was only that she had married an Iranian and lived in Iran for many years - no big deal - although in a country in turmoil, it is always tempting to write an alternative narrative.

On our way again, leaving conspiracy theories behind we head for Tehran, slowing down as sheep amble across the road followed by small lambs and goats urged on by a shepherd holding a baby black and white goat which he displays to children in the cars. We wound our way through green mountains up across the bridge over the river and up steep hairpin bends. I did not dare to look down. If there were an accident we would not stand much of a chance. It was very like the Kabul Gorge, which we had traversed during our short stay in Afghanistan.

Cars twisted perilously around corners and Niall closed his eyes (I am driving). Arriving at the narrow tunnel we wait for our turn as the traffic can only move in one direction. I can really understand how people were asphyxiated in that tunnel a few years ago. In the distance the lights of Karaj make a pretty picture on the hill.

We stop to look at the old mosque which has a picture of Beheshti at its entrance. He was a very powerful figure in the revolution but was killed in the bombing of the Majlis just after our arrival in Tehran in 1981. An old man is dismantling a prayer platform out in the garden. Several men gather around looking for pictures of the tomb tower. I show them some of the Friday mosque and they acknowledge Bobby Sands as we go out. It is amazing how his story has travelled the world and shows how, by refusing to give in to requests for negotiation, government policies can be ultimately counter-productive and produce some very powerful martyrs. The heavy door is closed behind us, prayers finished for another week.

84. TRIP TO REY
Friday June 27th 1986

Today is going to be a fairly simple journey, we hope. We are planning to travel to the town of Rey, the former Iranian capital just south of Tehran. The German and new Finnish Ambassadors arrive plus two Irish men working in Bandar Abbas. I get them all coffee just as Inge, the wife of Peter, the previous chargé d'affaires of Norway and our Finnish friends, the Franks, arrive. We photocopy pages from '*Travels with a Paykan*' and Pope's '*Persian Architecture*' and carrying Sylvia Matheson's '*Archaeological Guide*' we all set off for the Danish Embassy to pick up the Danish Ambassador who sits beside Niall in the front of the car while I sit in the back beside Clare.

The Ambassador points out the shops and says how they appear to be so well stocked. He thinks everything will be OK and the regime will remain in place because roughly a new revolution occurs only every one hundred years. We look a little horrified; thinking a hundred years of this cruelty is not good. He wishes to correct himself in case he is quoted - he has probably seen the notebook I always carry with me. 'Sorry' he says quickly, 'I think it will not be that bad.'

The Ambassador is quite new to Tehran. He is in fact the third ambassador from Denmark since we arrived and it seems, perhaps understandably, that recent arrivals are always more accepting of the regime than the ones who were here before the massive general crackdown of summer 1981. The new diplomatic wives also seem to have no problem with covering up because they did not see the vicious treatment meted out to Iranian women who did not wish to start covering their hair.

The calls to prayer in the Mosques seem to be everywhere as we drive through the south of Tehran. It is a sign of mourning for the martyrs at the war front. This reminds the Danish Ambassador of another kind of killing. He mentions three Bahais who have been persecuted. Two were killed for their religious beliefs and one escaped. It looks like executions are starting again or maybe they have never been discontinued. It was always difficult to work out exactly what the regime was doing. The European Community continually made representations to the Iranian Government but the Iranians were a law unto themselves.

Passing a horse and cart filled with huge, delicious, green watermelons, we reach the refinery. Everyone is looking eagerly for signs of damage from the reported Iraqi bombing but we see nothing, except that the usual flares from the refinery are not burning. Next we are surrounded by fields of giant sunflowers gold and brown, gleaming in the sunlight. A car ahead swerves to a halt as two men cross the road carrying a dead sheep. The men shout at the car driver but they were very lucky they were not killed too.

We pass the spot where the mausoleum stood which contained the body of Shah Reza Pahlavi. There is no longer any sign of the elaborate white marble tomb, which was desecrated after the revolution. A Pasdar car overtakes us with its siren screaming while in Rey children are playing without a care in the world. Khomeini's photos are everywhere and in the background smoke rises up from the cement factory. Wooden mats are hanging over the window of the old houses to protect the inmates from the burning sun. There is a huge model of a hand grenade in the centre of the square and on the wall of the shrine a painting of the leading mullahs, Khomeini and Rafsanjani, as well as pictures of the local *shahids* (martyrs).

It is difficult to imagine that Rey was anything other than a small suburban town on the edge of Tehran but, in fact, it was called Rhages and was a very important city from about 5000 B.C. until 1200 A.D. when it was destroyed by the Mongols. In the third century B.C., Alexander the Great passed through Rhages in pursuit of Darius III, the last of the Achaemenian kings.

The Danish Ambassador notices a Toyota Truck and asked what are they doing with these at the war front. This week they apparently sent hundreds of trucks down to the war front. No one knows the answer to that question. All around us hand-made rugs lie out to dry on the flat roofs of the houses.

85. FATH ALI SHAH

We move on to see the carpet washing at the spring, Cheshmeh Ali. This used to be a big tourist destination, watching men, women and children splashing around in the water, while energetically cleaning and scrubbing their rugs and carpets. We park our cars on the main road. Across the road a group of old men gather around a photo of a young boy surrounded by lighted candles. Feeling a little embarrassed at passing this scene of mourning, we try to move as quietly and quickly as we can but they are resignedly muttering kharaji (foreigner) and seem to be more interested than annoyed. Death, especially of the young, has now become the norm, unfortunately. We carry on along the dusty street past a group of children. "How are you?" They laugh as they test out their English reminding us once again of the friendliness of the majority of the Iranian people even at times of extreme suffering.

We climb up the sand hill behind the old city walls crumbling with age and lack of care. As we descend the hill to our surprise we see lots of screaming young boys jumping up and down in the pool. The party holds back, frightened in case they might be dangerous but we see that Inge, Niall and the men from Bandar Abbas are already there so the rest of us push through to the pool, which is very clear and clean. Young boys are jumping up and down in the water alongside a group of chadoris washing piles of sheep wool.

A Qajar relief dominates the scene on the rock face. Roger Stevens describes the scene. The central part of the relief depicts Fath Ali Shah 'seated on the Marble Throne and surrounded by ten of his sons; by the steps to the throne stand two diminutive soldiers…. While on the right Fath Ali Shah appears again standing with a falcon on his wrist under an umbrella held by a figure standing behind him.' The rock carving has the appearance of being quite old but in fact is only 19th century, not old at all for Persia. We are now surrounded by young boys and a small man dressed in black with a black beard. The man asks for somebody to lend him a car to go down to the *Jeppe* (warfront) but gets no response. He then asks me to show him pictures of the relief in Sylvia Matheson's archaeological book, which I am carrying with me. I say there are not any but we examine other pictures of archaeological sites and he seems quite happy.

A very friendly gang of half-dressed children surround us as we walk up the hill. Niall is chatting to a black-clad Komiteh member who says we must not take photos. Fortunately they are already taken. The Iranian man goes back to shout at the crowd especially the man in the black shirt. I stop with the Franks, our Finnish friends to watch all of this until we realise we are in the middle of a football game. We are told to leave by a small boy who wishes to continue his game. There is a pungent smell arising from the river and the streets are very dusty because there has not been any rain for a long time.

The next stop is the fluted Seljuq (Mongol) Tomb Tower. We park the cars outside as a chadori descends the steps and calls to the 'guardian' of the tower to let us in. A man emerges to let us in and as we walk through the vegetable garden, we pass his small house surrounded by tin cooking pots and squawking hens running around in all directions. The tower doors are open, so now we can walk inside but the unique conically shaped roof has collapsed and groups of small birds are perched its rim, while wooden beams poke through the holes in the old walls. This is a funereal tower dating back to 1139 just before Genghis Khan's invasion. It is called 'Mongol' because it is the only building in the city not destroyed by the invaders.

The German Ambassador wakes us from our reverie and tells us it is time to go out again onto the hot dusty road for the last part of our trip to Varamin. Hot and tired we reluctantly set off along the Varamin Road through a rather unattractive plain, littered with brick works. Seeing a small tower we stop outside a small hut. Uniformed police come out to inform us that we cannot take photos. We climb uphill and potter around picking through one or two archaeological shards, which are lying around everywhere.

We then turn off to find shade under the trees beside a covered well. We seem to have picked a construction site as tractors, workers and trucks back to and forth in front of us. At this point we are too tired and hungry to find anywhere else so we start to eat our lunch, which consists of salads and tandoori chicken washed down with copious amounts of water and a glass of punch. It's getting really hot now and I cannot stop drinking the cool water.

86. VARAMIN

Beautiful red pomegranate and flowering bushes surround us in a blaze of colour. The foliage really is quite stunning. Back on the road, we look for the site of a Sassanian hunting lodge, but are unable to find it. We swing into Varamin, the Danish Ambassador notes that it looks more revolutionary than Rey. In the central square a huge clenched fist rises out of a Tulip. On the top of this two hands hold up the world. Beside this piece of revolutionary artwork, is another small Mongol funereal tower dating from 1289AD. This one is intact with a conical roof and some lovely decoration of turquoise enamelled brickwork.

An angry-looking older man with a grey beard takes down the car numbers then asks our friends from Bandar Abbas the identity of everyone in the group. Basil hands over a peace offering of a pomegranate flower, which is immediately discarded. The angry man then calls over two smiling policemen and they all have to check the German Ambassador's papers. We have not been stopped so we drive off watching warily from a distance.

Finally everyone is allowed to go, so we stop and wait for them opposite a 14th century mosque built in 1332. A huge picture of a Shahid rising up to Paradise is on the front of the mosque. Standing in the courtyard we cannot understand why it is described as one of the most attractive mosques. There are some signs of intricate brick work but it is only when we enter and see around the Ivan decorated with fine bands of calligraphy and a frieze of turquoise, flower-decorated Kufic script, that we realise the full beauty of the old building. This beauty is marred somewhat by an Islamic stamp which now decorates the Mirab. Teardrops of red blood are painted on the walls and a picture of Beheshti is painted at the entrance. An old man is dismantling prayer platforms out in the garden. Two men gather around looking for pictures of the Mongol tomb tower. I show them some of the mosque in the guide book and once again the men acknowledge Bobby Sands as we leave and the door is closed behind us.

A policeman on a bike offers to escort us. A Pasdaran car hangs back. They both take us to the roundabout and the policeman points out the road to Rey. 'Look for the cement factory as a pointer' he says helpfully.

We can see that the flares in the refinery are now burning again. Finally we spot Yazid's tower on the mountain that used to contain a Zoroastrian tower of silence which has been demolished. Matheson's guide book informs us that Yazid was a 'Caliph who ruled between A.D. 683 and 690' and the tower used to contain the graves of two princes but is now destroyed probably by people searching for treasure. There is a small shrine above it. Stopping the cars we climb up and peer down into the now exposed tower and damaged interior. The road to the little brick building is very steep, muddy and slippery and we all slide back down to the cars and gratefully drink any remaining water. The little shrine above the tower is reputed, writes Sylvia Matheson, to be the tomb of Bibi Shahrbanu, the daughter of Yezdigird III and 'may only be visited by women (wearing an ankle-length veil or chador) or by Sayyids, descendants of the Prophet through the male line'. As none of us fitted into either of these categories we all split up at this point and our friends from Bandar Abbas come back for a swim in the embassy pool. We hear the news that the divorce referendum in Ireland has returned a 60 to 40 majority to maintain the ban on divorce. (A few years later divorce was finally approved by the narrowest of margins.)

87. VISA PROBLEMS

Wednesday August 6th

Raining all night. Very fresh in the morning. The thunder was so loud that Niall thought the Iraqis had started bombing again. In fact Mahmoud said there was a bomb at 2.30 a.m. in Azadi square. Later, when going to collect money for the embassy, the police told him there was a bomb in a suitcase near the bank but, sensibly, Mahmoud did not wait to find out if that was true. The weather is starting to cool down now that it is August. I always think it is still summer but the temperature drops dramatically.

Friday August 8th
Went to see Arus Teherantchi in the evening with Peter from the Norwegian embassy. The Doctor says she is quite ill and needs a visa for hospital treatment in London. Niall is still having a lot of trouble with the Irish Department of Justice and is finding it very difficult to get visas for anyone. It really is a dysfunctional department as the officials refuse to make decisions and delay everything interminably, even short-term medical problems.

Sunday August 10th 1986
Father Mulligan talking about how everyone who got Khomeini to power has been disposed of. He refers to the death of Beheshti in the Majlis bombing in 1981; other important figures, so it was said, left just before the bombing.

Kian has promised to try to help Teherantchi. It must be terrible to need medical help for a life and death situation and be unable to obtain it because of bureaucracy.

Thursday August 14th 1986
Esther's father also wants to go to England for medical treatment but he was kept waiting outside the British embassy for a day. And then his visa was refused. Niall tries his best to help him but in vain. There has been a changing of the guard and the new individuals are not so flexible and do not seem to take humanitarian needs into consideration. Like Teherantchi, Esther's father is seventy-six so I do not see what the problem is, as he certainly does not want to live in Britain.

I go down to Manucheri to show Mandy the copper shop although it is not so easy with Clare and Hannah investigating everything.
In the evening we go to dinner with Soli, his father and wife Farimah.

Kami's parents are there too and they fill us in on how Kami and Kristie are settling down in the U.S.A. We all really miss them so much.

Friday August 15th 1986

Swimming and sorting our belongings, Mahmoud comes in at 5pm and we drive to the Indian Embassy. The Ambassador looks very distinguished in a white military uniform and his wife very beautiful in a lovely brown and gold sari. The embassy gardens are filled with lights and little food stations which are dotted around the grounds. Devji has been 'borrowed' for the day by the Indian Embassy. Wearing a chef's hat he waves to us as he fries samosas.

The Yugoslav commercial counsellor wants to discuss the story of the Afghan chargé d'affaires who was attacked on the train to Moscow near Zanjan at 1pm last Monday, when armed men broke into his train compartment and demanded the diplomatic bag. When he resisted their demand they hit him and he had to go to hospital in Tabriz. When we saw him he had a big bandage around his head. The story was that two armed guards stood outside his compartment and there was also a getaway car. It all seems very strange and much too organised to have been carried out by Afghan terrorists. Maybe some Iranian groups were involved.

Saturday August 16th 1986

Our Finnish friend phones to ask what is going on. She tells me that the Finnish Embassy has told her not to go out as a Danish woman was beaten up downtown. She has been in Iran more than thirty years and this has never happened before. A friend of hers has also just committed suicide. What a week! At least Clare is enjoying her time in the pool, turning round and round and swimming like a fish which is a relief because on one occasion, she fell into the pool and had to be lifted out with the big net pool cleaner!

Tahgouti, the cat, also seems in good spirits. She disappeared for a few weeks, maybe she found a better restaurant, but anyway she certainly seems happy to be back. In Tehran, at the moment, the sight of any happy person or animal has to be appreciated.

The Dean of the diplomatic corps, the Ambassador of Romania, rang to say that 59 countries contributed to our farewell present and he would send the money and card with a message tomorrow. We were going to choose a piece of silver from Joseph's shop and the message would be engraved on it.

Devji arrived back from the Indian Embassy. He had heard the news on the Indian radio that there had been a car bomb in Qom. Gerry and the meat boys arrive for dinner just as the electricity goes off. They won't be too happy about that!

Sunday August 17th 1986

Niall goes down to the National Iranian Oil Company (NIOC) to meet a senior official for the last time. There is a guard at the gate holding a pistol. On either side of the entrance to the building are two ten foot coloured wall paintings. On one side Montazeri and Khomeini and on the other Khamenei and Beheshti. Niall sighs in despair as he leaves the car: 'to think this was the only place that was keeping Iran financially solvent.'

The BBC reported this morning that the Iraqis bombed two power stations inside Iran, near Desfoule and one plane was shot down. The UN Secretary General Perez de Cuellar asked both countries to stop bombing civilian targets. Both countries replied they could not guarantee that as long as the war was on. The newspapers admitted to a car bombing in Qom: 11 martyrs, 100 wounded, near the shrine but they do not mention any Iraqi bomb attacks. Kian managed to get visas for the Teherantchis but she, Hassan and their two children, Sanam and Arastu, are leaving this week to attempt to start a new life in Denmark. She speaks Danish and English fluently so I'm sure she will succeed wherever she goes and we will always keep in touch.

88. VALLEY OF THE ASSASSINS
September 1986

The doors of the embassy burst open and a gang of five arrived. Paper and packing tape were soon strewn across the floor as boxes were assembled. Another packing experience was about to take place. Whether moving house is really as close to the stress of divorce or a death as studies imply, I am not sure; but after so many moves in the last decade I am at last beginning to develop some immunity to the process.

The movers fell upon our possessions like a crowd of locusts, throwing clothes into boxes and carefully wrapping brass bowls, handmade Iranian glass and Persian rugs, all of which I had bought on shopping trips with Kian or Friday afternoon visits to Joseph. Fortunately on this occasion, unlike our departure from Japan, the packers did not wrap in tissue paper the empty eggshells, other remnants of our breakfast and half the embassy furniture. The whole procedure was less delicate but on the whole quite efficient. The only shock was when I realised how much I had collected over the years. My excuse would be that in Tehran there were no cinemas or concerts and consequently shopping was one of the few major sources of entertainment and stress-reduction! Finally, at the beginning of September 1986, five years of an amazing adventure came to an end. We had decided to drive back to Ireland but unfortunately we had not planned for a petrol shortage, which had occurred because of the bombing of the petrol refinery. This made the journey across Northern Iran much more anxiety-provoking as we could not be sure that the petrol stations on our route to the Turkish border would be open. I knew, of course, that this would be only one of many problems we would face – but I tend to respond much better when facing challenges. This is probably because of my five years in Belfast at the beginning of the nineteen seventies.

August had been a mad month of farewell parties. We tried to avoid as many as we could but, as we had been in Tehran longer than any of the other European diplomats, we had made a lot of friends and contacts. Maybe for most people the thought of glamorous dinners in moonlit gardens was fun and of course many evenings were. You can, however, have too much of a good thing and after a while I began to feel like a sacrificial lamb being fattened up as more and more food and drink were poured into us.

Many diplomats feel that the more farewell dinners, the more popular or the more highly regarded they are. In fact it is probably the opposite: the more serious the diplomat the less the fuss. Sometimes farewell parties can even be a celebration for getting rid of someone or perhaps just and excuse for using up the yearly entertainment budget.

Once again we packed up the car so tightly that we could barely fit ourselves inside. I had very mixed feelings about departing Iran, especially about leaving vulnerable friends behind in such a volatile situation. There were a lot of tears as we waved goodbye to the staff. Devji had been so special during all our problem times and had done an excellent job, cooking and looking after the embassy. Fathi had been wonderful with Clare, despite having so many problems with her own family and Mahmoud had been a good-tempered driver and guide on our many trips across the country. I would even miss Esther and of course Roya. We kept in touch by letter for several years. Mahmoud got a visa for his family to live in Sweden and Roya moved with her husband to Dubai.

Devji was sacked soon after we left, for no apparent reason, except maybe he had been too close to us. At least the Indian Embassy were sensible and delighted to have him back. Latif was reinstated and apparently died later of a drug overdose. We never saw any of them again but unfortunately that is a major part of the diplomatic life, especially before the advent of social media.

On the day of our departure our excitement at the idea of another adventurous trip back to Ireland was tinged with emotion as we crammed ourselves into our over-laden car and waved goodbye to the staff. Even the *ashrali* man came to see us leave but unfortunately there was no sign of Tahgouti, our favourite furry lady of the night. Maybe she had eaten a mouse dinner late the previous evening and was sleeping it off in the bushes or more likely she was not bothered by our departure. Clare, who always liked to be on the move, waved farewell happily to

Devji and Fathi not realising the significance of our departure on this occasion.

As we drove for the last time through the dusty streets of Tehran and headed past the imposing Elborz Mountains for the city of Tabriz, I sat beside Clare's seat in the back of the car. Driving along Ali Shariati we passed by the iron gates of the British Embassy summer residence at Golhak where we had spent some good times with our friends and their children. As we passed I remembered some of the writings of Gertrude Bell in the letters she sent in 1892 when staying at this exact location in Golhak:

'Say, it is rather refreshing to the spirit to lie in a hammock strung between the plane trees of a Persian garden and read the poems of Hafez – in the original mark you!...That is how I spend my mornings; a stream murmurs past me which Zoroastrian gardeners guide with long handled spades into tiny sluices leading into the flower beds all around.'

On our way we passed the ancient city of Qasvin, full of memories of our terrible car accident. It was also the starting place on our journey in 1984 to Alamut (Eagle's Nest) the Valley of the Assassins, an area made famous by the travels of Freya Stark in the 1930s. She describes as 'grim' the great Rock which towers over the valley where the castle 'looks down nearly a thousand feet of stone to the fields and trees of Qasir Khan.' In the 12th century in the inaccessible Elborz Mountains were groups of fortified castles used by the followers of Hassan Sabbah, the leader of the Ismaili sect. Marco Polo called him 'The Old Man of the Mountains'. The English name assassin probably came from the name Hassan or the word Hashasin. This feared group of men would, so it is alleged, kidnap and murder political figures while under the influence of hashish. Drugged in a secret garden they would be told, when they awoke, that they were in paradise. Whatever the truth of this story, it has fascinated explorers throughout the centuries. One other interesting fact was that Hassan Sabbah was a school friend in Nishapur of Omar Khayyam, who was under the patronage of Malik Shah and was famous for astronomy and poetry, not kidnap and murder.

Our journey to the Valley of the Assassins, with its ruined castles like birds' nests high up on top of the mountain, echoed the thoughts of

Peter Somerville-Large:

'However the site, so difficult to approach, on the steep cliff overlooking the whole valley, had a grandeur and a suggestion of all the sinister mystery which the Assassins deliberately cultivated.'

In the late seventies, however, Peter Somerville-Large, travelled around this area by mule rather than relying as we did, a few years later, on a jeep for at least some part of the journey. We travelled with our friends Peter and Inge to this incredible mountainous area and marvelled at the adventurous spirit of all of those who had climbed the Rock.

Now on our return journey to Europe, we were, once again embarking on what could turn out to be another hair-raising trip.

As explained earlier, Iran was experiencing a petrol shortage at the time. We accordingly had to pack a big plastic container of petrol in case we were stranded without fuel. The car was also overflowing with cases and bags and we would take turns to drive. As on this occasion I remembered to pack toys for Clare but she still liked to play the 'boggie' game where I threw strips of tissue in the air and she would try to catch them calling out 'boggie'.

On our arrival at Tabriz we went to visit the home for people suffering from leprosy who were looked after by Sister Maryam. The atmosphere in the home was very friendly and welcoming and we watched some women painting cards and other groups weaving their warm, colourful sock-slippers. The burden of this terrible illness was lightened by the kindness and compassion they experienced in the home and their self-esteem was increased by their ability to be creative and produce beautiful handicrafts. I bought several pairs of slippers and we said our goodbyes, confident that everyone was happy and well looked-after and that the small effort of the diplomatic wives over the last few years had been worthwhile. The newly arrived wife of the Swedish Ambassador had offered to continue the charity bazaars and I continued to support them from Ireland until a few years later when the French nuns were unjustly accused of being foreign spies and for their safety we had to break off all contact.

By the time we reached Tabriz, however, we were running out of petrol and did not know how we were going to proceed to the Turkish border. To our delight one of the patients in the leper clinic had his own business and was able to refill our tank from his personal petrol supply. So once again our problems were solved and we set off towards the mountainous passes of Northern Iran. Amid the stunning views of Western Azerbaijan, we passed a fortress hanging precariously on the soaring cliffs at Maku. These ruined fortifications were the buildings in which the Bab, the founder of the tolerant Bahai faith, had been imprisoned in the mid-nineteenth century.

89. TURKISH CAFE

At long last the sight of the border post at Bazargan greeted us. It was set against the multi-coloured hills now stripped of their covering of winter snow. The formalities were completed quite quickly and we breathed a sigh of relief until a young Revolutionary Guard came out to investigate the car, which appeared to be carrying all our worldly belongings. Through the open door he could only just see part of my head as the rest of me was covered in coats and teddy bears but his eyes lit up when he realised that I was clutching my handbag. Big mistake - this immediately drew attention to the bag which contained my grandmother's and mother's jewellery and some items of value from Joseph's shop. The guard thrust his arm inside the car and grabbed the bag, I immediately held on tightly and a tug of war ensued followed by a discussion about whether or not my handbag could be searched.

According to international law no diplomatic baggage can be searched but this rule was unlikely to be known by a young, eager Revolutionary Guard at the far-flung outpost of Bazargan. Another round of diplomatic jargon was put into motion until finally with assurances of goodwill and everlasting friendship between our two revolutionary countries, my bag was returned unopened and we were free to go.

We were going, of course, with very mixed feelings. We were glad to be leaving behind the violence and oppression of a dictatorial regime and heading for freedom but at the same time we were sad because Iran was such a wonderful country and our friends were left behind in very uncertain circumstances.

Soon we turned off the so-called 'main' road at Dogubayasit and onto an even worse 'main' road on the way to the ancient town of Van. Along the way there were few houses until at last we reached a little open-fronted cafe used by truck drivers on their way to Iran. Parking the car in front of the small tables we sat down surrounded by friendly drivers who were very happy to break the monotony of their long drive with pleasantries.

The strong black Turkish coffee was delicious after the long, hot, dusty journey and Clare was enjoying her orange juice when to our horror we heard an almighty crash and looked up to see that a huge Turkish truck had driven into our car! The distraught driver jumped out of his cab to examine the damage – a crushed back bumper and scratched side. It could have been much worse from the sound of the collision, so we were actually quite relieved. There was a feeling of nervous anticipation from the surrounding drivers as they tried to gauge our reaction when the offending driver came over to apologise. We knew that at that time there would be no insurance for local truck drivers just as we had no insurance in Iran or for our return journey. There was, therefore, no other choice than to be gracious, accept his apology and suggest that as recompense, he could pay for our coffee and orange juice. That done we drove away from the scene of the crime to the sound of the relieved cheers of the drivers.

Soon the amazing sight of Lake Van came into view. It is so large that it is more like a sea and is so salty that no fish can survive. Turkey's second highest mountain loomed in the background overshadowing the turquoise lake where several ancient royal tombs are hewn into the cliffs. Arriving in Van we booked into a small hotel and went to look around. Van has an interesting history having been vanquished many times over the centuries and had a largely Armenian population before the Turkish massacres in the First World War. Glubb Pasha tells us how 'Tamerlane marched against Van, the capitol of the Black Sheep Turkmans whom he put to flight, the citizens of Van being killed by being thrown over the mountain precipices.'

The next morning we took the ferryboat to Akdamar Island in the middle of the lake. On this island stood the ruins of an old Armenian church, which was completed in the year 915. Cengiz Alper in his book on Van describes the 'Brightly coloured wild flowers, clouds of thousands of snow-white gulls and the dark blue waters of the lake make a brilliant picture together with the 9th century church which is an important artistic monument.'

Our only companions on the ferry to this interesting island were a young Israeli couple who had just finished their military service. They appeared to be a nice couple but sadly they knew absolutely nothing about any important issues. Their understanding of the Palestinian problem was negligible as was their interest in Turkish culture. Nevertheless they were good companions on an exciting day trip.

Moving on to southern Turkey, we headed for Mount Nemrut to view the monumental remains of the Commagene kingdom located at the top of the mountain. These huge statues were built in 62BC by King Antiochus I but were damaged over the centuries with most of the heads removed, defaced and scattered over the site. At 5 o'clock in the morning we had to leave our hotel in order to join the group wishing to see the sun rise over the majestic statues of the local deities. A magnificent sight!

90. ISLAND OF RHODES

Our next destination was the Mediterranean coast, which I hoped finally might offer more of a holiday feeling and we were very pleased when we found a small motel with a tiny swimming pool. At that stage a shower and a pool would be a real luxury. Unfortunately the manager refused to give us a room because he had seen the Iranian registration plates on the car and he thought we were Iranian. After another tiring round of explanations everything was sorted out and we spent a relaxing few days there trying to recover from the stress of Eastern Turkey and Northern Iran.

We continued down the coast to the pleasant port town of Bodrun.

From there we boarded a small car ferry which would take us to the Greek island of Rhodes. As we entered the harbour surrounded by huge walls, the medieval city lay before us.

The traveller Ida Pfeiffer was very impressed by the sight of Rhodes harbour which is 'shut in on all sides by walls and masses of rock, leaving only a gap of a hundred and fifty to two hundred paces in width for ships to enter. …A round tower stands as a protection on either side of the entrance to the harbour.' She was interested in find out about the 'Colossus of Rhodes' one of the seven wonders of the ancient world but was unable to find any information, either from books or from the people she met.

We found a beach hotel and headed off to view the beautiful Crusader town depicted best by Ida Pfeiffer: 'The principal street, containing the houses of the ancient Knights of St. John is very broad, with buildings so massively constructed of stone as almost to resemble fortresses. Heraldic bearings with dates carved in stone, grace many of the Gothic gateways. The French shield, with the three lilies and the date 1402, occurs most frequently.' After several days resting and enjoying the ambience of the island it was time to leave. Like Ida Pfeiffer we also found no traces of the 'Colossus of Rhodes' but it was good to dream. Feeling refreshed, we finally took a large car ferry to Piraeus and then onwards to Patros for another ferry to Bari in Italy.

91. DEATH OF FATHER MULLIGAN

In Rome we stayed again in the Belgian embassy with Roger and Jennifer who were anxious to hear all the news of mutual friends in Iran. Roger took great delight in telling us that Belgium was to blame for the revolution. He went on to explain how many years ago the embassy building in Tehran had been guarded by an arrogant young Iranian soldier whose behaviour was so obnoxious that the Belgian Government had asked for his removal. He was transferred to another part of Iran and after a successful coup he overthrew the reigning monarch and installed himself as successor. He was Reza Shah, the founder of the

Pahlavi dynasty and father of the last shah deposed by the recent revolution. Roger felt that if this young man had been left as an army corporal, guarding embassies, he would not have staged a coup. That was an interesting theory but as we do not know too much about the personality and circumstances of Reza Shah, it is not an easy one to prove.

Our four days in Rome were really interesting as we discussed the political situation in Iran tossing backwards and forwards ideas on what had happened and what would happen in the future and most importantly what would be the effect on the rest of the world. None of us, however, dreamt that the revolutionary regime would go on for so long.

In later years we would go to stay with Roger and Jennifer many times in their different postings and they would come to stay with us; but our time in Iran would always be the central topic of conversation.

We kept in touch with as many friends as we could, including Father Mulligan who had once again been expelled from Iran and sent to Damascus. He came to see us in Dublin a couple of times but seemed quite unhappy in Syria because he missed Iran so much.

In August 1989 he phoned us from London to say he wanted to see us that evening on his return to Ireland. I said we would love to see him but that night was not really a good time because we had an Irish family of five coming to stay for the Bank Holiday weekend and a Spanish Diplomat coming to dinner. We felt we would not have time to concentrate fully on him and hear his interesting stories. He insisted, however, saying that he wanted to see Clare and our second child Andrew. We sat upstairs discussing Damascus and eating our dinner when suddenly Fr. Mulligan said he did not feel well. He had felt a little sick at Heathrow Airport and he had bought some pills but was now feeling worse.

I was worried and asked him had he felt this way before. He said no, so I looked at Niall and our Spanish friend for advice but assuming that there was nothing seriously wrong they continued to eat their meal. He asked to go to the bathroom and I helped him to leave the room but at the door he collapsed. At this point the men left their dinner and came to help and I ran to the phone to ring for an ambulance but it was too late - Fr. Mulligan had died within three minutes. Just as he was dying, the family who were staying with us for the August weekend arrived at the front door and the three children ran up the stairs. The ambulance men arrived very soon after but to no avail.

It was almost as if he had come to us to die because he knew that like him we loved Iran. He died on a Persian carpet on the fourth of August 1989 beside a photo of my mother who died on the second of August many years before and my great aunt who had died on the third of August the previous year 1988 and whose illness I had discussed with him in Iran. The *post-mortem* did not find any cause of death: no heart attack, no stroke, no blood clot, no brain haemorrhage and fortunately no poison from my food.

It was so sad and I was very distressed and shocked and sobbed until the funeral, but then standing beside the coffin I felt an amazing sense of peace. At the funeral, I apologised to his sister because he had come to see us first and consequently she had not had a chance to see him before his death. Her reply was that she had angina and could not have coped with his death so maybe he had saved her from her own heart attack and instead went to die with people who understood both countries he loved so much.

92. RETURN TO REALITY

On my return to Ireland I had to adjust to the fact that the most stressful daily experience I would undergo in the short-term would probably be standing in a supermarket queue (apart from the death of Fr. Mulligan). I also had to be careful when talking about our time in Iran because few people wanted to hear about it. Their own more pressing issues tended to be local. It would probably take another few decades before many people would begin to take an interest in foreign conflicts and appreciate how interconnected the world really is.

This lack of stress did not last long. As I mentioned earlier, Niall was dispatched to Baghdad in August 1990 after the Iraqis invaded Kuwait and started what became known as the first Gulf War. His task was to assist the Irish Ambassador there in evacuating the several hundred Irish citizens who were trapped and were being refused permission by the Iraqi authorities to leave the country. Many of these were doctors and nurses working in the Park Hospital in central Baghdad. The Iraqi strategy was to hold as many Western male hostages as possible in the vicinity of military posts in order to deter any attack on these locations by the United States and its Western allies. While based in Baghdad, Niall travelled down alone to Kuwait to locate the twelve Irish citizens who were known to be living there and to bring them out - at least as far as Baghdad. This he succeeded in doing (including the rescue of six Aer Lingus employees who had been providing what they had thought was a short two-week technical support trip to Kuwait Air). In the process, however, he ended up being arrested by the Iraqi army who broke in at gunpoint to the Canadian Embassy where he had been kindly provided with shelter for the night. Fortunately, his long experience dealing with Iranian bureaucracy had equipped him to handle the Iraqis effectively and to negotiate his release and that of the Aer Lingus employees and the other Irish citizens who had been arrested with him.

Meanwhile we had another child, Andrew, and I was appointed as the first official psychologist on the Irish Olympic Medical Committee to work and travel with the team for the 1992 Olympic Games in Barcelona. Sadly, although I had been developing my own approach to sport - using Japanese meditation techniques to aid concentration since the 1980 Moscow Games - several athletes still regarded psychology as something strange and many were unwilling to join my training sessions.

The one team who did use the techniques successfully was the boxing team under the guidance of their Cuban coach, Nicolás Cruz, who understood the crucial importance of psychology in most sports. I watched with pride in the Barcelona boxing stadium as Michael Carruth who was recovering from fractures on both his arms won a gold medal, the first in any sport for Ireland since 1956. The Belfast boxer, Wayne McCullough, also saw the importance of a focused mind and won a silver medal using a consistent meditation programme.

I worked as the official psychologist with the Olympics for many more years and even now continue to work with individuals involved in different sports.

We spent five interesting years after that when Niall was appointed to Irelands mission at the UN in New York during which time I was able to work with university sports groups, children with concentration problems and individuals suffering from stress disorders. While I was there I completed two books, one on sports psychology and one on education. Both of the books were published by Wolfhound Press. Seamus Cashman, Wolfhound's publisher, became a close friend and published my next two books on Palestine and on Mordechai Vanunu. New York was not the easiest posting with two young children, but at least I was able to concentrate a little more on my own work.

There then followed for Niall three years in Belfast, which, in the wake of the Good Friday Agreement, was a totally different place from the previous time when we were there at Queen's University. Niall's next appointment was as the Irish Representative to the Palestinian Authority in Ramallah. The leader of the Palestinian Authority at that time, Yasser Arafat, was a world-renowned freedom fighter or terrorist, depending on one's viewpoint. By then I was lecturing in Dublin at the American College so I stayed in Ireland with Clare who was at university - while Niall and Andrew lived on the Mount of Olives in Jerusalem.

During the long holidays, Clare went out to Jerusalem and worked on a psychosocial programme with UNRWA (she had studied human rights as part of her degree course). I went around the refugee camps in both the West Bank and Gaza training the psychologists and teachers for the UN. On several occasions I met Yasser Arafat and felt that our time in Palestine was one of the most inspirational of Niall's postings because there was so much interesting and useful work to be done. Furthermore, Seamus Cashman and I started a registered charity for orphanages and disabled children in Palestine, which eventually spread to other countries across the world.

Our final posting was a very interesting five-year stint in Saudi Arabia where I became involved in producing an Arabic collection of perfumes for our charity. Because Niall was also ambassador to four other countries – Iraq, Yemen, Bahrain and Oman – we had an amazing time travelling around the region.

93. AN UNCERTAIN FUTURE.

More than thirty years on, there was again new hope for Iran and regional stability with the success of the nuclear negotiations and the (partial) lifting of sanctions against Iran by President Obama and the EU. The only countries that were not seemingly pleased by the progress in these negotiations were Saudi Arabia and Israel. This is quite ironic as Saudi Arabia and Israel are in close proximity to Iran and would be the most affected if it did develop a nuclear weapon. Later, however, the U.S. under President Trump reneged completely on what had been agreed. In fact, it seems unlikely that Iran really desires to or is even capable of producing nuclear weapons but it can be expected that the regime will continue to use the threat of developing a nuclear device as a lever to achieve other ends. It was hoped that President Biden would start to renegotiate a new deal which would make the world a safer place and pragmatism would win out over ideology. That sadly did not happen and it's hard to see at the present time, any future American leaders behaving any better.

Many of those in power during our time in Iran – such as the Supreme Leader Ayatollah Ruhollah Khomeini who returned from exile in France in 1979 to lead the Islamic Revolution and Ayotollah Montazeri – are now dead. These were obviously central figures in our lives in Tehran. Their faces along with others such as Ali Akbar Hashemi Rafsanjani who only died a few years ago, were on huge posters across the capital city and their names and statements were constantly on the Iranian television and radio (although apart from the latest developments in the Iran-Iraq war, there was not much else reported at the time on the Iranian news broadcasts).

I find it interesting, however, that many of the old names are still there after forty years. Ali Akbar Velayati was Foreign Minister when we were there and is still an important figure in the current regime. Ayatollah Ali Khamenei, who was pulling the strings in the background for much of the time, took over formally from Ayatollah Khomeini when the latter died in 1989 and is still the Supreme Leader of Iran at the time of writing. I remember Niall returning from a meeting with Khamenei looking a little bemused as he described how he attempted to shake his right hand only to find it hanging limply at his side. Paralysed after a bomb blast at Friday prayers in 1981, his right hand was no longer functioning. Quickly recovering his composure, Niall shook the left hand. Years later we were to draw on our memory of some of these politicians to name our menagerie of household pets - including our birds and two goldfish.

Over the years there have been some periods when change may have been possible. In the 90's under President Mohammad Khatami, there was a small window of hope and optimism as journalist Sean Boyne suggested in his article for the Washington Post in 1999. Sean felt that the women appeared to be less restricted by Islamic regulations. Had the Clinton administration engaged in further negotiations at that time, it is possible that these significant changes could have been maintained. Sadly, that did not happen. In recent years, Hassan Rouhani who was President from 2013 to 2021 seems to have been fairly moderate and sophisticated, as was his Foreign Minister Mohammed Javad Zarif. Certainly their behaviour in the nuclear negotiations made a great contrast with the antics of the previous President Mahmoud Ahmadinejad. While the moderate factions have had some successes in recent elections, the hard line religious elements together with the Pasdaran (Revolutionary Guards) are fighting back to prevent change. Ibrahim Raisi, the next president was also a hardliner, but was killed in a helicopter crash in 2024. The latest president, Masoud Pzeshkian, a former heart surgeon, would appear to be more liberal and was voted in on the expectation that he would reduce the power of the Revolutionary Guards and the morality police. Regrettably, presidential elections in Iran cannot be regarded as free and fair as only those endorsed by the so-called Guardianship Council (and thereby the Supreme Leader) are permitted to stand as candidates.

Nothing seems to have changed since we were in Tehran forty years ago. Executions in Iran are still continuing and are now among the highest in the world. In 2024 the UN estimated at least 901 executions had taken place. The advent of social media, however, has highlighted some of the more atrocious crimes of the regime. Visitors to Iran - such as the high profile cases of Nazanin Zaghari-Ratcliffe and the Irish citizen Bernard Phelan (both of whom have recently been released) - have been held as bargaining chips against debts allegedly owed to Iran and in retaliation for grievances held against the UK, France and other countries. The tragic death of Mahsa Amini - who was killed because her head covering was not sufficiently Islamic - and other less well known women killed for similar offences, will only lead to even further protests against the regime.

The leaders of the Islamic Revolution have often tried to rid Iran of its ancient history and mythology, the more they do so the more the young people hold on to their pre-Islamic culture. Professor Llyod Llewellyn-Jones suggests that other empires, including the Roman Empire, who conquered different countries and forced their own rules and languages upon them could learn from the ancient Persians. He says it is also true that "the foreign powers who invaded Iran across many successive centuries - the Arabs, Mongols and Turks - eventually ended up being conquered by the culture they aimed to destroy. The sheer force of Persian civilisation, its deep historical legacy, overpowered them and they became thoroughly Persianised."

Iran is still being accused of involvement in terrorism and assassination attempts against its opponents around the world. Of particular interest was the revelation in the Sunday Times on 14 May 2023 that Mohammed Reza Kolahi Samadi had been killed in 2015 in the Netherlands by a gang organised by the Kinahan crime group from Ireland. This was apparently the same Samadi who was accused of planting the bomb in the Majlis which killed more than seventy people just after our arrival in Tehran in 1981. This would suggest that the Kinahans are more than just a drug gang and may even have moved their residence to Iran in order to avoid prosecution.

Nevertheless, for the sake of global peace and to prevent further destabilisation in the region, it would seem to be of vital importance to continue to talk to Iran and re-launch the failed nuclear negotiations at the earliest opportunity. Unfortunately, Israel's killing of six Revolutionary Guards in the Iranian Embassy in Damascus and the subsequent tit-for-tat missile exchanges are not conducive to a peace settlement. It seems that Israel would be only too happy to drag Iran into the current Gaza conflict. The world is clearly becoming an ever more dangerous place.

As I complete this book, however, there are increasing worries about regional wars in the Middle East. Not content with the near-destruction of Gaza, Israel has attacked its northern neighbour Lebanon. In Syria President Bashar al-Assad has now fled to Moscow and Damascus has been taken over by Islamist Rebels. The region has been raised to a new and dangerous stage which now involves violent confrontation with Iran.

On Sunday June the 15th 2025, Iran was due to hold nuclear discussions with the Americans. Only two days before this on the morning of Friday the 13th, Netanyahu ordered operation *Rising Lion* to bomb the nuclear facilities across Iran. Fearing that the nuclear facilities had not been sufficiently damaged, Trump subsequently launched Operation *Midnight Hammer*, bombing Iran's nuclear plants in Fordow and Isfahan with fourteen special "Bunker Buster" bombs carried by B-2 stealth bombers.

Netanyahu had intended not only to destroy the nuclear facilities but was also openly calling for regime change. This appeared rather foolish as - however much they might dislike their own government – the Iranian people would be unlikely to allow Israel to dictate their new leadership.

Life as the wife of a diplomat can be difficult, often superficial, sometimes dangerous and always challenging; but it is also interesting, exciting and truly a privilege to live in so many countries and meet such a cross section of people.

Definitely the trials and tedium of some aspects of a diplomatic life are outweighed by the inspiration provided by a caravanserai in the desert, the medieval mud-brick city of Bam, the eternal flame in the temple of the Zoroastrians in Yazd, the beautiful Islamic masterpieces of Isfahan and the archaeological wonders of Persepolis. It was, and still is, truly humbling to have experienced such a political, historical and sociological adventure, side by side with living within the magical culture and mystery of what is still the ancient land of Persia.

It is not possible to see what the future holds for Iran and its people but change will always come about at some point. The Iranians are a proud, talented and resilient nation who will continue to overcome their difficulties as they have always done. Lessons can be learned from the great history of Persia that dynasties or regimes, whether laudable or authoritarian, do not last forever. My hopes are that one day peaceful conditions will return and that the rest of the world will be able to visit and enjoy this fascinating country and culture once again.

> *"Think, in this batter'd Caravanserai*
> *Whose Portals are alternate Night and Day,*
> *How Sultan after Sultan with his Pomp*
> *Abode his destin'd Hour, and went his way."*

Rubaiyat of Omar Khayyam (1048–1131)
Translated by Edward Fitzgerald (1809 -1893)

Clare and I at the Tomb of Hafez, Shiraz, Iran

An Irish St Patrick at the camp in Bandar Abbas on the Persian Gulf

Caviar for Breakfast

Niall and I at St Patrick's Day Embassy reception, "Don't eat the Shamrock"

St Patrick's Day Embassy of Ireland - myself with Embassy Staff.

Niall at the Statue of Ferdowsi, Tus

Sheikh Lotfollah Mosque, Isfahan

Dome of Shah Mosque, Isfahan

Rooftops of the Zorastrian town of Yazd

Wind Towers in Yazd

The Tower of Silence in Yazd where the dead used to be laid out to be consumed by the vultures

Clare and myself with our Russian friends at the Grand Hotel Ramsar

Rudsar, Caspian Coast

Tomb of Kashef of Saltaneh, Lahijan (now Pasdaran H.Q.)

Weighing the tea leaves in Lahijan

At the Silk Farm, Caspian Coast

Hamid and Arus Teherantchi's house museum

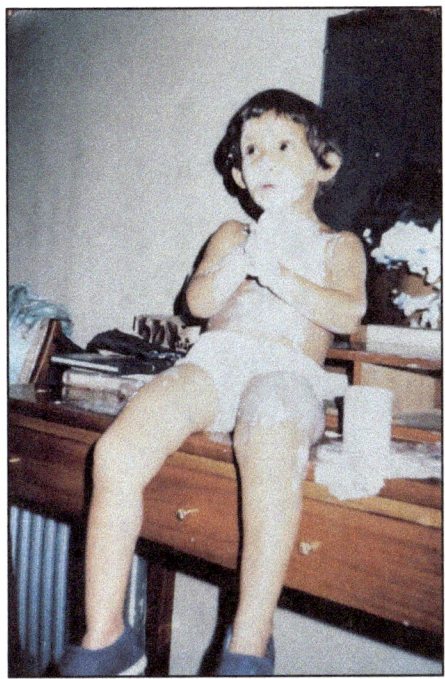

Ooops! – the end of the face cream

Kian's daughter Sanam with my daughter Clare Simran

Trade Fair in Tehran

Clare Simran at the Tehran Trade Fair with picture of Ayatollah Khomeini in the background

Diplomatic Farewell Party - Niall and I with the Dean of the Diplomatic Corps.

The Village of Alamut and the Assassin's castle

Peter in Alamut

The Leprosy Clinic in Tabriz

Clare in front of Armenian Church (915AD) on Akdamar Island in the middle of Lake Van, Turkey.

Niall and Clare climbing Nemrut Dag in Eastern Turkey

Our Children Clare and Andrew back in Ireland 1988

Acknowledgments

Thanks to our friends in Iran - especially Soleiman and Farimah Abdol Rasouli, Dr. Kami and Kristie Fatehi, Arun and Livleen Bhagat, Marina Niknejad, the Irish community and the many others who helped to make my stay there such a special experience.

To Bassem who helped with some of the translations.

To the many friends who put up with our visits during our travels to and from Iran, especially Niall's sister Renagh Holohan and his colleague Adrian McDaid.

To Dr Susan Mullaney who permitted me to use photographs taken by her late mother, Dr Joan Mullaney, when she stayed with us in Tehran.

To Monica Chambers who permitted me to use her photographs of Agatha Christie in Egypt.

To H.E. Roger Martin and H.E. Witold Smidowski for their expert advice.

To Seamus Cashman, publisher and poet, who published all my previous books and supported me throughout my writing career; he aided and edited this project from the very beginning to its end.

To Eoin Mulcahy, a wonderful musician, whose enthusiasm, tireless work and creative input were essential in organising and bringing this book to life.

To Sharon Crowley for her great title suggestion, Katrina Kenny, Daniel Cunningham, Myles Duffy and especially Michael Bevan whose creative ideas were invaluable.

To Jim, Rose and Carol of the Breffni and to Stéphane and Indi of the Encore Café, all of whom provided a haven for my writing over the years.

To my family: my husband Niall, whose love of history and politics helped to make every day an adventure into Persian culture. He also took most of the photos in this book and helped with endless advice and editorial support. To my daughter Clare Simran and my son Andrew for his creative and editorial input, and my grandson Ciarán who - along with my three rescue dogs and my African Grey parrot - gave me lots of enthusiastic encouragement over the years.

Caviar for Breakfast

References Consulted

Persia: An Archaeological Guide, Sylvia A. Matheson (Noyes Press 1973)
A visit to Holy Land, Madame Ida Pfeiffer (Incram Cooke & Co. 1852)
The Holy Land – An Archaeological Guide from Earliest Times to 1700, Jerome Murphy-O'Connor (Oxford University Press 1980)
Rubaiyat of Omar Khayyam - Translated by Edward Fitzgerald (Rupa & Co. 2008)
Iran Today, Jean Hureau (Jeune Afrique 1975)
A Journey to China, Arnold J. Toynbee (Constable & Co.1931)
The Lost Centuries, John Bagot Glubb (J.B.G. 1967)
Laughing Diplomat, Daniale Vare (John Murray London 1939)
Caviar Coast, Peter Somerville-Large (The Travel Book Club 1968)
Incidents of Travel in Greece, Turkey, Russia and Poland, J.L.Stephens Esq. (Edinburgh : Chambers 1839)
Iran Travel Survival Kit, David St Vincent (Lonely Planet 1992)
Jesuits Go East, Felix Alfred Plattner (Clonmore & Reynolds 1950)
The Great War for Civilisation, Robert Fisk (Fourth Estate an imprint of Harper Collins London 2005)
The Letters of Gertrude Bell Volume 1 (Earnest Benn Limited London 1927)
The Land of the Great Sophy, Roger Stevens (Methuen & Co LTD London 2nd Edition 1974)
The Majesty that was Islam, W. Montgomery Watt (Sidwick & Jackson London 1974)
Persepolis: The Archaeology of Parsa, Seat of the Persian Kings, Donald N. Wilber (Cassell London 1969)
Persian Architecture, Arthur Upham Pope (Oxford University Press 1969)
Archaic Egypt, W.B. Emery (Penguin Books 1961)
Palestine Past and Present, L. Valentine (Frederick Warne & Co. 1893)
The Nearer East, D.G. Hogarth (William Heinemann London 1902)
East of the Jordan, Selah Merrill – Archaeologist of the American Palestine Exploration Society (Richard Bentley & Son London 1881)
Seven Pillars of Wisdom, T.E. Lawrence (Jonathan Cape London 1942 - First published 1926)
The Road to Oxiana, Robert Byron (John Lehmann London 1937)
The Valleys of the Assassins, Freya Stark (John Murray London 1934)
Full Tilt: Ireland to India with a Bicycle, Dervla Murphy (John Murray 1965)
Sufism: An Account of the Mystics of Islam, John Arberry (George Allen & Unwin Ltd 1950)
Shiraz: Persian city of Saints and Poets, John Arberry (Norman: University of Oklahoma Press 1960)
Selected Sonnets from the Divan of Hafez (Eghbal Publications Tehran 1985)

Felonies of the MKO (Islamic Propagation Organization Tehran 1983)

Imam Khomeini, Pope and Christianity (Islamic Propagation Organization Tehran 2nd Edition 1984)

Persia by Richard Nelson Frye (Schocken Books 1969)

Balcony Over Jerusalem: A Middle East Memoir - Israel, Palestine and Beyond, John Lyons (Harper Collins 2017)

Persians: The Age of the Great Kings, Lloyd Llewellyn-Jones (Wildfire 2022)

Lords of the Desert, James Barr (Simon & Schuster UK 2018)

Travels with a Peykan, Roger Tagg (Rayka Printing Teheran 1975)

Rubaiyat of Omar Khayyam - Translated by Edward Fitzgerald, first and fifth versions (Hartsdale House New York 1952)

A Princess Remembers: The Memoirs of the Maharani of Jaipur, Gayatri Devi and Santha Rama Rau (RUPA 1976)

Selected Sonnets from the Divan of Hafez, English translation by Gertrude Bell (Eqbal Printing and Publishing Tehran 1985)

Van: a unique historical treasure in beautiful Eastern Anatolia, Cengiz Alper (Ankara, Turkey, 1986)

You Will Die in Prison by Bernard Phelan (Eriu 2024)

Prisoner of Tehran, Marina Nemat (John Murray 2008)

Passenger to Teheran, Vita Sackville-West, (Tauris Parke Paperbacks 2007)

DYNASTIES OVER THE CENTURIES
Some principal rulers and events mentioned in this book
(Some dates listed are approximate)

Achaemenians: B.C. 550 to 330
- Cyrus the Great – Founder of Pasargadae as military capital
- Cambyses (Son of Cyrus)
- Darius the Great (Son-in-law of Cyrus) founder of Persepolisas his capital
- Xerxes I (Son of Darius)
- Alexander the Great - Destroys Persepolis by fire and defeats Darius III, the last of the Achaemenian Rulers B.C. 331-330
- Alexander dies B.C.323

Seleucids and Parthians: B.C. 312 to A.D.224

Sassanians: A.D. 224 to 642
- Ardashir I
- Shahpur I
- Yazdegerd III

INVASIONS: AD650 TO 1502

Early Islam: A.D.651 to 1000

Saljuqs: A.D.1000 to 1018
- Toghril Beg
- Alp Arslan
- Malik Shah

Mongols: A.D.1218 to1368
- Mongol invasions
- Genghis Khan
- Hulaghu Khan (Grandson of Genghis Khan)
- Oljeitu founds new capital at Sultaniyeh near Qazvin

Timurids: A.D. 1370 to 1507
- Timur (Tamerlane)
- Ulugh Beg

Safavids: A.D.1491 to 1722
- Shah Ismail
- Shah Abbas I (Isfahan becomes his capital
- Shah Safi

1736 TO MODERN TIME

- Nadir Shah
- The Qajar Dynasty
- Fath Ali Shah

Pahlavis
- Reza Shah 1925 – 1941
- Mohamad Reza Shah 1941 – 1979

The Iranian Islamic Revolution
- Supreme Leader Ayatollah Khomeini 1979 -1989
- Supreme Leader Ayatollah Khamenei 1989 - present.

www.ingramcontent.com/pod-product-compliance
Lightning Source LLC
Chambersburg PA
CBHW052009070526
44584CB00016B/1674